Red Square, the heart of Moscow. The Kremlin wall is in lower right corner,
St. Basil's Cathedral in the middle and Lenin's tomb in lower center.

Russia and the Near Abroad

St. Petersburg: Church of the Resurrection on the blood.

RUSSIA
AND THE NEAR ABROAD
РОССИЯ И БЛИЖНЕЕ ЗАРЧБЕЖЬЕ

JOHN TOMIKEL – BONNIE HENDERSON

Allegheny Press

RUSSIA AND THE NEAR ABROAD
РОССИЯ И БЛИЖНЕЕ ЗАРЧБЕЖЬЕ

Address all correspondence concerning this work to

Allegheny Press
Elgin, PA 16413

Cover design and title page by Eric Tomikel

Library of Congress Catalog Card Number 96-84450

ISBN 0-910042-76-4 Trade Paperback

CONTENTS

Chapter   **Page**

Computer Maps and Graphics - Eric Tomikel
Chapter 21 by Baher Ghosheh, Ph.D.

Photo Credits

Photos by RIA Novosti on pages 8, 9, 41, 43, 46, 47, 120, 125, 127, 130, 132, 140, 143, 146, 148, 153, 159, 179, 187, 189

Photos by Baher Ghosheh on pages 4, 54, cover and title page

Photos by Donald M. White on pages ii, 50, 150, 172

All other photos from Allegheny Press archives or by John Tomikel

Arbat Street: Moscow - The Golden Arches come to Russia.

MAPS

MAP 1 Location and relationships of Russia and the Near Abroad.

RUSSIA AND THE NEAR ABROAD

Western Republics	Caucasus Republics	Central Asian Republics
Estonia	Armenia	Kazakhstan
Latvia	Azerbaijan	Kyrgyzstan
Lithuania	Georgia	Tajikistan
Belarus		Turkmenistan
Moldova		Uzbekistan
Ukraine		

1. A New Russia

On December 26, 1991 the Soviet Union officially dissolved. A union of fifteen "autonomous" republics, the country had endured for over seventy years, a bastion of communism and the arch-enemy of the United States and the West. The Soviet Union which began with the Russian Revolution in 1917 and Vladimir Lenin ended with Mikhail Gorbachev, *glasnost* and *perestroika*. Her people had suffered every horror imaginable: revolution, civil war, Stalinism, World War II, political repression, the KGB and shortages of every kind. Yet the Soviet people had also achieved much including almost universal literacy and a space program that once surpassed that of the United States. The Soviets also created an empire that stretched from the Pacific Ocean to Eastern Europe. At one time it looked as though Soviet Communism might be the wave of the future.

The Russian Federation is a huge country and, along with the countries of the New Abroad (former Soviet republics), covers one sixth of the earth's land area. The land contains vast plains, mountains, deserts, taiga and arctic tundra. There are hundreds of rivers including some of the largest in the world like the Volga and Lena. Russia spans eleven time zones.

Russians are only one of many ethnic peoples who inhabit this immense territory. Over 120 different ethnic groups live in Russia and the Near Abroad. Over 100 languages are spoken and some 25 religions are practiced Although westerners tend to view Russia as one huge homogeneous mass, the opposite is true.

Natural resources are abundant including vast oil deposits, natural gas, coal, timber and metal ores. Russia has the greatest mineral wealth in the world.

Russia and the old Soviet Union produced some of the world's greatest writers, poets, composers, musicians and scientists. But she also gave birth to autocratic czars and one of the world's most ruthless and bloodthirsty tyrants.

The Soviet Union was a collection of fifteen republics that for the most part had been forcibly incorporated either by the czars or the Soviets themselves. Nationalist sentiments in many of these republics had never completely died out. For 300 years the Russian Empire had been ruled by czars, authoritarian leaders whose rule was absolute. After the last czar was overthrown the communists imposed a "dictatorship of the proletariat."

When communist extremists attempted a coup against Gorbachev in August 1991, the three Baltic States (Latvia, Lithuania and Estonia) immediately declared their independence. The coup was unsuccessful but the drive for independence continued. On September 6, 1991 the Soviet Congress officially recognized Baltic independence. Nationalists in the other republics were encouraged and grew bolder with their demands. The Soviet Union, once perceived as an indestructible monolith, was quickly dissolving.

In an effort to gain some cohesion over the inevitable dissolution, Boris Yeltsin and Mikhail Gorbachev, with leaders from Belarus and Ukraine, engineered a new confederation of republics called the Commonwealth of Independent States (CIS). Eleven former Soviet republics agreed to join the CIS, four refused. Those refusing included Latvia, Lithuania, Estonia and Georgia. Economic chaos and a brutal civil war later caused Georgia to reconsider and agree to a working relationship with the CIS.

There are about 130 million Russians living in the Russian Federation and about 26 million Russians living in the Near Abroad. In Kazakhstan, for example, Russians (37%) are almost equal in numbers to the Kazakhs (40%). Russian president, Boris Yeltsin, said he would guarantee the safety of Russians living in the new republics. When the United States sent peacekeepers to Haiti in 1994, Yeltsin sent his own peacekeepers into Moldova, Azerbaijan, Tajikistan and Georgia.

The ethnic Russian population in the countries of the Near Abroad are listed in the chart below.

Country	population (millions)	percent Russian	No. Russians (thousands)
Armenia	3.6	-.1%	neg.
Azerbaijan	7.8	6%	450
Belarus	10.5	13%	1,365
Estonia	1.7	30%	510
Georgia	5.7	6%	342
Kazakhstan	17.4	37%	6,438
Kyrghyzstan	4.8	22%	1,056
Latvia	2.8	33%	924
Lithuania	3.8	9%	351
Moldova	4.5	13%	585
Tajikistan	6.2	-1%	45
Turkmenistan	4.0	9%	360
Ukraine	52.0	22%	11,440
Uzbekistan	23.1	8%	1,848

Russians in the Near Abroad
1996 - 25,732,000. 1994 - 26,367,000 (Source: World Almanac, 1994 and 1996 plus other sources.

In some of the Near Abroad countries, Russians tend to be concentrated in certain districts. These include eastern Ukraine, the Crimea, northeast Estonia, western Moldova and northern Kazakhstan. Here, Russian language and culture dominates.

Even in Kiev, the capital city of Ukraine, Russian is the dominant language.

1-1 Mikhail S. Gorbachev, the last president and general secretary of the communist party of the former Soviet Union, 1985 - 1991. Gorbachev resigned on December 25, 1991 and the Soviet Union was dissolved the next day.

The Russian Federation's administrative districts consist of 21 autonomous republics, 49 mostly autonomous regions, 6 territories, 10 autonomous areas and two federal cities (refer to Appendix V). A region is a self-regulating district and a territory receives its directives from the central government. If it were Canada, Alberta would be a region and the Northwest Territories would be a territory. The republics are technically self-governing regions with their own legislatures creating laws for their republics.

Ethnic Russians have a low fertility rate (0.7). Under present economic conditions Russian women are reluctant to bear children. The non-Russian ethnic groups in the Federation such as the Bashkirs, Tatars, Mordva and Chuvash have high fertility rates (3.6 - 4.8). This difference in fertility rates have implications for the future.

The Russian Federation is not entirely Russian but contains numerous ethnic groups. Many of these groups have started agitating for true autonomy or in some cases independence. The Federation republics of Tatarstan and Bashkortostan have negotiated treaties with the government which gives them more autonomy. They have been able to make trade agreements with foreign countries and have been able to keep most of the revenues from the sale of resources, especially oil and natural gas.

In 1992, Chechnya, a tiny republic in the extreme south of the Russian Federation declared independence. Two years later Russian troops were sent in and a bloody civil war resulted.

Russians are returning from the Near Abroad in large numbers and returning to the Moscow region, adding to the ranks of the unemployed. For example, of the 600,000 Russians in Tajikistan in 1991, only 45,000 remained in 1995. Russia set up The Federal Migration Service in 1992 to help returnees. High inflation and decreased funding has stymied their efforts to resettle the migrants and these people have become a destabilizing social group. Many Far East citizens are also returning to the Moscow area. The return of citizens from the countries of the Near Abroad diminishes Russia's rationale for interfering in the internal affairs of those countries.

The new Russia confronts many problems besides her ethnic diversity. The high crime rate forced President Yeltsin to reinstate the secret police. The economy suffers from a huge bureaucratic payroll, corrupt government officials and a lack of economic incentives like a systematic tax code. Environmental pollution is widespread. Alcoholism is rampant. Yet, side by side with these problems, there is the emergence of a market economy and an incipient democracy.

The Soviet Union's major problems before dissolution were the war in Afghanistan, the need to import huge quantities of food, the growing democratic movement, the arms race that led to bankruptcy and the decay of the nation's roads, bridges, railroads and buildings.

1-2 Boris Yeltsin: The first democratically elected president of Russia. Elected on June 12, 1991. He was reelected to a second term July 3, 1996.

Most Westerners, like U.S. President George Bush, were surprised by the speed with which the Soviet Union broke up. But, as to what will replace the old empire remains unclear. Reform remains incomplete.

The collapse of communism and the Soviet Union and the re-emergence of Russia and the newly independent countries of the Near Abroad may turn out to be the most significant events of the twentieth century. The Soviet Union is now consigned to history. The Russia of the 21st century will be a new country whose fate has implications for the entire world.

9

DAILY LIFE

Every adult Russian carries an internal passport which is used for a variety of purposes, much like an expanded version of the Social Security Number in the United States. The internal passport consists of a photo taken at age 15 when the passport is first issued as well as address changes, occupation and military service. Photos must also be taken and affixed at ages 25 and 45.

About three fourths of the Russian population live in an urban environment (1996 - 74%). This fact dominates the political, social and economic life of the country.

Most people prefer life in the city where the jobs and services are. Few people actually choose to live in the country.

Russians now have access to a variety of consumer goods. Some are provided by American companies like Proctor and Gamble, Pepsi, Coca Cola, Levi Jeans, Ben and Jerry's Ice Cream, Microsoft, Sprint, McDonalds, Pizza Hut, Legos, Wrigleys and all brands of American cigarettes.

A McDonald's hamburger, fries and a shake cost $6.50 in 1996. A 12 oz. can of Pepsi cost 80 cents. For most Russians these are high prices.

Life In The City

Most Russians live in cities. In many cities such as St. Petersburg and Moscow there are no individual houses and everyone lives in high rise apartment buildings. Most apartments are substandard and were built in the 1960s and 1970s. Russians call them "Khrushchevskies."

An average apartment consists of two bedrooms, a small kitchen which is sometimes shared with another apartment and a bathroom shared with two to three

other apartments. In 1965, there were an average of nine people living in such an apartment. Today there are an average of six people to each two bedroom apartment. Of course, newly rich Russians (called New Russians) live under better conditions.

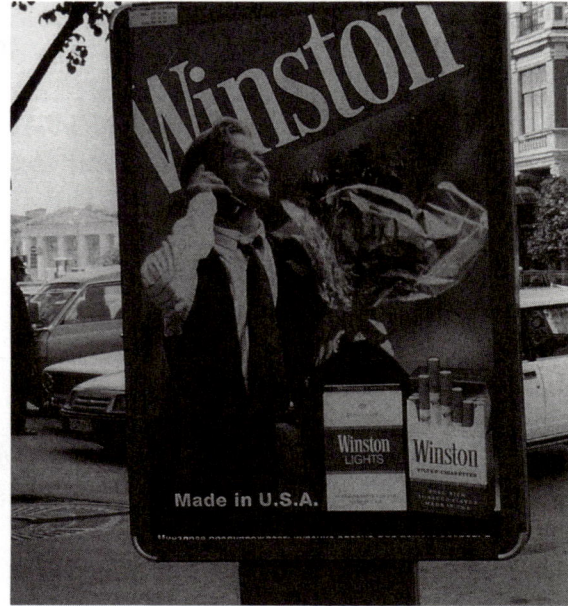

1-3 Advertisements for American cigarettes are everywhere in Russia.

It is possible for anyone with money to buy an apartment. In 1996 a two bedroom apartment in St. Petersburg was selling for $35,000. The same apartment in Kostroma sold for $30,000. At that time, the average wage of a fully employed worker was $1800 a year.

For now, most apartment dwellers pay rent to the city or federal government. If repairs are needed, the apartment dwellers must make them at their own expense. Rents are subsidized by the government. Most apartments have refrigerators, running water and television.

Russian winters are deadly cold and apartments are constructed with thick brick and block walls. New construction walls are at least 18 inches thick and some are up to

1-4 "Khrushchevskies" on the outskirts of Moscow.

three feet thick. Windows have at least a double thickness and some have triple thickness. Windows in most of Siberia are triple glazed.

Doors are thick with a high sill which prevents air and heat from leaking under the door. Public buildings usually have double doors with a high sill between. Visiting Americans find it difficult to keep from tripping on these sills.

Buildings are multi-storied and close together. Several buildings are usually connected to one central heating system. In large cities a city heating plant provides services to hundreds of apartment buildings.

Russians love dogs and on any summer evening the parks are full of apartment dwellers out walking their dogs. All breeds of dogs are found, from tiny poodles to huge mastiff hounds.

The criminal element, referred to as Mafia, has much influence on city life. They can provide goods and services more efficiently than the government. They are often involved in protection schemes and local businesses pay taxes to them instead of the government. In many cases local governments work with the Mafia.

Alcoholism is rampant and is one of Russia's biggest social problems. Vodka is very cheap. Vodka costs less than Coke or Pepsi and is cheaper than bottled water. There are more than three million registered alcoholics in Russia although the actual number is believed to be five times higher. Alcoholics who register are available for government medical assistance. Since they are known to local police they receive less harassment.

Enterprising individuals have become

11

rich through investments, restaurants, banking and buying merchandise from foreign merchants and reselling it. In the first six months of 1993 there were more top-of-the-line automobiles (Cadillacs, Rolls Royce, Mercedes etc) sold in Russia than in the rest of the world combined. However, most private cars are old and in need of repair. In 1996 there was one automobile for every 16 people in Russia. Moscow residents registered 575,000 private automobiles in that year.

Most cities are getting supermarkets which combine groceries and hard goods. They can deliver products cheaper than the conventional stores which specialize in one commodity. Products from around the world are available to those with money to purchase them. The long lines for which Russia was once notorious have disappeared.

There are still neighborhood stores in many cities which sell bakery goods, candy and snacks, beverages, cigarettes, fruits and vegetables as well as vodka. In summer, kiosks are everywhere selling ice cream,

cigarettes, soft drinks, souvenirs, baked goods, candy, fruit, flowers and paper products. Kiosks are found in many public buildings. Kiosks have not found their way into the major Metro stations but it is only a matter of time until they are there. Price fixing seems to be taking place in kiosk trade.

1-6 In summer kiosks are everywhere.

City people travel by subway (Metro), electric street cars, trolley bus, regular bus and private cars. Metro construction was perfected in Russia. The escalator leading down to the Moscow Metro is ten stories deep and the St. Petersburg Metro is fifteen stories deep.. The metro tunnels are hollowed out of solid rock. The metro is cheap and very crowded at all hours of the day.

A typical day in the city will find old women (babushkas) standing near the metro selling plastic bags, old coins, postcards, flowers, worn clothing, mushrooms or small household goods. In winter the homeless crowd into the metro despite police harassment.

Enterprising street musicians can be seen in every city. Many of these are university students who see an opportunity to

1-5 A drunk sleeps it off in St. Petersburg.

capitalize on their abilities, especially during the tourist season.

Life In The Country

Scattered between the large cities are countless villages connected by poor roads. Russia is a vast land and distances between settlements are great. Winters are long and the sun is low in the sky.

Life is much harder in the country. Unlike city apartments, rural housing is not subsidized. Most houses lack the modern conveniences found in city apartments. Income in the cities is higher because the best jobs are there. Villages often lack banks, schools, stores and medical facilities.

In the southern plain village houses are much like those found in an American small town. However, the houses have thick walls double windows and big chimneys. New plastic foam insulation has reduced wall thickness in new construction.

In the north there are log cabins as well as standard houses. Rural houses do not have running water or indoor toilets. In the larger villages (a population of five thousand or more) city water is delivered by pipeline to street intersections where residents can be seen filling containers at all hours of the day. In winter, water is obtained in one or two well heated town halls.

Some rural communities have cottage industries such as weaving, wood working, leather tooling and sewing. The long winter brings out the artist in the villager and many of them work at creating dolls, painted spoons, lacquered boxes and lacework to sell to city folk or tourists. Many rural homes have ornate window and door decorations.

Many villages are connected to the old collective farms (kolkhoz) which are now considered privatized. Most rural residents have an individual house on one-fifth acre of land and also part ownership in the former collective.

1-7 An ornate window decoration in a village east of Tver.

On each small household parcel there is always a garden. There are no lawns in rural villages. In the garden is a plastic covered green house or a low plastic covered hot bed where seedlings are started. The seedlings are then shifted to the regular garden once the weather warms. Typical gardens north of the Oka River grow cool weather crops such as cucumbers, red beets, tomatoes, onions, cabbages, carrots, garlic and potatoes. South of the Oka River watermelons and cantaloupes can be found.

Villagers often have goats living in lean-to sheds attached to their house. Cutting and drying winter hay for these animals begins as soon as grasses are high

13

1-8 A rural girl tends her flock of sheep and cattle south of White Lake.

enough to cut. Goats provide milk and meat.

Cattle and sheep are housed in communal barns, a hold-over from Soviet days. And most families have at least one milking cow in the barn.

Large farms are still run by the former managers of the collectives. A few farms are individually owned. Large farms produce sugar beets, grains, potatoes, sunflowers and meat for city markets. Many military vehicles have been diverted to these farms by the government. Enterprising villagers have been known to repaint and sell these vehicles illegally.

Getting crops to markets in the cities is very difficult. Rural roads are unpaved and almost impassable in wet weather. (For every 1,000 kilometers of rural roads, only 13 kilometers are paved.)

The large former kolkhozes are only now getting used to capitalistic practices of planning, buying seed and machinery and marketing products. Farm work is hard and entails long hours. Not many rural youths want to stay on the farm once they see their city counterparts with nice clothes, cars, television and glamour.

The Dacha

One of the great traditions of Russian culture is the dacha, a summer place in the country. Seventy-five percent of Russians live in cities and eighty percent of these have a dacha available to them. From the Black Sea to the Arctic Ocean the dacha seems to be a necessity.

The dacha is often a formerly abandoned home in a rural village or a small

14

1-9 A recently constructed dacha about 50 miles north of Cherepovets.

plot of land in a remote region accessible by train or bus. For New Russians the dacha is an expensive three story red brick structure. There are also many newly constructed medium priced wooden dachas that are of Pennsylvania Dutch design. Almost all new construction has roofs of sheet aluminum.

Many dacha owners leave the city and spend the summer tending their vegetable gardens at the dacha. The family is moved to the dacha and the wage earner joins them on weekends. Summer visitors to Russia will notice how quickly the cities empty on Fridays. People are anxious to get to their dachas for the weekend.

During the Soviet years, dachas were reserved for the communist elite. Many of these were plush estates with servants and central heating. Powerful bureaucrats had dachas in the Crimea, along the Don River and Black Sea or in the lake districts of Karelia and Belarus. Stalin had several dachas scattered around European Russia.

In small villages a dacha can be easily distinguished from the permanent village house. The permanent house has an elaborate chimney and a large stockpile of wood or coal outside. The dacha has a modest wood pile used for cooking. The dacha is not as well insulated as the permanent house and dacha owners do not raise animals for milk or meat.

Each dacha usually has an elaborate garden and orchard which provides the city owner with fresh fruit and vegetables. Cool weather crops are grown and everyone cans

1-10 An usually busy Moscow intersection on a Saturday morning in July. Where has everyone gone?

pickles and tomatoes. Herbs, garlic and spices are favorites.

Apartment buildings in April and May have green tomato plants on almost every window sill. Seeds are started in milk cartons or cans and the seedlings transferred to the country once the dacha is opened for the summer. Like the villager the dacha owner usually has a plastic covered hothouse to protect the plants from late frosts which go well into June. Sometimes these garden crops are sold in the city giving the dacha owner a little extra income.

A Personal Glimpse

It is difficult to generalize diverse peoples but sometimes a personal story can give an insight. "Ludmilla Ivanov" is an example of an urban woman. She is 32 years old and lives in a suburb of Moscow. It takes about an hour for her commuter train to reach the city and she spends another 45 minutes on trolley buses to get to her job as a cashier in a delicatessen. Even though she has a degree in geohydrology from the University of Moscow this is the best job she could find and considers herself lucky to have it. She supplements her income by working as a tourist receptionist on summer weekends. Like many Russians she finds she can make money in tourism.

She works an eight hour day at the delicatessen but sometimes longer on busy days. Her average time away from home is about twelve hours each day. She does not work weekends even though the deli is open on weekends. Her deli income averaged 40 dollars a week in 1996 but her tips from tourists can average 80 dollars per weekend.

Ludmilla has a young daughter and is divorced from an alcoholic husband. Ludmilla claims a lack of privacy in her cramped apartment created many of her domestic problems. (In Moscow, one out of every two marriages end in divorce.)

Ludmilla and her daughter live on the fifth floor of a "Khrushchevskie" with Ludmilla's grandmother, mother, father and sister. Their apartment has two bedrooms as well as a bathroom and kitchen. There is no living room. One bedroom is converted to a living room during the day.

Father works as a maintenance man for a state-run apartment complex and sister works as a chambermaid in a hotel. Sister also has a college degree. Grandmother receives 40 dollars a month pension from the government. Mother takes care of grandmother, the house and granddaughter who is in primary school.

Ludmilla and her family are fortunate. They do not have to share their kitchen or bathroom with any other family. Their combined income will probably allow them to eventually buy their apartment. There are over 500 banks in Moscow. Ludmilla may get a loan once she has saved the down payment, about twenty percent of the loan.

Sister has a boyfriend and they will get married as soon as they can work out living arrangements with his parents. When sister marries, it will reduce the amount of money available to Ludmilla's household. However, it will mean one less person in their tiny apartment.

1-11 Babushkas in a suburb of Kostroma.

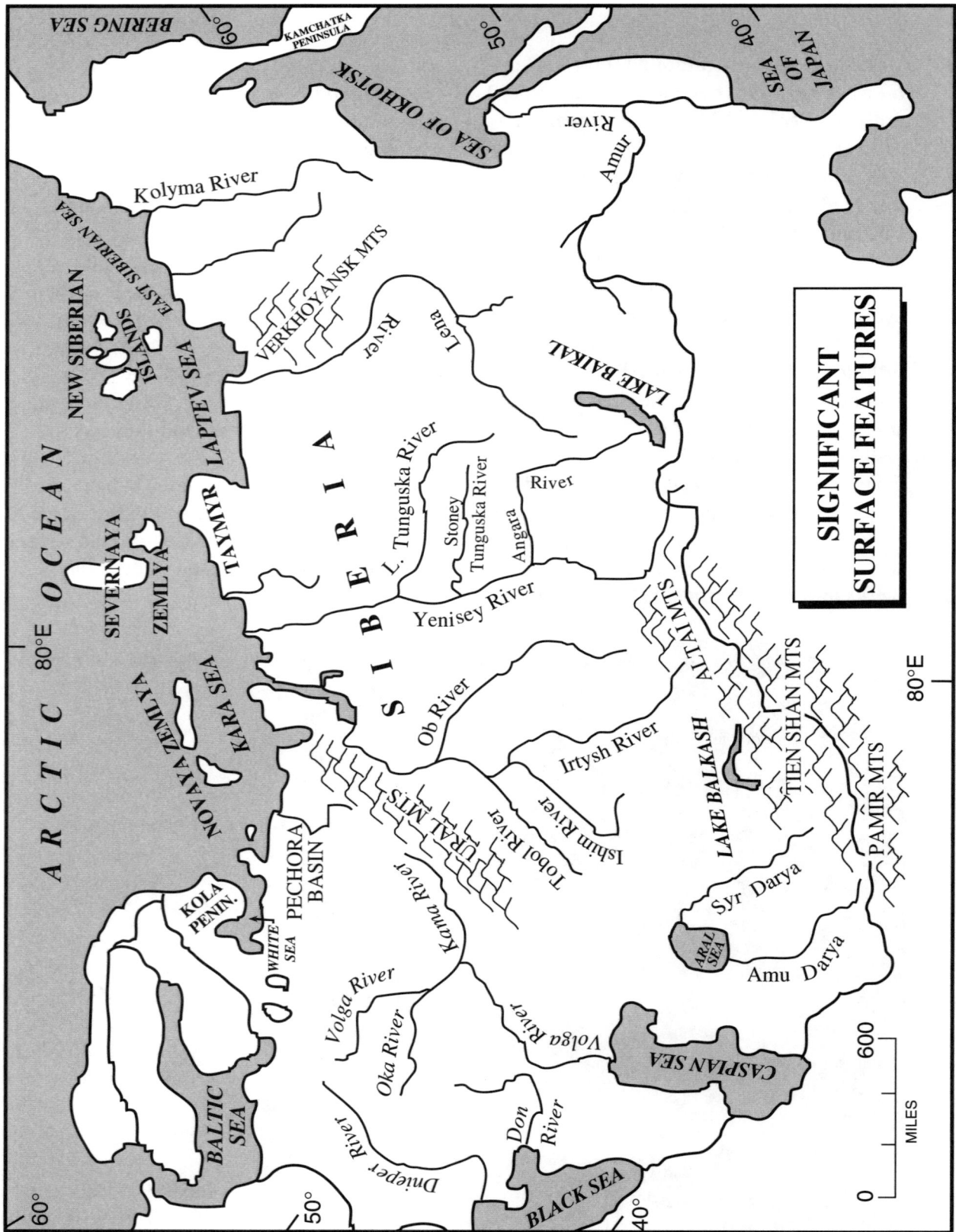

MAP 2 Significant Surface Features of Russia and the Near Abroad.

SIGNIFICANT SURFACE FEATURES

ARCTIC OCEAN

BERING SEA

KAMCHATKA PENINSULA

SEA OF OKHOTSK

SEA OF JAPAN

Amur River

Kolyma River

EAST SIBERIAN SEA

NEW SIBERIAN ISLANDS

LAPTEV SEA

VERKHOYANSK MTS

Lena River

LAKE BAIKAL

TAYMYR

SEVERNAYA ZEMLYA

S I B E R I A

L. Tunguska River

Stoney Tunguska River

Angara River

Yenisey River

KARA SEA

NOVAYA ZEMLYA

Ob River

ALTAI MTS

Irtysh River

LAKE BALKASH

TIEN SHAN MTS

KOLA PENIN.

WHITE SEA

PECHORA BASIN

URAL MTS

Ishim River

Tobol River

PAMIR MTS

Kama River

Syr Darya

ARAL SEA

Amu Darya

BALTIC SEA

Volga River

Oka River

Volga River

CASPIAN SEA

Dnieper River

Don River

BLACK SEA

80°E

60°

50°

40°

MILES

0   600

18

2. THE SOVIET UNION (USSR)

Communism lasted over seventy years in the Soviet Union. It began in 1917 with the overthrow of the last Czar, Nicholas II. Prior to the Revolution, Czars had ruled Russia for over 500 years. They were absolute rulers and dissent was not tolerated. There was a secret police system, and political dissidents were frequently arrested and exiled.

At the beginning of the 19th century, the people of Russia and those of eastern Europe were subjects of various dukes and barons who answered to the royal families. The Russian Empire was matched by the Austro-Hungarian Empire to her west and the Ottoman Empire to the south. Serfdom was the lot of the Russian peasants.

After serfdom was abolished in 1861, the lives of most peasants did not significantly improve, although some did become prosperous. Russia was still largely rural, relatively untouched by the Industrial Revolution that had transformed Europe and the United States. Russian attempts to became part of the industrial world centered around the building of railroads in the late 19th century. The Empire was finally united with the completion of the main segments of the Trans-Siberian Railroad at the beginning of the 20th century. But most of the country still remained underdeveloped and backward.

A disastrous war with Japan in 1905, along with periodic uprisings in the Empire, severely weakened the power and prestige of the Czar. This was coupled with one of the severest economic depressions in world history.

By the start of World War I (1914), the Russian economy, political system and society were in near chaos. It was only a matter of time until some well organized counter-militia would take over. The successful militia had the name of Bolshevik.

World War I ended with the defeat of the Austro-Hungarian Empire, Germany and Turkey. Their lands were split into many regions and a plethora of new countries emerged or re-emerged: Lithuania, Estonia, Latvia, Czechoslovakia, Yugoslavia and Poland.

After the Russian revolution in 1917, Vladimir Lenin, the Bolshevik leader took control. His Red Army went to the far reaches of the empire and subdued the many counter-revolutions and uprisings that were springing up. The Bolsheviks preached freedom but refused to grant freedom to the territories conquered by the czars.

Lenin organized the Bolshevik leadership into a tightly knit body. Under his guidance, the country took the first steps toward socialism. Following the writings and teachings of Karl Marx, the Bolsheviks attempted to create the ideal state where there was no class structure and each person would share equally in the benefits of productivity.

Perceived enemies, including Czar Nicholas II and his entire family, were destroyed while Lenin and other leaders mapped out the destiny of the Russian peoples and the lands that had been conquered in the past. One of the first steps was to prohibit any other political party, thus creating a single party dictatorship.

Under Lenin the move to socialism was slow. Private ownership of production continued, especially in agriculture. Peasants in the rich agricultural lands of Ukraine and Kazakhstan prospered.

While agriculture enjoyed a burst of freedom, other segments of the economy were nationalized, notably industry and mining. Trade unions were abolished.

According to Marxist philosophy, capitalist owners of industry had made huge fortunes by exploiting their workers. Marx called for revolution and rule by the proletariat (industrial workers). Workers themselves would own the industries.

What Marx had not foreseen was the rise of trade and workers unions and the power they gained through strikes and withholding of services. Workers in the west, through their unions, were able to win most of the benefits desired by Marx without resorting to revolution. With the prohibition of trade unions, the Bolsheviks eliminated one of the organizations which could have brought true socialism and democracy. Marx also did not foresee the opportunity to workers of buying individual stocks in the companies where they worked, thus giving them a stake in the industry's success (or failure). As a result, Marxism/Leninism was an anachronism almost from its inception.

2-1 Vladimir I. Lenin   Soviet leader 1917 - 1924

Lenin died in 1924. Although Lenin did not want Josef Stalin (a minor party official) to succeed him, he knew that Stalin would. Stalin went along with the policies of Lenin until he had organized a hard core of supporters.

Stalin was officially given command of the new Soviet Union in December 1927. He became a dictator who would rule Russia more cruelly than any Czar. By various maneuvers he was able to liquidate all the old Bolsheviks who had supported Lenin. Stalin ruled his inner circle with absolute terror. Lenin's communist ideal was replaced by a brutal, repressive dictatorship that would last until Stalin's death in 1953, and would influence later Soviet leaders.

Millions of people were arrested, then executed. Secret police and informers were not known, and everyone suspected everyone else of being an informer. By the time Stalin's terror was over, it was estimated that more than twenty million Soviet people had died as a result of his decrees and death sentences.

Those arrested for any reason were either shot or sent to forced labor camps. Forced labor was used to build the enormous canal projects around Moscow and the many hydroelectric installations in Siberia. If five thousand laborers were needed by the managers of a project, the word would go out and five thousand men (and women) would be arrested. Later as the Soviet Union entered into a long economic decline, the labor camp system, or *gulag*, would become the only successful, profitable part of the economy.

It seems unlikely that Stalin could have continued this brutality had it not been for World War II. Patriotic appeals to the Russian people were highly successful and cemented his authority. The Soviet people were mobilized into a great war effort. In 1941 Germany invaded the Soviet Union and advanced to the Volga River in the south but not quite to Moscow in the north.

The Red Army, after initial defeats and horrifying losses, regrouped and, aided by Allied supplies, counterattacked. The Germans were put to rout and eventually pushed back to Berlin.

After liberating Eastern Europe from Nazi Germany, the Red Army troops stayed. The "iron curtain" fell across eastern Europe and did not lift until 1989.

Stalin became more than a war hero. He became a Godlike figure, an object of intense fear and respect. Religion was outlawed by the communists and the press was strictly controlled. In this situation, the Cult of Personality was born.

2-2   Josef Stalin   (Soviet ruler 1927 - 1953)

During World War II, called the Great Patriotic War or War For The Motherland in Russia, the Soviet people responded with unparalleled effort and sacrifice. It was time for them to start enjoying the fruits of their sacrifices and their victory. Stalin responded by increasing the military budget and expanding the police state. He began an industrialization policy that ignored the consumer and the environment. Arrests continued and people disappeared into the gulag. Famous dissidents, like Andrei

Sakharov, who were too well known to be imprisoned, were exiled to remote cities.

Stalin died in 1953 and after a short skirmish for leadership, Nikita Khrushchev came to power. He had been a Soviet bureaucrat who had successfully managed the Ukraine. His success in agriculture kept food on the tables of many Soviets. Khrushchev was concerned about the quality of life for the people. He moved away from the harsh policies of Stalin and began discussing the excesses of his regime.

Khrushchev tried to ease Cold War tensions with the West. He visited the United States, the first Soviet or Russian leader ever to do so. Under Khruschchev's leadership there was an attempt to increase food supplies. He ordered the manufacture of more consumer goods, such as stoves and refrigerators. Automobiles were a top priority.

The "cult" mentality of the Russian people which made Stalin immortal began to switch to Khrushchev. This worried his jealous colleagues who had never forgiven him for caving in to President John Kennedy during the 1962 Cuban Missile Crisis. In 1964 Khrushchev was removed from power.
.   The next Soviet leader was Leonid Brezhnev, a conservative professional. Brezhnev revived Stalin's image as a war hero and increased military spending. Consumer goods virtually disappeared.

Brezhnev cracked down on dissident peoples whose numbers had grown under Khrushchev. The secret police, or KGB, was activated on a greater scale. Outspoken critics in literature, arts and science were investigated and harassed. Arrests were made and the population of the gulags increased.

Czechoslovakia, along with the rest of Eastern Europe, was considered an extension of the Soviet Empire. Czechoslovakia experimented with democracy in 1968. This episode was referred to as "socialism with a human face". The experiment was met with an invasion by the Red Army. The invasion of Czechoslovakia was followed by the invasion of Afghanistan in 1979 and led to world-wide condemnation. By 1980, the Russian people were beginning to demand more from the government.

The chronic shortages of consumer goods and continued political repression was causing widespread dissatisfaction. Communists, who made up less than seven percent of the population, simply were not delivering on early promises.

Brezhnev died in 1982 and the void was filled with old men who had no staying power. Leadership finally passed to the relatively young Mikhail Gorbachev in 1985.

It was obvious the people were in no mood to continue making sacrifices, and Gorbachev understood this. He granted more power to the people through his program of perestroika or economic restructuring and glasnost or political openness.

Glasnost demanded that government officials respond to public criticism. Anger from years of communist repression burst forth and stunned the leaders.

The Soviet constitution had technically acknowledged the republics could gain independence from the Soviet Union if they wished. Lithuania tested the waters of independence in 1989. Its efforts were met with a weak effort at intimidation. Fuel supplies were cut off to Lithuania and their major television station, the main channel of dissension, was captured by special forces of the Soviet army.

This was the beginning of the end, and by the summer of 1991 the Soviet Union was coming apart. In August 1991, the communist leadership tried to oust Gorbachev by holding him prisoner in the Crimea where he had gone to vacation. They set up an interim government but were thwarted by Boris Yeltsin, president of the Russian Republic. His association with the military made it reluctant to carry out the orders of the communist coup. Instead, the coup leaders were arrested on Yeltsin's orders and Gorbachev returned to Moscow. In all her history, Yeltsin was the first popularly elected leader of Russia

Several other republics followed Lithuania's lead and it was obvious that the Union would come apart unless the strong arm military tactics of the past were used again. The Parliament of the Soviet Union voted to end the Union on December 25, 1991. Boris Yeltsin became the president of the new Russian Federation.

Under Yeltsin's insistence, the new country of Russia began to shift from government control to private control of agriculture and industry. By New Year's Day 1994, more than a half million industries and about twenty percent of the land were in private ownership.

Russia still faces daunting challenges. Economic reform has led to high inflation and a high rate of unemployment. Capitalism and democracy are still in their beginning stages. There has been a surge of right wing nationalism that threatens the process of reform. Pollution and environmental degradation is an urgent problem. Many parts of the country seem to be controlled by organized criminals.

One of the biggest challenges facing Russia and the Near Abroad is the integration of multicultural peoples. In many republics ethnic civil wars have broken out. Former communists have been successful in several local elections. Shifting to capitalism and democracy has been uneven and even painful. Some former communist bosses still rule their regions like feudal lords.

3. THE PHYSICAL ENVIRONMENT

Russia is the largest country on earth with more than six and a half million square miles and extending through eleven time zones. The next largest country is China which is about half that size.

Russia trends east-west rather than north-south which is unfortunate climate-wise. The bulk of the country lies north of 50 degrees latitude giving most of the country an extremely cold winter and a relatively short summer.

While the broad physiographic provinces stand out plainly the subtleties within those regions are harder to delineate. A short description of the main provinces follows with more detailed analysis given later.

1. **The Russian Plain** extends from the western lowlands of the Baltic Republics east to the Ural Mountains. North-south, it reaches from the Caucasus in the south to the Barents Sea of the Arctic Ocean in the north.

The northern part was under ice during the last glaciation. The ice reached the Dnieper and Don river valleys. Glacier melting enlarged the Caspian Sea and combined it with the Aral Sea. An arm of this sea reached all the way north to the big bend in the Volga River at present-day Kazan.

Most of the region is extremely low with a highland crossing the Kola Peninsula from east to west and land somewhat higher than the plain found south and west of Moscow and along the lower reaches of the Volga River.

The bulk of the Russian Plain is drained by the Volga River and its main tributaries, the Kama and Belaya in the east and the Oka in the center. The Don River, flowing into the Sea of Azov, is an important waterway to the Black Sea. So many lakes have been created by locks and dams that the Don and Volga Rivers might be considered extensive lake systems.

Northeast of St. Petersburg there are several large lakes. Two of the largest are Lake Ladoga and Lake Onego which help to moderate the climate of this region.

2. **The Russian Caucasus** is a narrow belt of mountains in the extreme southern end of the Russian Plain. It runs from the Black Sea to the Caspian with very few low passes in it. The people who live here are closely associated with the people of the Caucasus Republics; Armenia, Azerbaijan, and Georgia.

There are two mountain ranges in the Caucasus, the Greater and the Lesser. These trend northwest to southeast. The Greater Caucasus, the highest range, is in the north. Mt. Elbrus, (18,510 ft.) in Russia, is the highest peak. The Lesser Caucasus spans the south, reaches through the three Caucasus republics, then extends into Turkey and Iran.

In Russia, the Caucasus range slopes gently to the north into Russia then falls steeply southward. The range has formed an important barrier, not only to invading armies but to important moisture laden air coming from the south.

The Caucasus ridges rise to 18,000 feet and the easiest passes through them are at 7,500 feet. The snowline is found slightly above 10,000 feet.

3. **The Ural Mountains** extend about 1500 miles north to south. It has been the conventional dividing line between Europe and Asia for centuries. In ancient times oriental people lived to the east of it and Caucasians to the west.

The northern section has the highest ranges, slightly over 5,000 feet with Mt. Naroda at 6,214 feet. The central section has many low passes and historically was the gateway to the east. It is traversed by the Chusavaya River Pass which leads to the city of Yekaterinburg, formerly Sverdlovsk, on the eastern side of the mountains.

The southern section again rises to over 5,000 feet. The Ural and Emba Rivers flow out of the southern section and find their way to the Caspian Sea. The Ural Mountains extend south into the steppe lands of Kazakhstan.

The Urals are quite low; most of them are less than 2,000 feet. They are comparable to the Appalachians of the United States.

4. **The Western Siberian Lowland** makes up the center of Russia. It extends from the Kazakh highlands to the Arctic Ocean Lowlands and from the Ural Mountains to the Yenisey River.

The southern highland is traversed by the Trans-Siberian Railroad and is the location for the most important Siberian cities - Omsk, Novosibirsk, Krasnoyarsk and Irkutsk.

The area is drained by the Ob River and its main tributary, the Irtysh. The Irtysh has two important tributaries, the Tobol and the Ishim, all originating in the highlands of Kazakhstan.

In summer the Ob River flows so slowly that in many places the water becomes warm and stagnant. Fish die for lack of oxygen.

When winter approaches, the northern waters of the Ob freeze in November and the natural ice dam which is formed causes flooding in the southern lowlands. The flooding and freezing continues until April. The Ob empties into the Obskaya Guba, a long narrow bay of the Arctic Ocean.

This is the largest flat area on earth. The relief drops only about 300 feet in almost 2,000 miles. The small pockets of highland in the north which rise above the flood waters are too remote for habitation.

There are several man-made lakes in the south. These were created when streams were dammed to create hydroelectric stations.

5. **The Central Siberian Plateau** is bounded by the Yenisey River on the west and the Lena River on the east. To the south are the Tien Shan and Altai Mountains. The southern edge is skirted by Trans-Siberian Railroad.

The plateau has been deeply dissected by the Lena and Yenisey Rivers and their tributaries. The topography is tableland with a few peaks reaching to 4,000 feet. Much of the north was glaciated.

The great bend in the Lena harbors the town of Yakutsk. The bend was created by the last glaciation when the ice sheet reached the Yakutsk Basin, a large high plain just west of the city.

The Lena's major tributaries are the Vilyuy which joins it from the west and the Aldan joining it from the east. All three are connected north of Yakutsk.

Yenisey tributaries include the Angara to the south and the two central Tunguska Rivers, the Lower Tunguska to the north and the smaller Stoney Tunguska to the south. These tributaries reach the main river from the east. Heavy population centers are located along the Angara. sometimes referred to as the Upper Tunguska.

The middle and lower Yenisey valleys are almost devoid of human habitation. Norilsk, a city of 300,000 people in the Yenisey Valley at 69 degrees north latitude is the most northern outpost in the region.

6. **The Central Asian Mountains** consist of the Tien Shan, Altai, and Sayan ranges, separating Russia from Mongolia and China. Among the eastern ranges is Lake Baikal, the deepest fresh water lake in the world. It contains as much water as all the Great Lakes combined. A large lake, the Bratsk Reservoir, was created when a

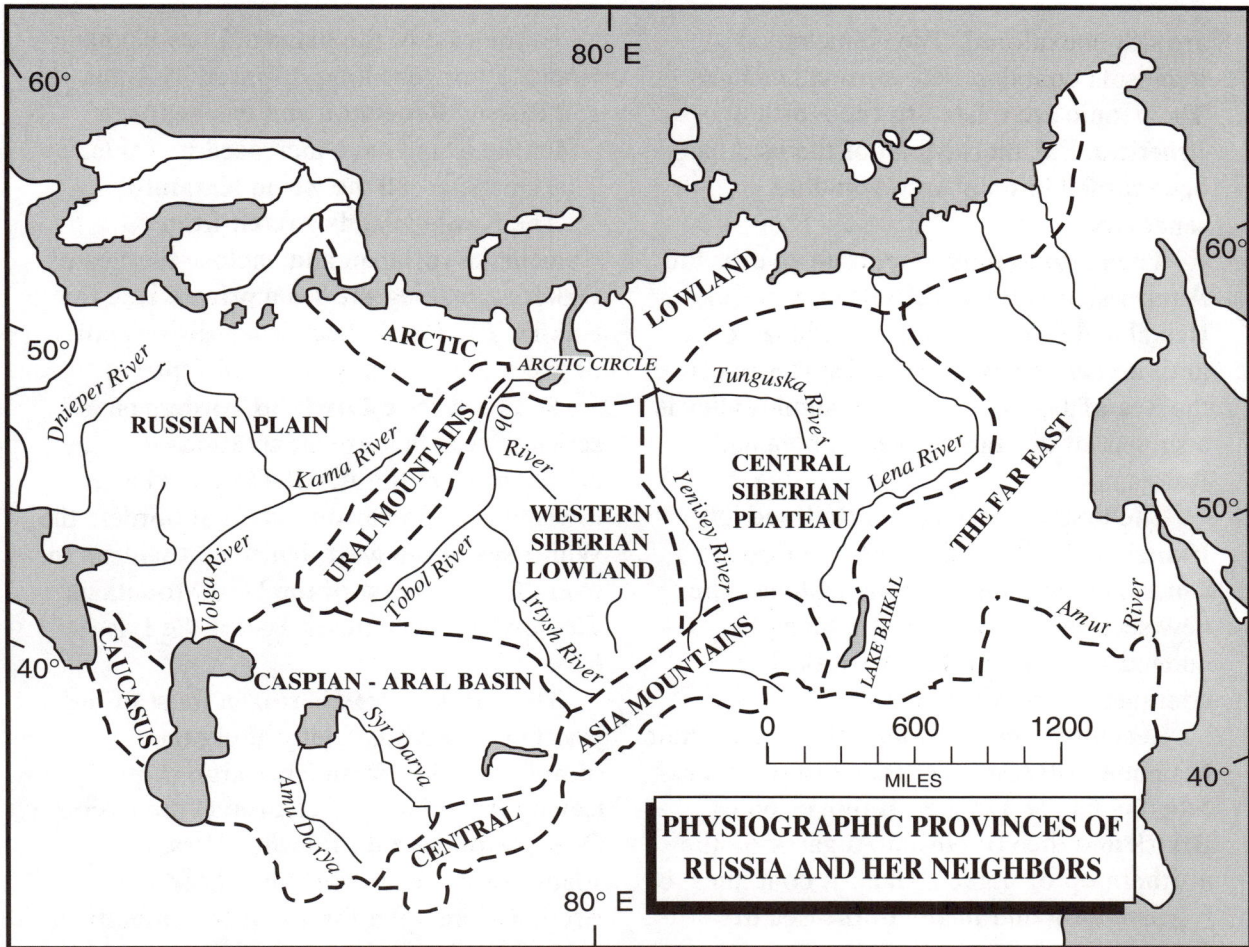

MAP 3   Physiographic Provinces

hydroelectric installation was built at Bratsk on the Angara River.

The Altai (Altay) Ranges extend into Mongolia and China. The highest peak in the Russian Altai is Belukha at 14,783 feet. Meltwaters from its ice and snow feed the Ob and Irtysh Rivers. Lake Teletskoye, with an area of 90 square miles, is the largest of more than 3,000 lakes found within the ranges. Rich mineral deposits of gold, silver, lead, mercury, zinc, copper and iron are found in the Altais.

The Sayan Mountains extend from the Lower Yenisey River to Lake Baikal. Its highest point is 11,686 feet above sea level. The Sayan forms the border between Russia and Mongolia.

The Tien Shan Mountain system extends from the Pamirs of Tajikistan north to the Altai. Its highest peak is Pobeda Peak at 24,406 feet. The Tien Shan snowline is above 11,000 feet due to its dry climate. Lake Issyk-Kul in Kyrgyzstan is one of the world's largest mountain lakes. The Syr Darya River rises from these mountains.

7. The Far East is a catch-all term for the rest of Russia. It stretches from the Lena River on the west to the Sea of Okhotsk and the Sea of Japan on the east. These connect to the Pacific Ocean.

The ranges in the Russian far east have not been totally mapped and many regions are still unexplored. The Kamchatka Peninsula contains several small villages. The people are related to the North American Eskimos. Much of the land has been turned into an Arctic wildlife sanctuary.

The region's most important river is the Amur rising in the highlands east of Lake Baikal and flowing along the China border until it veers north into the Tatar Strait of the Sea of Japan. The entire Amur Valley is a subject of dispute between China and Russia.

The first Trans-Siberian Railroad left Irkutsk and Lake Baikal, passed through Chita then continued through China. The new section is entirely in Russia and connects Chita with Khabarovsk. It continues on to Vladivostok.

Recently, a new rail line (the Baku-Amur Mainline or BAM) was added to the Trans-Siberian line at Tayshet. It moves on to Bratsk and then to Nishni-Angarsk on the northern tip of Lake Baikal. It continues to Komsomolsk and finally to the Sea of Japan at Sovetskaya Gavan.

Building the BAM forced engineers to contend with several great mountain ranges. The first after passing Lake Baikal is the Yablonovy Khrebet and the second is the Stanovoy Khrebet. A minor but formidable range was the Bureinskiy Khrebet which is just east of Komsomolsk.

The Zeya River is an important tributary of the Amur. It flows south from the Stanovoy Khrebet and joins the Amur at 50 degrees North Latitude. Its three cities, Svobodny, Zeya and Blagoveschchensk, though small, are important Far East agricultural centers.

The Zeya River valley connects to the northern Aldan River tributaries and forms an access way for the Yakut people to reach the Amur. One of the largest hydroelectric dams in the world is at Zeya.

To the east of the mainland lies Sakhalin Island, a territory long disputed by Japan and Russia. Recent oil and gas deposits under the island have increased its value. The Japanese call the island Karafuto.

The Kurile Islands stretch from Kamchatka to Japan and enclose the Sea of Okhotsk, making the sea a private lake for Russia. The Kurile Islands are also a source of friction between Russia and Japan.

8. **The Arctic Lowland** borders on a series of seas that are indentations into the continent from the Arctic Ocean. The lowland is quite narrow where it borders the White Sea in the west, but then it widens to over 200 miles east of the Ural Mountains. The lowland disappears east of the Lena River.

The Arctic Ocean is frozen most of the year but thaws out briefly along the shorelines in late summer. Cargo ships leaving the White Sea can travel the Arctic Ocean with the aid of icebreakers, to Vladivostok. Icebreakers can keep the Arctic Ocean open for about four months of the year and supplies can be brought to small coastal settlements.

There are small villages bays and inlets along the Arctic coast. At least eleven of them have more than three thousand inhabitants.

Ethnic groups living in the Arctic Lowland are the Lapps and the Komi who live west of the Urals and the Samoyeds (also known as Nentsy), who live just east of the Urals. Further east are the Yakuts, Tungus, Yukaghirs and Chukchis. These people have adapted to long daylight hours in summer and virtually no daylight hours in winter. They are related to North American Eskimos.

Novaya Zemlya, consisting of two main islands, lies off the Arctic Lowland. These are geologic extensions of the Ural Mountains. Two other important island

3-1 The Arctic Lowland

groups are the Severnaya Zemlya, north of the Yenisey River mouth, and the New Siberian Islands, northeast of the Lena River delta.

Novaya Zemlya (New Land) was an important coal fuel depot at the time ships used coal as fuel. More recently it was used for nuclear testing. The waters off its east coast were used as a dumping ground for spent nuclear fuel. The water is highly contaminated and has caused world-wide concern.

The Arctic Lowland receives the sluggish waters from the great rivers of Siberia - Ob, Yenisey and Lena. The interfluves, land between the rivers, seldom rise above thirty feet. When the spring thaws occur, the entire area is under water. Most of the small settlements are situated on high rocky ground and away from the river.

9. **The Caspian - Aral Basin** occupies an area once covered by a giant sea during the Ice Age. It is not in Russia. The northern fringe of the region is an area of slight relief-the Kazakh Uplands. It separates the waters flowing north into the Ob River and then to the Arctic Ocean from the interior drainage to the Aral Sea. The Syr Darya and Amu Darya empty into the Aral.

The interior basin is a region of desert steppe and sandy desert. Desert climate characterizes the entire region and the vegetation is xerophytic except for irrigated areas along the Syr Darya and Amu Darya Rivers.

Two large deserts are separated by the Amu Darya River. To the north is the Kyzyl-Kum (Qyzylqum) or red sands desert and to the south is the Kara-Kum (Garagum) or black sands desert. These deserts are dry alluvial plains with scattered sand dunes throughout. January temperatures average 17 degrees Fahrenheit and July temperatures 92 degrees F. Daytime temperatures stay above 100 degrees for almost all of July and August.

The Aral Sea is now a mere shadow of its former self because of heavy irrigation. The maximum Aral depth is 180 feet but its average depth is only 35 feet. Twenty five years ago it was 225 feet deep. Since 1940 the Aral has lost 60 percent of its volume. The water table for a one hundred mile radius was severely affected by this drop in water level. The dry lake bed has been the source of salty dust storms which has caused havoc to nearby villages.

Lake Balkash (Balqash) in the eastern end of the basin is located on a plateau extending down from the mountains. It is a shallow lake with a maximum depth of 60 feet. Its western end is fresh water, fed from a mountain river and its eastern end is saline due to intense evaporation. (Climate data for the city of Balkash, located north of the lake, is given in appendix IV).

The Russian Rivers

Getting large amounts of goods, people and material from one place to another is a necessity of modern society. Since early times, Russia has had excellent rivers on which to do this. The development of the country has been east-west and most of the rivers flow north-south and many historians and geographers have presented this as a handicap. However, many rivers trend east-west and these have been a major focal point of development. This has also facilitated the development of canals. Such important east-west rivers include the Oka, Upper Volga, Western Dvina, the three Tunguskas and the Amur.

The problems with river navigation has not been the direction of river flow but the length of the season. North flowing rivers freeze for seven months of the year and when they do thaw, subsequent flooding halts traffic. Runoff is rapid due to permafrost. In summer, precipitation is scant and the water levels are diminished making shipping hazardous. By damming the rivers, navigation has been enhanced, but this has caused problems with water levels in landlocked seas such as the Caspian and Aral. Dams also prevent rivers from flushing out pollution.

3-2 Ice breaker in the Arctic Ocean.

4. VEGETATION AND CLIMATE

Vegetation zones are indicators of soil and climate conditions. Vegetation and climate have a direct impact on a region's settlement patterns and agricultural.

1. The Tundra is a cold forbidding landscape stretching along the Arctic Ocean from Finland to the Pacific Ocean. Tundra implies both vegetation and climate. Most of the year the average monthly temperature is below the freezing point. Winters are long and very cold. Summers are short; the warmest month might see just one day with temperatures reaching 60 degrees Fahrenheit. The average monthly temperature does not exceed 50 degrees F. .

The Russian tundra is a treeless plain lying along the Arctic Ocean and extending south along the Pacific to the neck of the Kamchatka Peninsula at 60 degrees North. However, it is mainly within the Arctic Circle.

Beneath the tundra and under much of the land south of it there is **permafrost** or permanently frozen sub-soil. This frozen ground prevents root development. During the brief summer most of the land is covered with pools of water which further inhibit plant development. Permafrost prevents the sparse rainfall from infiltrating into the earth. This creates a floating surface which can turn into a sea of mud when humans and animals tread on it.

Even when the temperature rises, permafrost ground does not thaw except for a few inches at the surface. Precipitation is scant but evenly distributed throughout the year. In a good year rainfall total may reach 12 inches. This is enough to bring tundra plants to life - lichens, mosses and low flowering grasses. In the southern portions of the tundra there are some dwarf willows and birches but these seldom grow over 12 inches high.

Tundra animals include caribou, fox and arctic hare. Polar bears are rare. Summer insects are numerous, feeding a large population of migratory birds that come to the tundra to feed and breed.

The few human settlements have valiantly tried to engage in agriculture, and in some seasons barley and millet can be raised. However, most food has to be shipped into tundra settlers. Native Eskimo, Komi, Nentsy, Evenki, Samoyeds, Yentsi, Yakuts and Lapp peoples are self-sufficient and live off the reindeer, much as their ancestors did. Reindeer are a type of caribou.

Some experiments with greenhouse vegetables have been successful, but it is unlikely large numbers of people can be sustained this way. Greenhouses are products of man-made soils and delicate engineering. Biotechnology might offer help in the future.

The tundra is an extremely fragile environment. Footprints on it may last as much as fifty years. For an example of the tundra climate refer to Novaya Zemlya's temperature and precipitation data in Appendix IV.

2. The Taiga (Tayga) is a region of dense trees and possibly the largest extent of a single forest on earth. It covers about half of Russia. Much of the taiga is coniferous.

The taiga is bordered on the north by tundra and on the south by a mixed forest of broadleaf and coniferous trees with broadleaf dominating. It reaches to 53 degrees North in the Urals and covers most of Siberia.

Taiga is created by a continental climate where winters last from six to seven months. The growing season is short although summer temperatures in the Siberian taiga have been recorded at 90 degrees F. in July

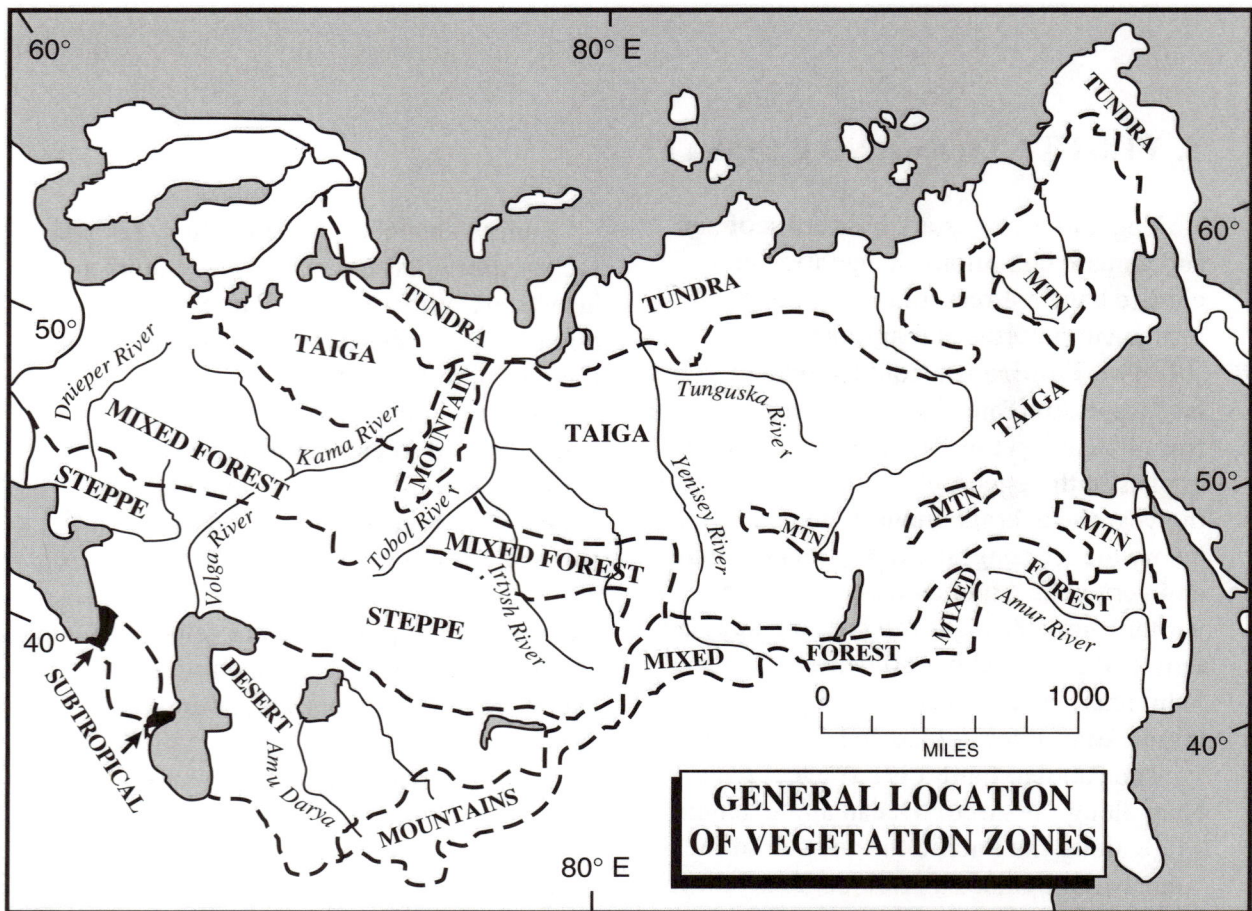

MAP 4 The Natural Vegetation Zones

and August. Day temperatures might be high but there is a quick chilling at night and frosts are common, even in July.

Podzols, or gray earths, are the soils. Barley, oats and potatoes are grown in the southern areas of the taiga. Agriculture is at best a risky enterprise.

Taiga trees are cedar, spruce, pine and larch with some aspen and birch intermixed in the southern portions. In spring, much of the forest floor is covered with water and transportation is difficult.

The taiga in European Russia has been extensively cut-over from St. Petersburg on the Baltic to Perm on the slopes of the Urals. This area once had an abundance of good fur bearing animals such as mink and ermine. These animals have mostly disappeared along with the forest and in their place are fox, squirrel and some hares.

Except for scattered mining camps most of the taiga is uninhabited. An agreement between the Buryat people who live east of Lake Baikal and Japanese lumber interests was made in 1993. Most logging is carried on in winter. Commercial logging has resulted in overcutting in some parts of the eastern taiga. Overcutting has already caused ecological problems in the Asian taiga. Taiga trees do not readily reproduce themselves. The weather is cold making seed germination difficult. Summer flooding drowns out seedlings. Attempts at growing seedlings in nurseries and transplanting them when they have reached sufficient size have proved expensive. The seedlings simply do not adjust readily to the poor soils and harsh climate.

3. The Mixed Forest lies south of the taiga. It begins just south of St. Petersburg and extends into northern Ukraine and westward to Novosibirsk. Although the

30

forest west of the Volga is large, it becomes a narrow belt toward the Urals and into the southern end of the Siberian Lowland. There is another patch of mixed forest along the Amur River. Forest vegetation consists of oak, linden, fir, boxwood, spruce, birch, ash and maple. Low vegetation here is similar to that of the American Great Lakes region. Wild plants include dandelion, dock, thistle, burdock, colt's foot, red clover, daisy, lamb's quarters, yarrow, plantain, buttercup, wild mustard and black berries.

As the mixed forest was cut over the soil was put to the plow. Leaves from deciduous trees have added humus to the soil and made them fertile. However, the soil fertility is being depleted and chemical fertilizer use has created some serious environmental problems.

The mixed forest is sometimes referred to as the southern taiga, but the mixed forest region receives more precipitation than taiga and its soils are more fertile. The mixed forest is a transition zone between trees and grassland.

4. The Steppe is a vast grassland separating the mixed forest from the desert. This is the area of **chernozem** or black earth soils. Chernozems are the most desirable soils on earth. They have high fertility and excellent texture.

Steppe weather is cold in winter and hot in summer. Precipitation is less than 20 inches annually in the best location and around 10 inches in the worst.

Steppe is a temperate grassland with trees in stream valleys. The steppe stretches from the Danube River in the west to the Altai Mountains of Asia in the east.

In Russia, the steppe consists of three vegetation zones due to differences in climates: wooded steppe, grassland steppe and semi-desert or desert steppe. Obviously, the differences are due to precipitation.

4-1 Snow removal in Moscow's Red Square. Moscow receives about sixty inches of snow in winter.

The wooded steppe in the northernmost region has deciduous trees with close to twenty inches of precipitation. Grassland steppe has the chernozem soils and precipitation reaching fifteen inches. The semi-desert or desert steppe is suitable for limited grazing. With irrigation, the desert steppe is very productive. Its soils vary from chestnut to brown.

Grassland steppe is most desirable for tilling. It is found in Moldova and Ukraine and stretches across the lower Volga into Kazakhstan.

As the forest begins to dwindle due to the limited precipitation in the southern plain, it gives way to wooded steppe, called lesostep in Russia. This is an area of clusters of trees, separated by wide expanses of grassland.

Wooded steppe in turn gives way to classic steppe- excellent grasses with some trees found in stream valleys. In the south, the chernozem soils give way to chestnut and brown.

Further south, the classic steppe gives way to desert steppe. This grassland is brown most of the year but turns green with the light summer rains and the return of the sun. Wild horses and antelopes were once numerous on the desert steppe. Today sheep and goats are the dominant animals.

Maize is the dominant crop which is grown on about one third of the steppe in Ukraine. Further east, wheat is grown. The southern Ural steppe supplies most of Russia's wheat.

In southern Siberia and Kazakhstan the steppe has separate names. The Ishim Steppe is found along the river by that name. The Baraba Steppe is centered around Omsk and the Kulunda Steppe is around Barnaul. Of the three, the Kulunda Steppe has the best climate and soils.

5. The Desert is not found in Russia except for a few areas near the Mongolian border. However, desert makes up a large part of the Central Asian Republics.

As rainfall decreases in the south, the desert steppe gives way to absolute desert. Vegetation becomes scarce and only drought resistant varieties can survive.

Desert soils called **sierozem**, need irrigation in order to be productive. Some desert fringes in Kazakhstan have produced wheat crops without irrigation but this is too risky to be practical.

The desert encompasses an area from the Caspian Sea to the base of the Tien Shan and Pamir Mountains. Americans tend to look on the desert as a hostile environment, but thousands of Central Asian peoples have lived on it for centuries, developing a unique nomadic way of life based on the raising of sheep, goats and camels.

Desert people have learned to follow the rains. When rains occur, they move their livestock to that area. After the rains, wild flowers and grasses spring forth.

6. Other Vegetation Zones include small semitropical areas along the Black Sea coast in western Georgia and Russia's Kuban region. Tea, tobacco, lemons, oranges, pomegranates, rice and other sub-tropical plants grow here.

Other **sub-tropical** patches include the Caspian coast of Azerbaijan and the southern tip of the Crimea. Rainfall on the Caspian is not as heavy as the Black Sea so less crop variety is found here.

Mountain vegetation is unique since it has vertical zonation of plants. Mountain zones include the Caucasus, the Urals, the zone from Tajikistan to Lake Baikal and several high areas of the Far East. The windward side of the mountains is moist and the leeward side dry. The high mountains, with snow and ice cover, supply streams which flow into the valleys and support agriculture and people.

Climate data are given in Appendix IV.

5. A BRIEF HISTORY

The Baltic region was inhabited at least three thousand years ago, the Caucasus at least eight thousand and the central Russian Plain at least two thousand years ago. To trace the history of these people and the lands they occupy would be an enormous undertaking and beyond the scope of this work. Therefore, the history presented here is a selection of events that influenced modern Russia.

In ancient times the land along the Dnestre and Dnieper Rivers was inhabited by Slavic tribes who lived off the land by hunting, gathering, fishing and trapping. Scandinavian Vikings used the Russian Plain as a crossroads. They traded with Finno-Ugrian peoples who migrated from the central mountains of Asia.

A series of nomadic people (Persians, Mongols, Turks and Germanic Goths) came from the southern areas into the lower Volga lands. In the 7th century, the region was controlled by Turkish Avars. During that same century they were overrun by the nomadic Khazars who ruled the steppes well into the 10th century. Their dominions stretched from the Black Sea to the Ural Mountains and along the Volga River to present day Kazan.

The Slavic people moved further north into what is now Belarus. They were influenced by the Scandinavian Vikings in the region who were also known as Varangians or Rus. These Varangians traded along the river and lake routes and built small settlements along Lake Ilmen, the Western Dvina, Lake Ladoga and the Dnieper. By the end of the 8th century Viking traders had made connections with the Byzantine Empire centered at present-day Istanbul. The Varangian Rus dominated the Slavic tribes and organized them into small principalities. The main leader of this loose federation was Rurik. Two of their chief city centers were at Novgorod on Lake Ilmen and Smolensk on the Dnieper. These rivers formed a water route from Sweden to the Black Sea.

At the end of the 9th century the Rus had settled in Kiev, an excellent city site on the Dnieper. Here the forest met the steppe and trade from both areas was advantageous. Oleg, the Scandinavian leader of Kiev, united Kiev with the northern cities of the Rus domain. Kiev, due to its superior trading position, became the cultural center for the Slavs.

The Vikings were later absorbed by the Slavic groups, and ultimately the region became Slavic in custom and culture. Slavs traded furs, wax, salt, honey, hides, hemp and slaves. Kiev was the "Mother of All Russian Cities". It's history as a Slavic city began in 482 A.D.

Kiev, on the western edge of the great steppe plain, was an easy target for nomadic horsemen who wandered in groups among the grasslands. The vulnerability of Kiev led the Slavic peoples to rely more on their northern outposts than on Kiev. In the middle of the 13th century there was a great migration north from Kiev to Novgorod and the new region of Muscovy. In the seclusion of swamps and forest, new, stronger principalities began to form. Moscow princes were able to take control of Muscovy and strengthen their hold on it.

The armies of Genghis Khan, or the Golden Horde, had conquered much of Asia and Eastern Europe in the 13th century. Their holdings extended westward through Kiev all the way up the Danube River to Hungary. While Kiev Rus was under Mongol control Moscovy Rus went into isolation.

5-1 The ancient walled city of Novgorod

Due to isolation of the various Rus groups the Slavic language evolved into "white" Russian (Belorussian), "little" Russian (Ukrainian) and "great" Russian (Moscow area).

To the west of Moscow lay the Baltic lands controlled by the Germanic Teutonic Knights. In the 15th century the Letts and Lithuanians were able to overcome the Knights and establish control over their own territories as well as that of the western Slavic peoples near their region. These Baltic peoples were later taken into the principality of Poland (1569).

Moscow emerged as the leader of all the Rus peoples under Ivan The Great (Ivan III) who ruled from 1462 to 1505. At the beginning of his rule Novgorod was the principal Rus city. By the end of Ivan's rule momentum had shifted to Moscow. Ivan III was the first ruler to be called Czar (Tsar). a shortened Slavic form of the Roman "Caesar."

Under the rule of Ivan the Terrible (Ivan IV 1547 - 1584) the Mongol (Tatar) hold was broken and a period of unsteady cooperation began between Moscow and Kazan. Ivan IV won a decisive victory over the Tatars at Kazan in 1552. This was followed by the defeat of Bulgars at Astrakhan in 1556. However, the Crimea Tatars were numerous and well armed and they kept the Russians from the Black Sea. Ivan IV created a new land holding Aristocracy whose position was based on service to the Czar. Beginning in 1581

34

laws were passed prohibiting the free movement of the peasant tenants who farmed the lands. During the reign of Peter I the peasants became bound to the landowner rather than the land. They became virtual slaves, much like black slaves in the American south. Serfdom reached its peak under Catherine II.

At the time of Catherine The Great (II), the noble landowner could sell serfs or settle debts by transferring them. The entire peasantry was enslaved - about 34 percent of the total population. Some landowners permitted their serfs to operate small industries such as flour milling and lumbering but such enterprises were officially in the landowner's name.

Eventually the majority of Russians began to criticize the system. The serfs were finally freed by Alexander II in 1861, two years before President Lincoln issued the Emancipation Proclamation in the U.S. that finally freed the black slaves.

During the reign of the two Ivans, Ukraine became heavily populated with Russian serfs as well as Poles who were escaping the tyranny of dukes and barons and seeking a better life. Many of them joined Khazar groups and became known as cossacks, the renowned fierce horsemen of the steppes. These *kazaki* were not the Kazakh of Kazakhstan but a different group related to the Slavs.

The cossacks concentrated around Kiev and the Dnieper. Becoming frontier soldiers in the armies of the Czars, they protected Rus from Turkic and Persian invaders to the south. As a reward, they were given their own autonomous district by the Czar. Later, Stalin took the district away from them. Today they want it back.

Under Ivan IV traders and trappers headed east into the Urals and Siberia. They traveled freely to the Arctic Ocean, setting up small forts and trading posts along the way. Periodic conflicts erupted with the Tatars who considered these lands a part of their kingdoms. Russian traders moved along the southern fringes of Siberia, the path later taken by the TSR.

It took one hundred years after the rule of Ivan IV for Russian traders to reach the Pacific in 1647. The biggest opposition came from the Mongol Buryats, east of Lake Baikal. They were defeated in a series of skirmishes beginning in 1641. Treaties with China in 1689 acknowledged Russia's right to the Pacific Coast. The final closing of the Pacific Territory with China came in 1860 when China gave up its claims to the Amur River valley and the coast up to Vladivostok. In 1867 the United States purchased all Russian claims to Alaska for 7.2 million dollars.

Peter the Great (Peter I, 1682 -1725) forcibly turned Russia away from the East and westward toward Europe. He proclaimed Russia an Empire, visited England and spent much time studying ships and sailing there. Under his rule Russia emerged as a leading European power.

5.2 Czar Peter The Great, Founder of Modern Russia (ruled 1682 - 1725)

Sweden was the power that blocked Russian advancement along the Baltic and Arctic coasts. Peter was able to defeat the Swedes and gain uninhibited access to these waters. He ordered the building of St. Petersburg on the Gulf of Finland and moved his government there in 1713. It remained the capital of the Empire until 1918 when the Czar was overthrown in the Bolshevik Revolution, and the capital returned to Moscow.

One of the outstanding leaders of Russia was Czarina Catherine the Great (Catherine II, 1762 - 1796). She concentrated her armies and empire expansion on the Black Sea. The Byzantine Empire had been replaced by the Ottoman Turks who were overpowered by the Russians. The Russians took the Crimea as well as the important port city of Odesa. Soon the entire northern Black Sea coast was in Russian hands.

5-3   Catherine the Great (ruled 1762 - 1796)

Catherine's armies moved into the Caucasus and overpowered the strongholds of Baky, Yerevan and Tbilisi. Her troops expanded westward and took over Poland. In 1804 they took Finland from Sweden.

During most of the 19th century, Russia spent much of her military strength subduing the Mongol horseman and other peoples of Central Asia. Assimilating this territory brought Islam to Russia.

Conflict emerged between Russia and Imperial Japan which was starting to flex its muscles in international affairs. China, preoccupied with its own internal problems, had agreed to let Russia build the Trans-Siberian Railroad (TSR) across Manchuria to the Sea of Japan. Japan saw this as a threat and the treaties between China and Russia led to the 1905 Russo-Japanese War. To the world's surprise, Czarist Russia was defeated easily and Japan took possession of southern Sakhalin Island. Russia was humiliated. This was her first defeat since the days before Ivan III, and seriously weakened Czar Nicholas II and his government.

Ten years later World War I broke out. Although Russia's initial response was enthusiastic, the war quickly turned into a nightmare for the country. Among other hardships, the war showed the weakness and inefficiency of the Czarist system. Many also thought the corrupt monk, Rasputin, had an undue influence on the monarchy. When Nicholas II refused to make a separate peace with Germany, his fate was sealed. After a series of uprisings and revolts, he was forced to abdicate. He was murdered, along with his entire family, on July 16, 1918.

For a brief time Russia was a democracy, but once again revolution broke out and the Bolsheviks seized power. In 1917, after 500 years, Imperial Russia came to an end and a new country was born - The Union of Soviet Socialist Republics. The Russian Federation, with all her achievements and problems, is a product of both her Czarist and communist legacies.

5-4 Garish buildings and grounds of the Czar's summer palace at Peterhoff (Petrodvorets), twenty miles south of St. Petersburg.

The Monastery

Monasteries are found scattered throughout the Great Russian Plain and into Siberia. Although Soviets suppressed religion, the monasteries survived and are valuable tourist attractions today. The Trinity Monastery, northeast of Moscow, had more than three million visitors in 1995. The first monasteries were constructed in the 12th century. These are mostly gone. Those built during the 15th and 16th centuries still remain. Soviets destroyed many monasteries or used them for storage and other purposes. Some of the more elaborate monasteries were preserved since they were designated as museums.

Some exceptionally well preserved monasteries are the Trinity Monastery at Sergiyev Posad (formerly Zagorsk) northeast of Moscow, Ipatyevsky Monastery at Kostroma, the Kirillo Belozersky Monastery south of White Lake and the Monastery of the Transfiguration at Yaroslav. There are also many well preserved convents throughout the Great Plain. Excellent examples of convents can be found in Goritsky and Moscow.

Monasteries served as stopping places for travelers and places of refuge for royalty. They were walled cities. Many of them had moats and all were protected by armed soldiers. Monks of the Orthodox faith maintained the monasteries and the elaborate churches within them.

Buildings and grounds were constantly added to the monastery. For instance, the first building at the Kirillo Belozersky

5-5 One outer wall containing monastic chambers at the 15th century Monastery of St. Cyril of the White Lake. (also Kirillo - Belozersk)

Monastery south of White Lake was started in 1487 and the last in 1782.

Many monasteries were used as prisons for royalty who fell into disfavor with the ruling Czar. Almost every convent held within their confines some royal woman who was forced to take the veil. Ivan the Terrible forced his sister-in-law to do so at the Resurrection Convent in Goritsy.

Michael Romanov was hiding at the Ipatyevsky Monastery in Kostroma when he was notified that he had been elected Czar by the **boyars** which were wealthy merchants who ran the country along with the Czar and his family.

Czars and Czarinas poured money into their favorite monasteries. Ipatyevsky Monastery had 55,000 acres of land and 17,000 serfs and more than 70 villages under their control at the end of the 17th century. Monasteries were the wealthiest institutions in Russia up to the Bolshevik Revolution.

The priests and prelates had great influence and power over the rulers of the country. Ivan the Terrible was not permitted in the church and was forced to listen to proceedings from a specially constructed balcony outside the church. Ivan had been married seven times.

Most monasteries operating today are understaffed and a great recruitment drive is underway to find new initiates. Many of the monasteries are still owned by the federal government which recognizes their economic value and is reluctant to return them to the Orthodox Church. Three million foreign visitors at three dollars a head is a lot of money.

6. PEOPLE AND CULTURE

More than 130 ethnic groups live in Russia. Russians are the most numerous at about 132 million out of a total population of 150 million. However, the percentage of Russians in the population has been steadily declining. Second are the Tatars who once dominated the region from the Middle Volga to the Crimea. Ethnic groups living in the Russian Republic with over one million individuals in 1991: Russians 132 million, Tatars 7.0, Germans 2.0, Chuvash 2.0, Jews 1.6, Poles 1.6, Bashkirs 1.6 and Mordvinians 1.3.

These numbers remained constant in 1995 except for Germans who decreased to about one million due to emigration to the unified Germany, and Jews who were about 800,000 in 1995 due to emigration to Israel and the United States.

Other ethnic groups in the Near Abroad with populations over one million are Ukrainians 46.5, Belorussians 10.2, Kazakhs 8.3, Azeris 6.7, Armenians 5.6, Georgians 5.2, Tajiks 3.6, Moldavians 3.6, Lithuanians 3.3, Turkomen 3.1, Kyrgyz 2.9, Latvians 1.7 and Estonians 1.4. Although most of this number reside in their individual republics, many of them are also in Russia. There are 26 million Russians living in the 14 other republics.

Internal Republics

The Russian Federation has 21 internal republics, many populated by non-Russians. The following list identifies the internal republics and their approximate location. The spelling is taken directly from official translations of the Russian Constitution. **Adygeya** - northern foothills of the Greater Caucasus. **Altai** - borders on the northeast corner of Kazakhstan. **Bashkortostan** - between Middle Volga River and the Ural Mountains. **Buryatia** - bordering on the eastern shore of Lake Baikal. **Chechen** - in Caucasus Mountains north of Georgian border. **Chuvash** - on the western bank of the Middle Volga. **Daghestan** - west of the Middle Caspian Sea. **Ingush** - west of Chechen. **Kabardin-Balkar** - north of Caucasus Mountains. **Kalmykia-Khalmg Tangch** - northwest along the Caspian Sea. **Karachai-Circassian** - Greater Caucasus along the Kuban River. **Karelia** - borders on Finland. **Khakassia** - northern border of Altai Republic. **Komi** - north Russian Plain, west of Ural Mountains. **Maril El** - north bank of Volga, north of Kazan. **Mordovia** - north bank of Volga, north of Nizhny Novgorod. **North Ossetia** - just north of central Caucasus. **Sakha (Yakutia)** - Lena River to the Arctic Ocean. **Tatarstan** - Middle Volga, Kazan is its capital. **Tuva** - borders on Mongolia. **Udmurtian** - west of Urals, between Kama and Vyatka Rivers.

6 - 1 Komi Women

Languages

The Slavic family of languages dominate the Russian Plain and extend along the TSR all the way to the Pacific Ocean. Because of Russification programs undertaken by the Soviets and the Czars, Russian is still the second language in most of the Near Abroad republics despite the dissolution of the Soviet Union. In Ukraine, Russian is the language of business and everyday conversation in Kiev.

Northern peoples in the western Tundra speak a Finnish-Uralic tongue. The Caucasus has about thirty different languages. For instance, the languages of Georgia include Circassian, Kabardinian and Abkhasian. The Armenians have their own distinct language while the Azeris speak a tongue closely related to that of the Turks.

In the Baltic region Estonian is closely related to Finnish while Latvians and Lithuanians speak an ancient form of Slavic. Many Lithuanians speak Polish as a second or first language.

Altaic languages are spoken in the mountains just north of the Chinese and Mongolian borders as well as to the frozen far northeast. A distinct tongue, the Paleosiberian, has been identified in the Kamchatka Peninsula, and in areas just north of it. This is an isolated region with less than ten thousand people. It's possible the early ancestors of the native Americans might have spoken a similar language.

Religions

The Soviets not only discouraged religion but periodically outlawed it. However since 1991, there has been a religious rebirth. The Eastern Orthodox faith dominates with its various offshoots of Russian, Armenian, Greek and Ukrainian. It is found in the Russian Triangle from St. Petersburg to Rostov extending east to Vladivostok. The Evangelical Lutheran faith dominates in Estonia and Latvia.

Islam dominates in the central Asia Republics and Azerbaijan. Islamic peoples have the highest birth rates (see Appendix VI). The third largest religion is Roman Catholic which is found in Lithuania, Belarus, Moldova and western Ukraine. Some of the recent ethnic strife may be traced to differences in religion, such as the conflict between Christian Armenia and Islamic Azerbaijan.

After the Soviet Empire dissolved a flood of Evangelical Protestant missionaries descended on many of the republics. Their zeal was overwhelming and the Orthodox, Lutheran and Roman Catholic clergy panicked, lest they should lose some of their newly gathered flock. Although these new groups were welcomed at first, once they started winning converts on a large scale, they became a serious threat. Russia, Estonia and Ukraine passed legislation curtailing the activities of the evangelists. Evangelist television programs, successful in the United States, have been restricted or banned outright.

In 1993 Russian lawmakers voted to ban foreign missionaries from proselytizing on Russian soil. This was an amendment to Russia's new law on freedom of religion. It applied specifically to foreigners and banned missionary work, publishing, business deals and advertising. The move was strongly backed by the Russian Orthodox Church which in 1993 claimed 60 million members.

The Mormons once had an active team of missionaries around Moscow, and the Hari Krishnas were once quite visible on the streets of Moscow and St. Petersburg.

In 1996 the Russian Orthodox Church officially refused to recognize the Church at Constantinople (Istanbul) as their superior. This is the prelude to a complete break with other groups of Eastern Orthodoxy.

6-2 An Orthodox priest gives the Eucharist to children. The Orthodox Church survived 70 years of harassment by the communist government. Today, religion is having phnomenal growth.

Education

Public education was one of the Soviet Union's greatest achievements. Under the Soviet system, education was free from primary school to the university level. As a result, literacy is over 90 percent in the fifteen republics. In Ukraine and Russia, literacy is 99 percent. In the other republics literacy in Russian is fairly high with more than fifty percent having proficiency. Many are also proficient in English which school students in large cities are required to study.

The quality of education in Turkmenistan, Uzbekistan, Tajikistan and Azerbaijan has declined since the dissolution of the Soviet Union. More children are put in the labor force in these countries which deprives them of education. In Georgia and Armenia, education has been severely interrupted by armed conflicts.

Many of the newly independent republics considered the Cyrillic Alphabet as part of Russian domination. After independence many republics passed laws making their own language the official language along with the Latin Alphabet.

Generally, Russian children can still get free education through high school and many go on to the university. With the collapse of the Soviet police state, Russian students are now free to study in foreign countries. The fastest growing numbers of foreign students in American universities are Russian.

Individual Accomplishment

Russia has always had noted scientists, writers, artists and philosophers. They were

41

encouraged since the time of Peter the Great and came to international recognition under Catherine II. Many of these accomplished individuals and thinkers eventually ran into trouble with the Czars and later Soviet because their ideas were often critical of government policies. Often the result was exile, imprisonment or even death.

One of the keenest Russian minds of chemistry was Dmitri Mendeleyev (1843-1907) who invented the Periodic Table. He was a professor at the University of St. Petersburg.

A leader in experimental psychology was Ivan Pavlov (1849-1936) who founded the Institute of Experimental Medicine in St. Petersburg. In 1904 he received the Nobel Prize in Physiology and Medicine.

Mikhail Kalashnikov, who settled in Izhevsk, invented the most used automatic rifle in the history of warfare. His automatic weapon known as the Automat Kalashnikova 1947 (shortened to AK-47) was cheap and effective. Had he lived in a country of copyright and patent laws he would have become one of the wealthiest people in the world. Instead, in his later years, he was living just above poverty level.

Andrei Sakharov (1921-1992) is outstanding among modern scientists for his work as a peace activist. As a nuclear physicist, he helped develop the Soviet hydrogen bomb. He, along with other world nuclear scientists, realized the horror of the creation and became a spokesman for peace. In 1975 he was awarded the Nobel Peace Prize. In1980 he was exiled to Gorki (Nizhny Novgorod) where he was forbidden to write or talk about anything scientific or political. In 1986 Mikhail Gorbachev pardoned him. In 1990 Gorbachev himself, was awarded the Nobel Peace Prize.

When one thinks of Russian writers two giants come to mind: Dostoyevsky (1821-81) and Tolstoy (1828-1910). They have written works that transcend time and will live forever. Fyodor Dostoyevsky was born and raised in Moscow by Russian Orthodox parents. Most of his long list of works are continually in print. Many of them were composed in the Czar's prison where he endured the most barbarous treatment. Two of his works are *Crime and Punishment* (1866) and *The Idiot* (1868).

Leo Tolstoy is equally celebrated as one of the towers of world literature. His great work *War and Peace* (1869) took seven years to write. Another famous work *Anna Karenina* (1876) took three years.

More recent Russian writers have won the Nobel Prize for literature: Aleksandr Solzhenitsyn (1970), Mikhail Sholokhov (1965), Boris Pasternak (1958) and Ivan Bunin (1933).

The person who set the stage for all Russian literature was the poet and prose writer Aleksandr Pushkin (1799-1837). He started his writing career while still a student. He was exiled to Southern Russia in 1820 partly for his poem "*Ode to Liberty.*" Books of his poetry are still published annually. His historical poems were the basis of many operas, plays and poems by other poets. Today, there is an active network of Pushkin Societies among the literati of Russia and his birthday is celebrated every year. His namesake city Pushkin (97,000) is a suburb of St. Petersburg.

The most celebrated Russian playwright is Anton Chekhov who was the grandson of a serf. He began writing under an assumed name while he was studying for a medical degree. Of his many plays and stories, the most notable are *Uncle Vanya* (1899), *The Three Sisters* (1901) and *The Cherry Orchard* (1904).

The artist Marc Chagall was born in Vitebsk, Belarus, and studied in Paris. His subject matter is drawn mostly from Jewish

6-3 Ballet.

life. His famous paintings include *I and the Village* and *The Rabbi of Vitebsk*. The former is in the Museum of Modern Art in New York City, and the latter is in the Art Institute of Chicago.

Other famous Russian artists include Vasily Kandinsky and Ossip Zadkine.

Kandinsky is usually recognized as the first abstract artist. Zadkine was a Russian sculptor who worked in France. Originally a cubist, he exerted considerable influence on modern art after World War II. Among his best known works is the public monument *The Destruction of Rotterdam* (1954).

Artist and jewelry designer Faberge is known for the ornate bejewelled porcelain Easter Eggs which he created for Czar Nicholas II and his family. His works in porcelain, gold, silver and precious stones are priceless.

Russian composers have also had world-wide influence. Modest Moussorgsky (1839-1881) is famous for *Boris Gudunov* but his *A Night On Bald Mountain* and folk songs received more public attention. Nikolai Rimsky-Korsakov (1844-1908) is best known for his orchestral work *Scheherazade*. Peter Tchaikovsky (1840-1893) composed famous ballets including *Nutcracker Suite*, *Swan Lake* and *Sleeping Beauty*. Every day, somewhere in the world, his ballets are performed.

Other notable composers are Alexander Borodin, Alexander Glazunoff, Mikail Glinka, Serge Prokofiev, Sergei Rachmaninov, Aleksandr Schiabin, Dimitri Shostakovich and Igor Stavinsky.

Russia is also famous for her ballet. The renaissance in romantic ballet began in Russia around 1875, but ballet was first organized in 1738 under the Imperial Theater. It was patronized by the Czars up to and including Nicholas II.

The impresario, Sergei Diaghilev, took his *Ballet Russe* to Paris in 1909, and from that debut dominated the world of ballet for the next quarter century. Among his performers were Anna Pavlova, Bronislava Nijinski and George Balanchivadze or George Balanchine, who later became the founder and director of the New York City Ballet.

The Bolshoi Ballet is the principal company of Russia. It began as a dancing school for the Moscow Orphanage in 1773 and opened as the Bolshoi Theatre in 1856. It has made numerous world tours with its celebrated productions of *Giselle, Nutcracker* and *Swan Lake*.

The Kirov Ballet began as the Imperial Russian Ballet in St. Petersburg in 1889. Today it is known as the Mariinsky. The company is famous for its performances of *Sleeping Beauty* and *Swan Lake*. The great teacher, Agrippina Vaganova, trained the company's dancers. Her work became the foundation of modern ballet instruction. .

6-4 Balalaika player - Moscow.

In 1994 Nikita Mikhalkov won an Academy Award for best foreign language film for his film *Burnt by the Sun*. Another noted movie director Vladimir Menshov won an Academy Award in 1980 for his *Moscow Does Not Believe In Tears*. The director Vladimir Khotinenko said, "Russian history is tragic, bloody and contradictory. It is up to us to bring to it an artistic approach and humor."

44

7. INDUSTRY AND TRANSPORT

Russia manufactures more steel than any other country in the world. It produces more coal, natural gas and petroleum than any other country. Large industrial complexes were built from Kazan on the Volga River south to Volgograd. The largest automobile complex in the world was established at Tolyati (Togliatti) just north of Samara. The world's largest roller bearings plant is in Samara. In 1949 Volgograd became the site for the first Soviet tractor factory, and it is still producing tractors today.

The largest truck manufacturing complex was built at Naberezhnyye Chelny. Large truck and army transport vehicles are produced in Simbirsk. Engels, across the river from Saratov, is the largest manufacturer of electric trolley buses.

The Soviets designated Nizhny Novgorod for new factories. Its location on the Volga River, as well as its railroad junctions, make it an ideal site for the distribution of its manufactured products. Here was the heart of the Soviet aircraft industry. Buses and trucks are also manufactured here. Its huge paper mill is the largest producer of newsprint in the country.

These Volga River cities make up the second most industrialized part of Russia. The leading district is Moscow's central core between the Oka and Volga Rivers.

All roads lead to Moscow, as do all railroad and airline routes. Moscow is linked to the Caspian, Black, White, Azov and Baltic Seas by a series of canals and rivers. Cities surrounding Moscow are heavily industrialized. Yaroslav produces tires, Ivanovo textiles and Tula iron and steel.

Another large though outdated industrial complex is found in the Ural Mountains. The Ural industrial belt stretches from Perm in the north to Orenburg in the southwest to Orsk in the southeast.

The Ural Mountain complex has been a major producer of iron and steel since Stalin planned its development in 1949. Tractors are produced at Chelyabinsk as well as iron ore processing and steel production. Plutonium is also produced at Chelyabinsk. Nizhniy Tagil produces railway cars, a valuable commodity for Russia's extensive railway system. Mining equipment is produced at Yekaterinburg.

A fourth industrial complex is located in the Kuznetsk Basin, or "Kuzbas", in the center of populated Siberia. This area has its own iron ore deposits and rich bituminous coal deposits. Lead, copper and gold are also mined here.

In the Kuzbas iron and steel products are manufactured at Barnaul, Prokopyevsk, Kemerovo and Novokuznetsk. The manufacturing area begins in the Kuzbas and stops at Tomsk on the north. Novosibirsk, the largest city in Siberia, is part of this industrial zone.

In the Far East there is an integrated unit of manufacturing and steel production at Khabarovsk, Komsomolsk and Vladivostok, but nothing comparable to that along the Volga, or the Urals or Kuzbas. Products from the eastern manufacturing district are mainly for local consumption although some products are exported from Vladivostok and Nahodka. Far eastern cities are finding it more profitable to deal with Japan, South Korea and China than to deal with European Russia.

The Soviets also constructed an industrial district in Ukraine, centered in the Donetsk Basin or "Donbas", and north to Kharkiv. The largest iron and steel manufacturing plant in the world is at Kriyvyy Rih. It has the capacity to produce 22 million tons of steel annually. (The largest plant in the United States is capable of

7-1 A dam and hydroelectric generating station on the Volga River north of Saratov.

producing 6 million tons.) Other large steel works are located at Donetsk and Kerch.

In the industrial Kuzbas, agricultural machinery is produced at Kharkiv, Kiev and Rostov-na-Donu. Oil tankers are produced at Kerch. Rostov is in Russia, the other cities are in Ukraine.

Kuzbas industry is based on its large deposits of anthracite and bituminous coal plus its iron ore and manganese deposits. With the dissolution of the Soviet Union, Ukraine now possesses one of the world's foremost industrial complexes. However, much of this industry depends on natural gas which is supplied by Russia. This has put Ukraine in debt to Russia which is causing Ukraine serious political problems.

While all of this heavy industry may sound impressive, it is mostly outdated by late 20th and early 21st century standards.

Russian heavy industry was a legacy from economy that has become increasingly unproductive in the new information, computer based, high tech world economy. Stalinist industrial policy ignored the consumer and the environment. As a result, the Soviet Union has a history of consumer shortages, and Russia now faces enormous cleanup costs from 70 years of unrestricted industrial pollution.

The Soviets were keen on developing hydroelectric power. Seven of the world's twenty largest hydroelectric stations were built by the Soviets. Most of the other thirteen were built by Russian engineers in other countries. These giant Russian hydroelectric stations are located at Tunukhansk, Sayano Shushensk, Krasnoyarsk, Bratsk, Ust-llimsk and Boguchany in Siberia. The highest dam in the

46

world, over one thousand feet, is at Rogun in Tajikistan. Other large dams are found at Nurek, also in Tajikistan, in Georgia and Chirkey on the Sulak River in Dagestan.

Most of the giant hydroelectric stations have created huge lakes with multi-purpose uses. The largest of these is at Bratsk on the Angara River. Other large man-made lakes are found at Krasnoyarsk on the Yenisey River, Samara on the Volga and Zeya on the Zeya River of the Far East.

Hundreds of other smaller hydroelectric stations are scattered around the country-just about anywhere there are people and a flowing stream. However, these power plants have not come without cost. Diverting rivers and streams for these dams has caused extensive erosion and silting as well as the destruction of some natural lakes.

Despite extensive hydroelectric development, Russia still gets 80 percent of its electric power from fuel - coal, oil, wood, peat, natural gas and nuclear. Russia has one fourth of the world's coal reserves. Although inefficient, burning coal is still the cheapest method of producing electricity.

The Soviets also emphasized nuclear energy and built 28 atomic plants in Russia, 15 in Ukraine, two in Lithuania and one in Kazakhstan. But their reactor designs are seriously flawed. The nuclear accident at Chernobyl in northern Ukraine (Chornobyl in Ukraine) on April 26, 1986 was the worst in history. A Chernobyl-style reactor would never have been licensed in the United States or any other industrially advanced country.

Russia has two basic nuclear reactor types in operation. The RBMK is graphite based and the VVER is a pressurized water type.

The Chernobyl RBMK reactor has a "positive void coefficient". (Sweet 1994:29)

7-2 Inside a nuclear reactor station.

Its energy can actually increase with the loss of water and higher temperatures. The RBMK also has poorly designed control rods that are so slow they initially increase, rather than decrease, energy in an emergency insertion. Its containment core has a design flaw that allows "small increments of excess pressure to lift the reactor's lid". (Ibid)

There are still RBMKs operating at Chernobyl as well as near St. Petersburg and in Lithuania. The other type of reactor-the VVER-is considered to be almost inadequate as the RBMK. VVERs still operate in most of Russia.

Upgrading these reactors would cost tens of billions of dollars, money Russia simply does not have. Officials say they must have nuclear generated electricity and so millions of people as well as the environment remain at serious risk.

Russia has the largest reserves of natural gas in the world. In Siberia only a small portion of the vast reserves have been tapped. The energy value of Siberian gas is more than the total energy value of oil reserves in the Middle East. The biggest problem is getting the natural gas to the major markets in western Russia and Europe. Building pipelines across Siberia is difficult and very expensive.

One of the Siberian gas fields, the Urengoy, outproduces the entire North Sea field operated by Great Britain and Norway. However, the gas presently produced in Siberia takes a full week to reach industries and homes in Germany, its biggest foreign purchaser.

Until the Siberian discoveries, the largest natural gas reserves were found in central Turkmenistan. Much of this gas was transported to the Urals and Moscow but with the dissolution of the Soviet Union this will probably change as more republics exercise autonomy over natural resources. Russia has the largest deposits of minerals in the world. However, much of these are also in remote areas such as the Arctic Lowland where mining and getting them to market is a problem of logistics and high cost. Only when world prices increase and foreign expertise is made available will it be profitable to exploit most of these resources.

In 1995, Russia claimed that 60 percent of its industry was privatized along with 70 percent of its retail outlets. The government gave its citizens 144 million vouchers which they used to invest in privatized enterprises.

Despite major shortcomings, Russia and Ukraine together still lead the world in the production of wheat, barley, rye, sugar beets, cabbage, flax, hemp, sunflowers, potatoes, butter and milk. They are among the leaders in the production of maize, oats and tobacco.

Russia and Ukraine are among the world leaders in the numbers of beef and dairy cattle raised. There is a conflict of interest in the disbursement of grain production between human and animal consumption. Over 30 percent of cultivated land in Ukraine is in maize production and most of this goes to the cattle industry. Ukraine ships maize to Belarus where it is used to feed cattle.

Sheep and goats have always been important in this region of the world. The grazing lands of the steppe, the mountain meadows and southern Siberia were ideal for sheep raising. Woolen products are a major export. Historically, Russia was second only to Australia in wool production.

Russia ranks second to Canada in lumber production and lumber exports. Along with the paper and pulp industry, lumber is one of Russia's most profitable enterprises. However, much of the western forests of the Russian plain have been overcut and once again transportation costs will become a factor in sustained production of timber resources of Siberia.

Russia is second to China in harvest from the sea. Russia still operates a whaling fleet

7-3 Lock # 1 on the Moscow Canal where it joins the Volga River. The drop to the Volga is 35 feet.

to the disdain of world environmentalists. It is one of the few countries that refused to sign international treaties. The others are Japan, Iceland and Norway. The few treaties that were signed by these four countries were circumvented with the loophole of taking whales for "research purposes."

The Russian Atlantic fishing fleet catch herring, cod, haddock, pollock and redfish as well as the harp seal. In the Pacific, the fleet takes ocean perch, pollock, sablefish, halibut, mackeral, hake, herring and flounder. King crabs are taken from the Sea of Okhotsk. Salmon are caught near the Pacific river mouths as they come back to spawn.

Arkhangelsk and Murmansk are important fish processing cities on the Arctic Ocean. Other important fish processing cities include Kerch and Zhdanov on the Sea of Azov, Astrakhan on the Caspian and Khabarovsk and Vladivostok in the Far East.

There were 650 million tons of material shipped on Russian waterways in 1995. The Volga-Kama system had 44 % of this volume. The rest was shipped by Ob-Irtysh 9%, N and W. Dvina 8%, Don 5%, Yenisey 4%, Amur 4% and Lena 2%.

Rail and pipeline are the major methods of transporting large volumes of products. In 1995, the major products hauled by rail included coal and coke 20 %, oil 10%, ores 8%, iron and steel 5%, grain and milled products 4%, forest products 4% and fertilizers 4%.

In 1996, 45% of all products were shipped by rail, 35% by pipeline, 11% by sea, 6% by vehicles, 3% by river and canal. The amount shipped by air was negligible. As foreign trade increases it is assumed more products will be transported on the sea.

8-1 Bell Tower of Ivan III and the Czar Bell, in the Kremlin, Moscow. This, the largest cast bell in the world has never been rung. It weighs 200 tons. The Bell Tower has three tiers and twenty one bells in each tier. The tower is 240 feet high and can be seen from a distance of 22 miles.

8. MOSCOW AND THE CENTRAL CORE

Moscow and its satellite cities occupy the central portion of the Great Russian Plain. Moscow, the capital city, is also the national nerve center. Moscow has a population of ten million. Over fifty million people live in the central plain, about one third of the population of the entire country.

During the 9th century fortified trading posts grew up around key rivers and roadways. These were built by Scandinavian traders who were interested in the products of the Arab lands and those further east.

Novgorod, on the edges of Lake Ilmen, just south of present day St. Petersburg, reigned supreme. It was the most important fort and trading post of its day. Travel throughout the region passed through its streets.

From Novgorod, the road led south to the headwaters of the Dnieper River and then on to Kiev. It was Kiev's position on an excellent waterway to the Black Sea that led to its formation as the Kievan Rus Kingdom.

Kiev began to decline in the 11th century, but Novgorod continued to be a bustling trading post and way station. Even when Moscovy rose to prominence, Novgorod was still the most populated city in Russia.

Although the central region is devoid of any significant natural resources, it began to grow as the Kievan State began to decline. Slavic peoples, escaping the Tatar invasions, migrated from Kiev to the safety of the central plain's swamps and rivers.

Moscow's location at the center of four great water systems proved to be its fortune. It had easy access to the Volga, Oka, Don and Western Dvina Rivers and was a short way from the headwaters of the Dnieper. It was easily defended as Napoleon and Hitler were to discover.

To the north of Moscow are the headwaters of the mighty Volga River. To the south is the **Oka River**, the major tributary of the Volga. The 920 mile long Oka is the lifeblood of the region. It is a dividing line between the mixed forest and the forest steppe. It also divides the good soils to the south from the adequate but poorer soils in the forested north.

Snow stays on the ground only four months of the year south of the Oka but six months north of it. Much of the land north of the Oka is swampy and wet while south of it the land is dry and ready for planting in spring.

Glaciers left their imprint on the region. The land in the north is swampy with inadequate drainage. The swamps are easily converted to lakes by damming up their drainage outlets.

The land around the Oka and this section of the Volga was probably inhabited by Scandinavian trappers and fur traders before the coming of the Slavs. The area was restricted from expansion by the Tatars and Bulgars to the east, the forerunners of the invading Mongols under Genghis Khan.

When the Mongol horde arrived in the middle of the 13th century they set about destroying the existing towns. Most of the villages along the Oka and Klyazama Rivers were sacked and leveled. This included Ryazan, Lipetsk and Vladimir.

The Moscow merchants were able to save themselves from annihilation by paying tribute to the Mongol Tatars. By the fifteenth century, the Moscow Rus was strong enough to refuse payment of tribute. This established Moscow as the Slavic leader in the Central Plain.

Muscovy's growing population in the 16th century depended heavily upon the good farmlands to the south. In return for

MAP 5   The Russian Plain: Central - The Moscow Core Area.

grain, Muscovites traded wood, flax, hemp and hides. A good business relationship developed between Moscow and Kiev.

By the seventeenth century there was an iron works at Tula, using local ore and charcoal. In the eighteenth century cotton was imported from the south, and the local mills using hemp and flax shifted to manufacturing cotton textiles.

In the late 19th century railroads began to replace the slow river traffic. Railroads connected Moscow with the raw materials of eastern Russia as well as other lands. Russia went out to conquer new territories - Central Asia, the northern Black Sea and the Caucasus.

Serfdom was abolished in 1861, followed by a short period of chaos as the peasants began migrating to new homesteads east of the Volga. Most new developments at the end of the 19th century were not in the Moscow region.

Despite the lack of foreign capital industry continued to expand. The most important industry in all of Russia at the beginning of the 20th century was cotton textiles with the Moscow region producing almost all of it. It is still among the top three industries today.

Large cities developed along the northern Volga and the Oka: Ivanovo, Nizhny Novgorod, Tula, Tver and Yaroslav. Outside the Central Plain, the Russian Empire had expanded to the Caucasus and to the Pacific Ocean.

When the Soviets came to power in Russia they placed a premium on industrial expansion, and Moscow became the center. They also scattered industry among the chief cities. Nizhny Novgorod's name was changed to Gorky and it became the center of the automobile industry. Its population then doubled.

The Soviets dug deep canals from Moscow to the Volga and the Oka Rivers. The Moscow River was deepened and widened to accommodate larger ships.

At first the region relied heavily upon imported coal and oil from other areas. Today the main fuel is natural gas. However, the old sources of lignite from Tula still play a major role as does wood from the forested areas north of Moscow. There are hundreds of hydropower stations along all the rivers surrounding the central plain. There are four atomic electric generating stations - Nizhny Novgorod, Voronezh, Kursk and Smolensk. Three others are in the planning stage.

Among the region's limited natural resources are lignite, peat, phosphate rock and iron ore mined around Tula and Lipetsk. The Kursk region, 300 miles south of Moscow, produces a high grade iron ore that has been only recently exploited. The delay in extracting the iron ore was due to the extremely heavy lower grade ore that rested above the higher grade.

Today the most economically important activity is engineering, followed by textiles and chemicals. Engineering which is associated with all industries to some extent, is centered at Nizhny Novgorod. Chemicals and the important plastics and synthetic rubber industries are scattered throughout the region but most production is in Yaroslav and Nizhny Novgorod. Energy is provided by oil from the south and wood from the nearby forests.

Textile manufacturing is found in almost every city with the heaviest clustering around Ivanovo. Cotton for these mills comes from far away irrigated lands southeast of the Aral Sea.

Agriculture does best south of the Oka. The cold lands north of the Volga has periodic droughts and a short growing season. However, people with small backyard plots are able to produce enough food for themselves and possibly their neighbors. Chickens, goats and pigs are common backyard animals.

A dairy cattle industry north of the Oka is maintained by the growing of hay. People here also produce rye, barley, cabbages, oats and potatoes which is their main food.

South of the Oka, grain is the main product but there is a sizable dairy industry which requires hay. Beef cattle is important as are sheep and pigs.

Although grain is the dominant crop, the southern fringes of the region also produce sugar beets, sunflowers, hemp and tobacco. Since the building of the railroads, the inland waterways have fallen to secondary importance, but nonetheless remain important economically. Moscow has become more accessible to the seas, north and south, by the building of the Volga-Baltic waterway which connects the area to

8-2 The channeled Moscow River as it flows through the center of the city.

the Baltic Sea and the White Sea. The Volga-Don Canal connects Moscow to the Black Sea. Thus some geographers refer to Moscow as the "Port of Five Seas."

Moscow (10,004,000) is located on the Moskva River and a junction of the Moscow Canal. It is the country's largest city and leading economic and cultural center as well as the hub of all communications, railroads and airlines. It is the headquarters of all government agencies.

The city has five major airports and one of the world's best subway systems which first opened in 1935.

Moscow's major industries include wood and paper products, brewing, film-making, oil refining, metalworking, machine building, automobiles, trucks, aircraft, textiles, clothing and shoes. It also has a large military industry.

Moscow was first mentioned in literature in 1147. The Kremlin marked the city limits. A **kremlin** is a walled city. It became the seat of the grand dukes of Suzdal-Vladimir who later took the title of Grand Dukes of Moscow. The walls of the Moscow Kremlin were first built in 1367.

Muscovy, or Moscow, achieved dominance over the Russian lands because of its strategic location at the hub of four great river systems. The history of Moscow is basically the history of Russia.

The University of Moscow was founded in 1755 by the scientist M. V. Lomonosov. It is one of the most prominent universities in the world. There are over 70 other institutions of higher learning in Moscow.

The city is politically divided into five major sections with the Kremlin at the center. Next to the Kremlin is the huge Red

8-3 Moscow suburb. Velyaminovo village. Individual houses are rare in the suburbs.

Square, an original meeting and market place. It gets its name, not from the communists, but from the color it was painted in the 16th century. At that time each market area in Moscow had a characteristic color which identified it.

Moscow is also home to the **Bolshoi (large) Theater** which specializes in ballet and opera and the **Maly (small) Theater** which specializes in drama. The city has one of the largest sport stadium (Dynamo formerly Lenin) complexes in the world.

The city has a huge agricultural exhibition complex, a conservatory, a state historical museum, a museum of oriental culture, an art gallery and the large Lenin Library, second in holdings only to the U.S. Library of Congress.

Moscow is a country within a country with its 2,500 historical and architectural monuments, 70 museums, 125 cinemas, 50 theaters, 4,500 libraries and 540 educational and research institutions.

Moscow is home to the leader of the Russian Orthodox Church which is rapidly increasing its membership and is beginning to wield political power.

There are many parks in Moscow. The main park is Gorky Central Park but two other parks are equally busy, the Izmailovo and the Sokolniki. There is a botanical garden at Ostankino Park.

The Sparrow Hills (formerly Lenin Hills) in southwest Moscow is the most desirable residential area. Many residents provide their own security forces.

A 70 mile highway circles Moscow. Around this is a seven mile wide green belt. There are thirty cities with populations from 50,000 to 80,000 within 40 miles of Moscow's center. There are also isolated housing estates which are a group of high rise apartment buildings which are more than twenty stories high. These island estates house anywhere from ten to twenty thousand people and are connected to Moscow by good roads and trolley lines. Individual houses, like those depicted in Figure 8- 3 are rare.

Stalin used prison labor to demolish

55

8-4 Nizhny Novgorod is at the junction of the Oka River (left) and the Volga River (right).

much of the old city of Moscow and build seven ominous skyscrapers. These are referred to as "Stalin Gothic" architecture.

After Stalin's death, Nikita Khrushchev tried to alleviate the housing shortage by constructing residential dwellings on the cities outskirts. These huge concrete block structures are known as "khrushchevsky".

In recent years Moscow has been plagued with homeless people migrating in from the former Soviet Republics. In December 1995, 148 homeless "drunks" froze to death within the city limits.

The city also has problems with crime, trash and littering, as well severe pollution.

Nizhny Novgorod (1,445.000), formerly Gorky, also, Nizhniy and Nizhnii, was built at the junction of the Oka and Volga Rivers. It is a major river port and center of rail transport. The site of the second largest

automobile industry in Russia, it also produces heavy machinery, steel, chemicals and textiles.

The city was founded as a frontier post in 1221 by Prince Vladimir. This was to protect Moscovy from the Tatars and Bulgars who dominated the Lower Volga.

Nizhny Novgorod was famous for its annual trade fairs which brought together silks, brassware and rugs from the orient as well as furs, honey and paper from the north. The fairs continued uninterrupted from 1817 to 1930.

After the Soviets came to power the city was renamed Gorky for Maxim Gorky a famous writer who was born here. With the dissolution of the Soviet Empire the city voted to return to its old historic name.

The city has a turreted stone kremlin dating from the 13th century. It also has several 13th to 18th century cathedrals and castles. There is a major university.

several 13th to 18th century cathedrals and castles. There is also a major city university.

There are several large satellite towns around Nizhny Novgorod : Bakna Bor, Pravinsk and Kstovo.

Voronezh (905,000), in the black earth agriculture region and on the Voronezh River (a navigable tributary of the Don) developed early as a river port. Today it produces locomotives, synthetic rubber, oil and food products. It has one of the first nuclear power stations ever built in Russia.

The city was founded in 1586 as a fortress against the Crimean Tatars. It became a shipbuilding center where Peter the Great launched a military campaign to the Sea of Azov. It was largely destroyed in World War II and then rebuilt. Its famous Nikolsk Church and 18th century Potemkin Palace were restored.

There is a university in the city. Several Scythian burial mounds are in the suburbs.

Yaroslav (638,000), located on the Upper Volga River, is a major rail junction and an industrial and commercial center. Linen and leather factories date back to the 17th century, and textile mills date from the 8th century. Russia's first textile factory was built here.

Among the city's industries are oil refining, shipbuilding, printing, tobacco processing, synthetic rubber and the manufacture of diesel engines. These products are shipped by rail and water.

Yaroslav is one of the oldest cities in Russia, dating back to the 11th century. On the main route from Moscow to Archangelsk, roads and later railroads

8-5 Yaroslavl. Bride and groom traditionally pose before a World War II monument. Most couples are married in a civil ceremony.

crossed here. The city has a 12th century monastery and several 17th century churches.

One of the oldest structures in Yaroslav is the Church of St. Elijah the Prophet built in 1647-50. It is located on Soviet Square, the center of the city.

While other cities were destroying statues of Lenin and renaming streets after the dissolution of the Soviet Union, Yaroslav chose to retain these. Citizens explain that this is part of their history and people must not deny their history.

Tula (554,000) is located on the Upa River, a tributary of the Oka, Tula is a highway crossroads for the Moscow industrial region. It is Russia's oldest metallurgical center and today produces mining equipment, deepwater pumps, boilers, ventilators and military armaments. Peter the Great built the first Russian arms factory here using nearby iron and coal. One of the city specialties is the production of samovars, the famous Russian teapot.

During World War II, Tula was the first line of defense against the German invaders. It withstood heavy German bombardment and held its ground. There is a well preserved 16th century kremlin with turreted walls. Russian author Leo Tolstoy is buried near the city limits.

Ivanovo (540,000) is a great cotton textile center located in the Moscow industrial region. It is the leading textile city in Russia. It produces 20 percent of the country's product..

Ivanovo has a history of labor unrest. It was one of the first industrial cities to see organized workers attempting to negotiate with management. During the troubled times of 1905, 60,000 city workers went on strike and formed one of the first labor unions. Although the strike was crushed after six weeks, it demonstrated the latent power of the workers.

Ryazan (527,000), on the Oka River, was founded in the 11th century. It makes diversified chemical products, has an oil refinery, lignite processing works and a canning factory. It manufactures machine tools and agriculture equipment. One of its specialties is the manufacture of electric light bulbs.

Ryazan is connected to Moscow by an electric rail system. It uses the Oka River for trading agriculture products.

The city was known as Spassk-Ryazanski when it was destroyed by the Mongol Tatars. It has a medieval flavor with many richly ornamented buildings and churches. Its 12th century kremlin houses two old monasteries. A former Archdiocese Palace is now a museum.

Lipetsk (468,000), on the Voronezh River, is in an iron ore mining district. It produces steel, fertilizers, food products, cement and tractors.

There are several mineral springs in the city and this has formed the nucleus of a health spa industry. Like the other cities of the south, it was destroyed by the Mongol Tatars in the 13th century.

Tver (455,000), formerly Kalinin, was located on the main road between Moscow and Novgorod and St. Petersburg. A major port on the Upper Volga, it is situated at the junction of the Volga and Tver Rivers. The construction of the Moscow Canal to the Volga greatly increased its trade.

Tver is the center of a small farming area and manufactures linen textiles, light machinery and rail equipment.

The city grew around a 12th century fort and has an ancient cathedral and castle.

Bryansk (455,000), on the Desna River, a tributary of the Dnieper, is an important center for phosphates, peat, chalk, sand and timber. Its industries include glass, cement, fertilizers, iron and locomotives. It was once known as Brinyu and also Debryansk. The

740 mile long **Desna River** is the major tributary of the Dnieper. It joins that river just north of Kiev. The Desna is navigable to half its length.

Kursk (430,000) is near the Kursk Magnetic Anomaly just north of Ukraine. The anomaly is a distortion of magnetic directions in a standard compass. The city manufactures iron products, light machinery and synthetic fibers.

Vladimir (358,000), on the Klyazama River manufactures chemicals, cotton textiles and plastics. It was attacked by Mongol Tatars in 1240.

Vladimir has many old buildings and a museum of religious art. It also has the tombs of the early Princes of Vladimir.

Smolensk (335,000) is at the headwaters of the Dnieper River. The name is derived from "smola" which is the pitch produced from pine trees.

This is the largest flax processing city in Russia and a major producer of linen textiles. Flour milling and production of electrical appliances are other specialties.

The city, on a major trade route between Europe and Russia, was used by Napoleon as a staging area to attack Moscow. Later he used it as a retreat base.

Smolensk was traded between Russia and Poland through the centuries. It has many old buildings and several historical museums.

Orel (325,000) is at the junction where the Moscow-Kharkiv Railroad crosses the Oka River. It is an agriculture city trading in grain and livestock as well as a major producer of clothing. Orel has one of the largest breweries in Russia.

Cherepovets (315,000) , on the northern end of the Rybinsk Reservoir, is an important port on the Volga-Baltic Waterway. Its industries include the manufacture of fertilizers and lumber products.

Kaluga (280,000), an important railroad junction on the Oka River about 90 miles southwest of Moscow, manufactures diesel locomotives, telephone equipment, glass, leather, bricks and is known for its matches.

Kostroma (278,000), at the junction of the Volga and Kostroma Rivers, is a center of linen textile manufacturing. Textile machinery is manufactured here.

The city has a 13th century cathedral and a 16th century monastery. Most famous of Kostroma landmarks is the Trinity Cathedral of the Ipatyevsky Monastery built in 1580 with the financial aid of the Godunov family. This is where Michael Romanov, the first Czar and leader of the Romanov Dynasty, was elected to the throne.

Rybinsk (258,000), formerly Sheherbakov and also Andropov, was a center of the timber industry before a giant hydroelectric installation was built here. It now has one of the biggest man-made lakes in the world. Rybinsk is located at the junction of the Volga and Sheksva Rivers.

The city produces ships, road building equipment, printing presses and steel cable.

8-5 Trinity Cathedral - Kostroma

8-6 Open air market in Kostroma.

The **Rybinsk Reservoir** was created at a big bend in the Volga River. Until the reservoir was constructed boats had to be pulled into the Mariinskaya Canal System by horses. Many of the stretches of the system became so dry in summer a person could wade across them. Stalin authorized the reservoir in 1932 and construction started in 1936. The reservoir began filling in 1941. Political prisoners died at the rate of one hundred a day during the first two years of construction.

In the end more than 700 villages were flooded and almost 10,000 acres of farmland inundated. The houses are still under the water. About 60 rivers flow into the reservoir.

Rybinsk gets its name from the Russian word "ryba" or fish. However, since the reservoir bottom was not scraped there has been decaying trees and other vegetation

which has depleted the oxygen in the water making it difficult for fish to live.

The **Mariinsk Canal** built in 1810 linked Rybinsk with the Baltic Sea. The completion of the Volga-Baltic Canal increased its importance since it is a major route between Moscow and Archangelsk.

Podolsk (212,000), 20 miles south of Moscow, is a center for smelting tin, magnesium and titanium.

Kolumna (170,000), at the confluence of the Moscow and Oka Rivers, is an important locomotive manufacturing city.

Rostov (30,500) is a small city northeast of Moscow located on Lake Nero. Records of the city date back to 860 A.D. It has many old buildings and specializes in flax and linen spinning. It is mentioned here to avoid confusion with the large city **Rostov-na-Donu** to the south.

9. THE RUSSIAN PLAIN: NORTH

The Russian Plain north of the Volga River is a desolate place. Few cities of any size are found here and most of these are isolated from each other. The north plain is bounded by Finland and the Gulf of Finland on the west, the Ural Mountains on the east and the Arctic Ocean on the north. To the south is the Volga River.

The north is connected by a series of waterways and railroads. The Volga-Baltic Waterway connects St. Petersburg to the Rybinsk Reservoir. This is the renovation of the old Mariinsk Canal System. The system also connects St. Petersburg through the two big lakes to the White Sea.

Another series of waters connects the Sheksna River to Lake Kubenskoye, then to Sukhoma River and then to the Northern Dvina to the White Sea.

The water route from Moscow to the White Sea is still open despite the fact that most bulk material is shipped by rail. The waterway serves the military as well as an expanding tourist industry.

The system starts at Moscow where the canal connects the Moscow River to the Volga. A half million paid workers as well as prisoners and volunteers worked in the 1930s on it. More than 100,000 prison laborers died in the construction.

The Volga River flows from the canal northeast to the Rybinsk Reservoir. From there boats cross to the city of Cherepovets on the northern end of the reservoir. Here boats move into the Sheksna River which is dredged to handle them. The river canal leads to small lake Beloye (White Lake) where the canal continues northwest to Lake Onega. After crossing Onega a new canal takes boats to Lake Vyg. Another canal leads to the ocean.

St. Petersburg is joined to the canal system by the Svir River flowing out of Lake Onega to Lake Ladoga. From here the dredged Neva River transports boats to the Gulf of Finland. The Neva River is one mile wide as it flows through St. Petersburg.

In the northwest corner lies the **Kola Peninsula** with several highland areas. It is an eastern extension of the Scandinavian Mountains and the principle area called Lapland. It lies between the Barents Sea of the north and the White Sea indentation. The northern area is tundra and the southern area is forested.

The Kola Peninsula has rich mineral deposits, notably apatite and nickel as well as vast timber resources. Several hydroelectric power stations have been built along its various rivers.

The ice free port of Murmansk is on its northern shore. **Kirovsk** (45,000) in the interior, the second city of the peninsula, has an aluminum and superphosphate industry developed from local raw materials.

Two thirds of the world's nuclear waste is buried in the waters off the Kola coast. This includes 17 nuclear reactors and at least one submarine.

The region of **Karelia** lies south of the Kola Peninsula and borders Finland. Karelia was taken from Finland by the Soviet Union prior to World War II and more than 400,000 people emigrated to Finland at that time. Today, seventy percent of the inhabitants is Russian with Finnic peoples at eleven percent. Belorussians make up eight percent. There are also many Lapps who prefer to be called Nentsy and Samoyed.

Native Karelians never had a written language. Today they use a combination of Finnish and Russian.

The Karelian legislature does not consult Moscow in its dealings with Finland. For the present, this situation is tolerated by Moscow.

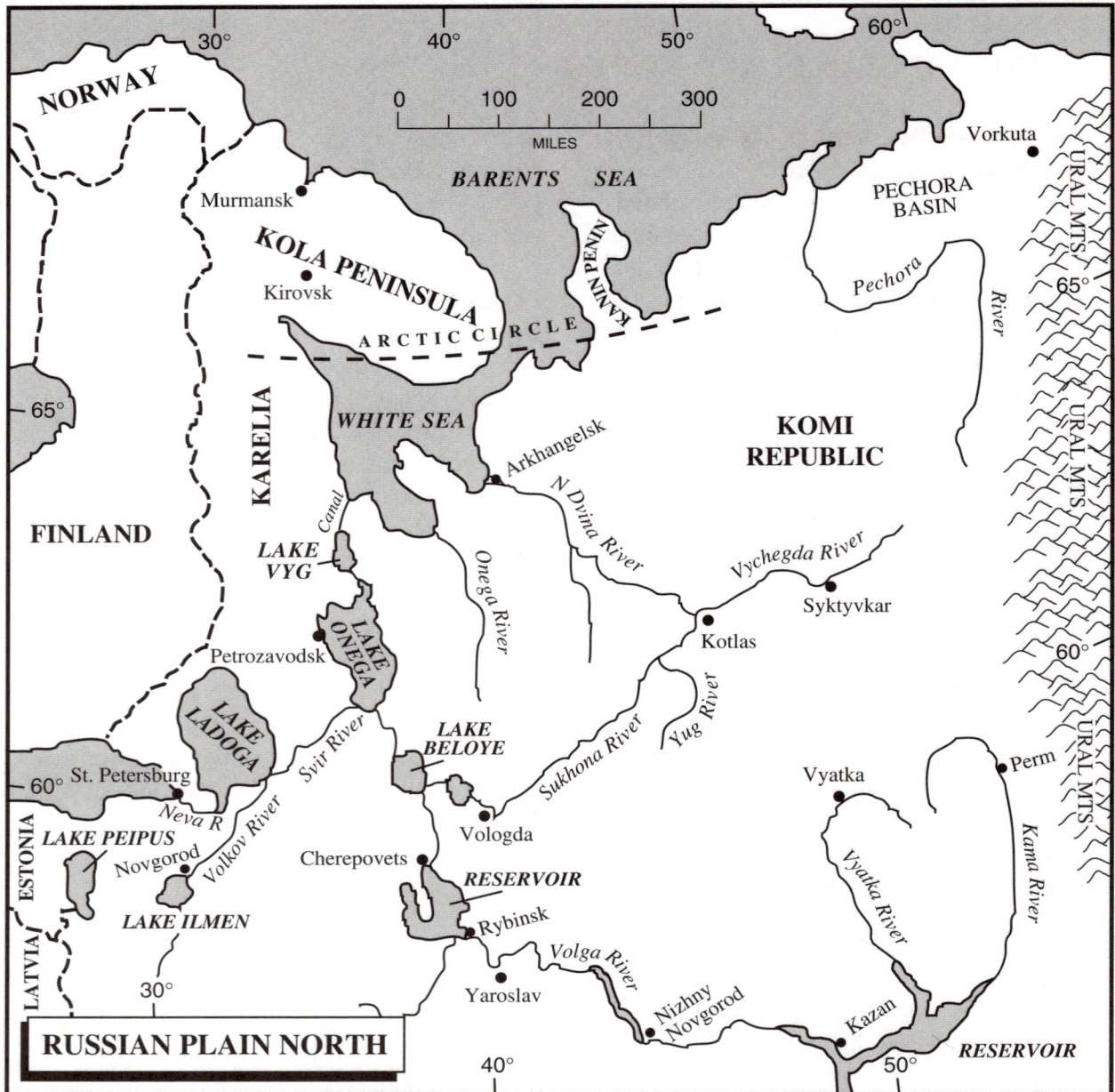

MAP 6   The Russian Plain: North

Petrozavodsk, on Lake Onega, is the capital city of Karelia. There are over 50,000 lakes in the region. Building transportation routes here is difficult because the lakes freeze early. Karelians have a saying. "We have nine months of winter and for three months we look for warmth."

Lake Ladoga, covering some seven thousand square miles, is the largest lake in Europe. It is roughly 130 miles long and 80 miles wide. Its southern shore is low and marshy and its northern shore is rocky. Many rivers empty into the lake, the largest being the **Vuoska** coming from Finland and the **Svir** coming from Lake Onega and the **Volkhov** coming from Lake Ilmen. The only outlet is the **Neva River** which flows to the

Gulf of Finland and through St. Petersburg.

There are several islands in the northern part of Lake Ladoga. A 12th century monastery on Valamo Island is a tourist attraction.

Lake Onega at 3,800 square miles is the second largest lake in Europe. It is between Lake Ladoga and the White Sea where its water forms an important connecting link between them. Like its big neighbor, Onega's shore is marshy in the south and rocky in the north. Both Ladoga and Onega are frozen from November to April.

Water flows to Onega from the **Vytega** and **Vodla** Rivers and exits with the **Svir** River. The 45 mile long Onega Canal connects the Svir River with the Vytega.

Forest products, fishing and lumbering are major Karelian industries. Farming is

9 -2 Logs float down the North Dvina River to be processed at Arkhangelsk.

almost impossible but potatoes and some vegetables can be grown. Hay is the basis for a small cattle industry.

Karelia has good deposits of iron ore, lead, zinc, copper, titanium, magnetite, nickel, marble and pyrite. These ores are smelted with the aid of the electric hydropower stations developed here. Karelia is crossed by the Murmansk Railroad from St. Petersburg and the Baltic-White Sea Canal.

Arkhangelsk is situated on the White Sea, a branch of the Arctic Ocean. It is isolated from the rest of Russia by large swamps and rivers which often overflow their banks. It is located where the Northern Dvina River empties into the White Sea. The eastern portion of the Northern Russian

9-1 Fishing is great in Lake Onega. The water is pure enough to drink.

Plain is a series of small plateaus surrounded by swamps. Most of the area encompasses the Komi Republic with its capital at Syktyvskar.

9-3 Policeman - Karelia

The **Komi Republic** is part of the Russian Federation. It consists of a wooded lowland stretching across the **Pechora** and **Vychegda** River basins and the upper reaches of the **Mezen** River. The northern part is permanently frozen.

There are major coal fields in the Pechora Basin and oil fields along the Ukhta River. Most of the coal and oil are shipped to St. Petersburg.

The Komi, formerly called Zyrians, speak a Finno-Ugric language and their religion is Russian Orthodox. Komi make up 25 percent of the population and Russians 70 percent. There are also Ukrainians (6%) living here. The people live mainly by hunting and trapping because agriculture is almost impossible in this harsh land. Lumbering is a major industry.

The Komi Republic was given a boost when the Kotlas-Vorkuta Railroad was built to haul away the coal and oil. This gave the Komi transportation to the outside world. The city of Vorkuta (120,000), north of the Arctic Circle is a coal mining center. A nuclear power plant is located near the small town of Pechora.

In 1994-95 an oil spill on the Upper Pechora River tributaries, especially the Kolva, caused much environmental damage to water, land and wildlife. The oil spilled from antiquated oil pipes. The region's entire pipeline system needs complete renovation and the government is inviting foreign investors to do this. Conoco, a subsidiary of Dupont, operates an oil extraction system under the title Polar Lights. Russians required Conoco to put up 100 percent of the money, but the company had to give Russia a 51 percent partnership.

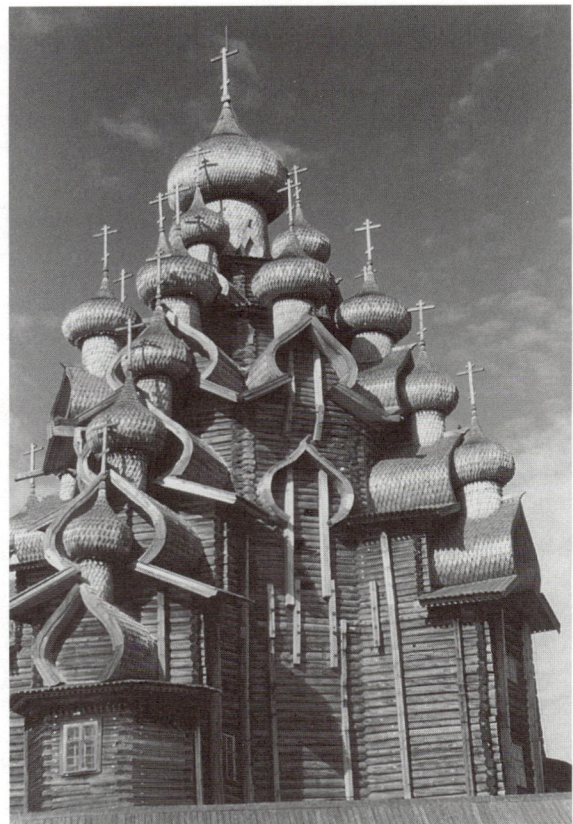

9-4 Church of the Transfiguration on Kizhi Island Lake Onega. (17th cen.) It was built without nails.

64

9-5 Section of the Winter Palace

The new pipelines lead to Yaroslav where the oil is distributed to western markets, mainly through Ventspils, a Latvian seaport.

When Komi declared its sovereignty in 1992, the word Autonomous was dropped from its official name. About a million people live in the district.

Most of the people of the northern plain live in an area fanning out from St. Petersburg. Their occupations are mostly lumbering and mining. They plant rye, oats, barley, flax, potatoes and cabbages. Dairy cattle and pigs are raised. Fishing and reindeer herding are also prominent occupations. White Sea fish are mostly cod, herring and sea perch. Cod liver oil and fish meal are exports. Timber is turned into lumber, plywood, cardboard, paper, pulp, furniture and electric poles.

Native people include about 35,000 Nentsy who live on the tundra and 350,000 Komi who live in the Taiga. Most of the northern people are ethnic Russians.

St. Petersburg (5,040,000) once Petrograd, then Leningrad, is located on both sides of the Neva River and the Gulf of Finland. Most of the city is low and high tides flood parts of it. Many intellectuals live in this historic center of learning and literature.

More than any other Russian city, St. Petersburg has been influenced by the fashions and ideas of Europe. It is Russia's most cosmopolitan city and is its major tourist spot.

All large buildings are set on piles driven into the earth. The Neva River is frozen from late November to April. Winter days

9-6 Teen-age girls - St. Petersburg

are short. In December daylight is from 10 a.m. to 3 p.m. It rains or snows 200 days of the year. In mid-summer the city is noted for its "summer nights" which is an extended period of lingering daylight.

St. Petersburg is a major seaport and naval base for Russia. Although it is one of the largest ports in the world it handles little ocean traffic because Russia does not trade with the rest of the world on a large scale. Generally, ice covers the harbor for three months of the year. Icebreaking ships can keep it open for all but one month.

St. Petersburg is at the terminus of two great canals, the Volga-Baltic and the Baltic-White Sea. These carry considerable cargo.

Industries include shipbuilding, oil refining, metallurgy, woodworking, rubber goods, turbines, tobacco processing, printing, pharmaceuticals, textiles, electrical equipment and plastics.

Peter the Great ordered the city to be built in 1703. He wanted a port on the sea in order to trade with Europe. He also wanted a classical European city. It was the capital of Russia for the next 200 years.

A rail line linked the city with Moscow in 1851. With the completion of the railroad, the canals became less important to trade but remained important to the military.

During World War II, in 1941, the city was surrounded by German troops and the siege lasted for two years. Thousands of residents died of famine and disease. During the extremely cold winters some supplies were brought into the city across frozen Lake Ladoga.

Today St. Petersburg remains a center of literature, music, theater and ballet as well as political liberalism. It's reckless social life in the 19th century has been the subject of many novels. Two revolutions erupted here, one in 1905 and another in 1917.

The main thoroughfare of the city is Nevsky Prospect which is the address for the Winter Palace, the Hermitage Museum and the Cathedral of Saint Isaac with its 333 foot high tower. Many 18th century buildings are also located on the street.

9-7 A hero of the seige of Leningrad.

The **Hermitage Museum** of St. Petersburg is full of world treasures. It expanded from the original pavilion palace built by Catherine the Great. It contains over 40,000 drawings, 500,000 engravings and 8,000 paintings including many by Rembrandt, Rubens, Picasso and Matisse. There are two paintings by DaVinci. The Hermitage has more Rembrandts than any other museum in the world. There are also tapestries, ivory carvings, gold artifacts and furniture. To look at every exhibit for one minute would take more than five years.

The Ethnographic museum located on Arts Square is little visited but it is a must for geographers who visit the city.

Murmansk (470,000) is located on the Kola Gulf of the Barents Sea. It is an ice free port, enjoying the somewhat warm ocean currents that drift across the Atlantic Ocean from the Caribbean.

Murmansk is the largest city north of the Arctic Circle. A leading freight port and naval base, it is linked by rail to Moscow and St. Petersburg.

Coastal waters off Murmansk are polluted with nuclear wastes dumped by the Soviets. Today, several nuclear ships, including an icebreaker and a submarine, no longer in use, are berthed in the harbor where their rapid deterioration is threatening the safety of the city.

Vyatka, (445,000) formerly Kirov, is a northern outpost on the 850 mile long Vyatka River, a tributary of the Kama. It is a rail crossroads between east and west and on the route from Perm to St. Petersburg. It was founded in 1174 by colonists from Novgorod. Today, it is a center for saw milling and metal fabrication.

9-6   A canal in St. Petersburg, "Venice of the North". The city is built on the delta of the Neva River.

Arkhangelsk, (425,000) also Archangel, is located where the Northern Dvina empties into the White Sea. Although icebound most of the year, the port can be kept open by icebreakers.

Timber and wood products from the hinterland make up the bulk of its exports. The city produces paper, turpentine, resin, cellulose, building materials, prefabricated houses and pulp. Fishing and shipbuilding are also important industries.

After the Bolshevik Revolution, civil war erupted between "whites" and "reds". White Russians, including many officers from the Czar's old army, opposed communism. Army units from several Western nations, including the U.S., landed at Archangel to aid the whites in their unsuccessful campaigns against the Red Army.

The city is named after a monastery dedicated to the Archangel Michael (1613) which is still standing. Much of the slave labor used to build the Baltic-White Sea Canal System was housed here.

The 465 mile long **Northern Dvina River** is formed by the waters of the Sukhona, Vychegda and Yug Rivers. Frozen from December to late April, it is connected to the Volga-Baltic Waterway by several canals.

Vologda (286,000), at the head of navigation on the Vologda River, a Northern Dvina tributary, is a crossing point for two major railroads: Moscow-Archangelsk and St. Petersburg-Perm. It is an important collecting and distribution center for dairy products, oats, hemp, flax and timber. The city is famous for its linen lace. There are many 13th to 18th century buildings in the city.

Vologda was an early outpost (1147 A.D.) between Moscow and the north. With the founding of Arkhangelsk in 1583, Vologda became a portage city from Moscow.

Petrozavodsk (274,000) on Lake Onega, is the center of a timber industry and an important iron smelter. It manufactures tractors and lumber products and has one of the largest mica processing plants in the world. It also has fish canning factories. Peter the Great founded an iron works here in 1703 which formed the city's nucleus. The city name means "Peter's Foundry". It

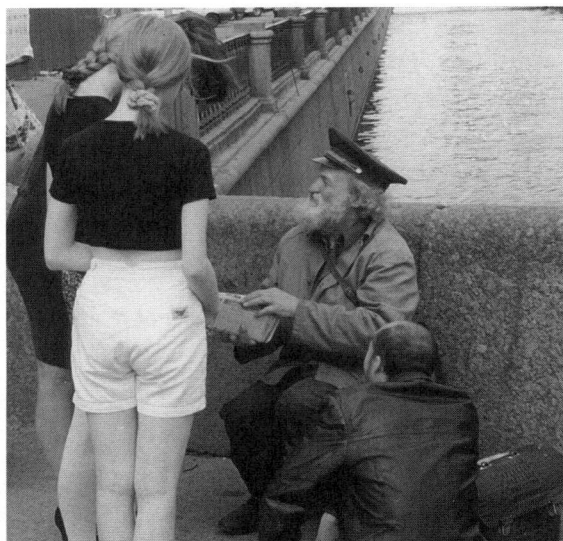

9-9 An old sailor tells his story-St. Petersburg

has a university. A main business attraction in the city is Ben and Jerry's Ice Cream.

In the 19th and early 20th century Petrozavodsk was used as a place of political exile. After the Bolshevik Revolution the city was turned into an economic and cultural center with forty-six induatrial enterprises and several educational and research institutes. The city still maintains its communist monuments and street names.

Syktyvskar (240,000) on the Sysola River near where it joins the Vychegda. It is the capital of the Komi Republic. Near the city, on the Vychegda River is Russia's, if not the world's, largest wood working complex. The city was isolated from the rest of Russia until the railroad connecting Moscow with the Pechora Basin was built.

Novgorod (234,000), just north of Lake Ilmen on the Volkhov River, was an important trade center of ancient Rus. Novgorod has wood and food processing factories and a major nitrate fertilizer plant.

Novgorod was on the old trade route from Scandinavia to the Black Sea. In 862 A.D. Novgorod asked Rurik to rule and protect them. The city was a rival of Kiev and one of the four chief northern trade centers of the *Hanseatic League*.

The city was nearly destroyed by Germans in World War II. Since then some of the ancient buildings have been restored, especially those in the kremlin. The city is often referred to as "museum city".

Pskov (205,000), on the Velikaya River, is in the center of a flax growing region.

Thus, linen is an important manufactured product. The city also engages in food processing and the manufacture of machinery and building materials. Pskov was an outpost of Novgorod in 903 A.D. It was a flourishing trade center in the 12th through 15th centuries. Its importance was diminshed when it came under Moscow rule in 1510.

When World War I was going badly for Russia it was at the Pskov railroad station Nicholas II announced abdication in 1917.

Vorkuta (120,000) is another outpost above the Arctic Circle. Its position in the Pechora Basin makes it an important processing center for regional trade. The city was founded as a prison colony and forced labor camp in 1932. Prisoners were still held here as late as 1985.

9-10 Ben and Jerry's Ice Cream factory.   Petrozavodsk

10. THE RUSSIAN PLAIN: SOUTH

The only portion of Russia below 50 degrees North Latitude is found south of Saratov along the Volga and Don Rivers. Here the land stretches down to the Caucasus Mountains and widens out to meet the Black and Caspian Seas. These lands were brought into the Russian Empire by Catherine the Great.

The **Volga River** flows south to Volgograd and then on past Astrakhan to the Caspian Sea. Over 2,300 miles long, it is Russia's principal waterway. Its entire length has locks and dams, and the river is really a series of lakes and reservoirs.

The Volga begins in the north at an elevation of 750 feet, and there is not much drop as it flows to the sea. It begins near Tver, flows east, then turns south. Its chief tributaries are the Oka, Sura, Vetluga, Kama and Samara.

The Volga is connected to the Baltic Sea by a series of waterways and canals, and to

MAP 7   The Russian Plain: South

70

the Black Sea by the 105 mile long Volga-Don Canal. It is connected to Moscow by the Volga-Moscow Canal.

The Volga valley is hilly on the west and low steppe on the east. Its easternmost point is at Samara. The river is navigable from April to November in the north and from March to December in the south.

A dam north of Moscow creates a 125 square mile reservoir which helps to regulate the level of the Moscow-Volga Canal. There are hydropower stations at Nizhny Novgorod, Samara, Kama, Volgograd and Votkinsk.

The Volga moves lumber downstream and fish, oil, and salt upstream. The main artery of Russian travel for centuries, it is referred to in folklore as "Mother Volga". The term **povolzhye** is used by Russians to mean "Along the Volga".

The **Don River**, little developed in the north, has a large dam and hydroelectric station just before it reaches Rostov and empties into the Sea of Azov. It begins its 1,200 mile journey just north of Voronezh, south of Tula.

Flooding of the Don is controlled by a dam creating the Tsimlyansk Reservoir. The river is navigable for 850 miles and is used to carry grain, coal and lumber. Its main tributary is the Donets which is 650 miles long and drains the Donetsk Basin (Donbas) of Ukraine. The Donets begins near Belgorod in Russia.

The area around Astrakhan receives less than 8 inches of precipitation a year, but the Kuban River basin toward the southwest may receive as much as 90 inches in some years. North of the foothills, maize, cotton and sunflowers are grown. Tea and grapes are grown at the foothills and on the mountain slopes.

There is natural gas and oil in this region. Molybdenum, zinc, tungsten and copper are also important minerals in the foothills and

mountains. The east bank of the Volga produces salt.

Russia gained control of the Volga when troops of Ivan the Terrible captured Astrakhan in 1556. The river became the main route for silk traders from the south and fur traders of the north. It is still the main thoroughfare between Russia and the Caucasus.

The **Kuban River** rises from the north slope of the Caucasus near Mt. Elbrus and flows north in a wide arc as it makes its way to the narrow straits separating the Sea of Azov from the Black Sea. It meanders through one of the rich black-earth grain and sugar beet producing regions of Russia. The 570 mile long river is only navigable for its last 150 miles.

The southern region is cossack country. These mounted hunters and warriors ruled the region from the 18th century until 1920. After the Bolshevik Revolution the cossacks proclaimed their independence, and Stalin responded by sending in the Red Army. The Soviets abolished the cossack government and revoked their traditional privileges. Today, cossacks are making a bid for an autonomous region.

Along the Volga River, from Volgograd north to Kazan, is one of the heaviest industrialized regions of Russia, second only to the Moscow Core. The Volga River carries about 50 percent of Russia's entire water traffic tonnage. With the completion of the Volga-Baltic Canal system and the Volga-Don Canal, the importance of the Volga was considerably increased. The dry summer period, when river water levels are low, has been overcome by the construction of many dams and the creation of many lakes.

A railroad runs parallel to the Volga, reducing much of the river traffic. Railways are less affected by floods and droughts than rivers. However, rail transportation costs are triple that of water transportation. So river traffic will probably expand in the future.

Large cities such as Samara, Kazan, Simbirsk, Saratov and Engels have grown wherever rail lines cross the Volga. Oil, once transported by rail, now moves across the Volga by pipeline.

Bulgars were the first ethnic group to populate the southern Volga. Then came the Mongol Tatars, followed by Khazars. To counteract these groups Catherine the Great invited ethnic Germans to settle here. Their descendants still live along the Volga.

The **Volga-Don Canal** is 62 miles long and has thirteen locks, many with a 30 foot lift. The locks are 460 feet long, 60 feet wide and have a low water depth of 15 feet. A dam on the Don River creates the 216 mile long Tsimylansk Sea which assists the canal. The Volga is below sea level at the first lock and ships must be raised about 400 feet to reach the Don River.

Rostov-na-Donu (1,030.000) is at the mouth of the Don River where it empties into the Sea of Azov. Rostov is an important industrial, scientific and cultural center. It exports grain and wool and produces agricultural machinery. There are ship and railroad repair yards and industries manufacturing electrical equipment, road construction machinery, furniture, clothing and shoes. It is also a center for fish, vegetable, grain and tobacco processing. The best European tobacco comes from the Caucasus region and much of it is processed locally.

The city grew around a fortress erected in 1761. It is regarded as the "Gateway to the Caucasus". Heavily damaged in World War II, the city has since been rebuilt.

Rostov is the principal city on the **Sea of Azov**, the northern arm of the Black Sea, which is also shared by Russia and Ukraine. The sea is shallow with the deepest part

only 45 feet. It connects to the Black Sea by the Kerch Strait. The Don and Kuban Rivers bring fresh water to the Azov as well as tons of silt each year. Azov trade was greatly increased by the Volga-Don Canal.

10-1 Mother and child; Rostov-na-Donu.

More Don and Kuban River water is being used for irrigation and industrial purposes. This has increased salinity in the Sea of Azov by 35 percent from 1970 to 1975. This has resulted in a decline of sturgeon and carp stocks and an increase in undesirable species such as jellyfish. However, fishing is still an important occupation of the Azov.

Volgograd (1,010,000), formerly Stalingrad, is an important port on the Volga River and the terminus of the Volga-Don Canal. The port handles oil, iron ore, lumber, coal and fish. It is a major rail center with direct connections to Moscow. One of the world's largest hydroelectric dams is on the Volga River just north of the city.

Volgograd has shipyards, oil refineries, steel and aluminum mills. Its workers build tanks, tractors and machine parts. There is also flour milling, vodka distilling, tanning and sawmilling.

In September 1942, a German army unit composed of more than 500,000 troops attacked the city. A bloody battle ensued with Germans losing 300,000 men and the Red Army losing 200,000 men. The rest of the German unit were captured. This defeat severely depleted the Axis forces.

The city was named Stalingrad in 1925 after the Soviet dictator. It was changed back to its historical name in 1961 as part of the denunciation of the Stalin personality cult. The original name of the settlement was Tsaritsyn.

Saratov (920,000) was founded in 1590 on the east bank of the Volga. It slowly shifted across river and, after a hundred years, is now completely on the west bank. The city is an important rail and river junction, distributing grain, timber, oil, fish, tobacco and salt. Its industries include aircraft, agriculture machinery and food processing. It has an important roller bearing factory.

Saratov was the center of German settlement during the reign of Catherine the Great but they were removed from the area during World War II. Now, many have returned and are seeking autonomous status.

A large highway bridge crosses the Volga at Saratov. The city has a university and a museum.

Krasnodar (630,000), on the Kuban River is not only a river port but an important rail junction. It has petroleum refineries and metal fabrication, chemical and textile factories. It was originally founded by cossacks upon orders from Catherine the Great who called it Yekaterinodar. It was renamed Krasnodar in 1920 by the Bolsheviks.

There is a large Philip Morris tobacco factory in Krasnodar which produces Marlboro, Chesterfield and L & M cigarettes.

Penza (556,000) located on the Sura River, a tributary of the Volga, is in the black earth agriculture district. It is an important railroad junction west of the Volga River. Its main industry produces agriculture products. There is also a significant paper industry. Several engineering firms are located here.

The city was founded in 1666, captured by Tatars in 1717 and by the cossack rebel Pugachev in 1774.

Astrakhan (526,000) is on the Volga River delta as it empties into the Caspian Sea. It obtained more river and sea traffic by the dredging of a deep channel. It has shipyards, ship repair facilities, a fish processing industry and is also a major exporting port for oil, fish, grain and wood.

Of interest is a special cloth called **astrakhan**, produced here and in other area cities. It is a woolen fabric woven to resemble the **karakul** Persian lamb fur. The cloth is woven on a cotton base entirely covered with a pile of closely curled mohair which is steamed to give it the tightly curled look of genuine karakul.

Astrakhan's kremlin was built in 1587 and a cathedral was constructed in 1765. After the Volga-Don Canal was built, river trade decreased by more than fifty percent.

Sochi (339,000) is an important subtropical port on the east shore of the Black Sea at the foothills of the Caucasus. It is a major center for a budding tourist industry and has several mineral spas and resorts. Russians hope it will someday be their Miami.

Stavropol (322,000), on the plateau north of the Caucasus, is a machine tool manufacturing city. It processes wool, leather and food stuffs. Its strategic position, centered between the Sea of Azov and the Caspian, was the base of operations for the Russian conquest of the Caucasus. It was briefly named Voroshilovsk from 1935 to 1943.

One of the big investors in the Stavropol region is the H.J. Heinz Company which has a baby food factory in Georgievsk just southeast of Stravropol. Heinz is the first foreign company to build a baby food factory in Russia. The company merged with a local agricultural firm to comply with Russian law. At full capacity the factory will rely on local agriculture products and produce 5,000 tons of processed food.

Belgorod (310,000), on the Northern Donets River was founded in the 13th century. Today it is the center of a large cement and construction materials industry which relies on nearby limestone and the Kursk iron ore deposits. It was an important fortress town in the 17th century, defending against the Crimean Tatars.

Novorussiysk (189,000) is a Black Sea port and naval base which handles grain and oil. It has ship repair facilities and is an important producer of cement which was first made here in 1882. Novorussiysk has an important meteorological facility where weather data for southern Russia is collected and predictions are made.

Engels (183,000), on the Volga River manufactures synthetic fibers. It was settled by Ukrainians and Germans during the reign of Catherine II. It was the capital of the German Volga Autonomous Republic before the republic was dissolved and many Germans were forced to move further east. Germans have petitioned the Russian Federation to restore the republic. Engels was known as Pokrovsk until 1931.

Tuapse (70,000) is a small important port north of Sochi on the Black Sea. It is a major petroleum port and terminus of a pipeline from the Grozny oil field. The city manufactures machinery and equipment for the oil industry and has a large oil refinery.

The **Caspian Sea** is the largest lake in the world. Its surface is 92 feet below sea level and its area is 3,200 square miles. In the north the depth averages only 17 feet. Water is brought to it by several rivers including the Volga (75% of its water) Ural, Emba, Kura, and Terek. Its large bay, the Kara-Boguz-Gol, is drying slowly and is exploited for salt.

Dams and municipal-industrial extraction have reduced the water flowing into it and over the years has lowered the water level. The lower water level is also partly due to changing climate. However, human activity has been mainly responsible. Salinity has also increased - a 30 percent increase since 1939 when data was first collected.

Building reservoirs and irrigation ditches plus municipal withdrawal, industrial withdrawal and agriculture practices have all contributed to the lowered water table and increased salinity. Creating reservoirs increased evaporation by increasing exposed surface.

The Caspian Sea produces 95 percent of Russian sturgeon and the prized black caviar. A female Beluga Sturgeon may weigh a ton and her eggs may make up ten percent of her weight. The average size caught is 700 pounds with 70 pounds of caviar. Three types of sturgeon are in the Caspian - -beluga, sevruga and osetra.

Today the entire Caspian is covered with at least a quarter inch of oil, mostly from mishaps and poor industrial practices around Baky. Damming the Volga concentrated the contaminants as the water volume decreased. Today the Volga sends thousands of tons of raw sewage, heavy metals and chemicals into the Caspian. The dams prevent sturgeon from swimming upstream to spawn in fresh water. The oil slick has caused the Caspian to rise slightly since evaporation from the sea surface has been retarded. The sea has risen seven feet

10-2 Astrakhan on the delta of the Volga River.

from 1985 to 1995, and it flooded hundreds of acres of newly developed farmland. It also inundated a railroad as well as thousands of new homes.

Overfishing has caused a sturgeon decline. Once only the USSR and Iran fished the Caspian and fishing was regulated by treaty. Today there are five countries on the Caspian and no fishing agreements. Each country has fishing limits but poaching accounts for 20 percent of the catch. In 1995, caviar that sold for eight dollars an ounce in Moscow could be bought in Baky for eight dollars a pound.

Poachers now face a tactical squad which hunts them down with infrared night scopes, assault weapons and fast boats. But there is still a lot of money to be made by poaching; one large fish might be worth as much as one hundred thousand dollars.

In 1977, the Caspian was an even 100 feet below sea level. By 1994 it was 92 feet below sea level even with the seven foot rise. Its deepest area, 90 miles north of Iran, is 560 feet.

ETHNIC REPUBLICS IN THE RUSSIAN CAUCASUS

The Russian Caucasus extends for about 750 miles from the Black Sea to the Caspian Sea, The mountains are the southern border between Europe and Asia. The Caucasus is divided into the northern Greater Caucasus and the southern Lesser Caucasus. Russia controls the Greater Caucasus, its highest point is Mt. Elbrus at 18,481 feet. The southern Caucasus with the Kura and Rion Rivers is known as Transcaucasia, and contains the countries of Georgia, Armenia and Azerbaijan.

75

The Caucasus has a tremendous mixture of different ethnic groups. There are at least a hundred of them with about 30 having populations of 50,000 or more. These include Mingrelian, Circassian, Svan, Ingush, Abkhazi, Adzhari, Kabardino, Dargwa, Lexghi, Avar, Adyge, Kartvelian and Zan. These are unified by a history of conquest and persecution by Russia. The Caucasus is a melting pot of nationalities which refuses to melt. Intermarriage, for example, is rare.

Most of the ethnic groups are and were followers of Islam. They terrorized Moscow and the Middle Volga region for generations. Their strength waned in the 16th century as Russia expanded. Under Catherine the Great most of the Caucasus was conquered.

Russians have never quite trusted the Caucasus ethnic groups. They tended to treat them as second-class citizens. Even today, in Moscow, they refer to Caucasus people as **chyorni** (blacks) or **churki**, a derogatory term which translates as chunks of wood. It is therefore not surprising that conflict broke out here, particularly in Chechnya and Dagestan after the Soviet Union breakup.

Circassia was a historic Black Sea region that extended into the Greater Caucasus to the Kuban River. The people were Muslims, called "Cherkess" by Russians. They referred to themselves as Adygey and their descendants are divided into Kabarda, Cherkess and Adygey. The

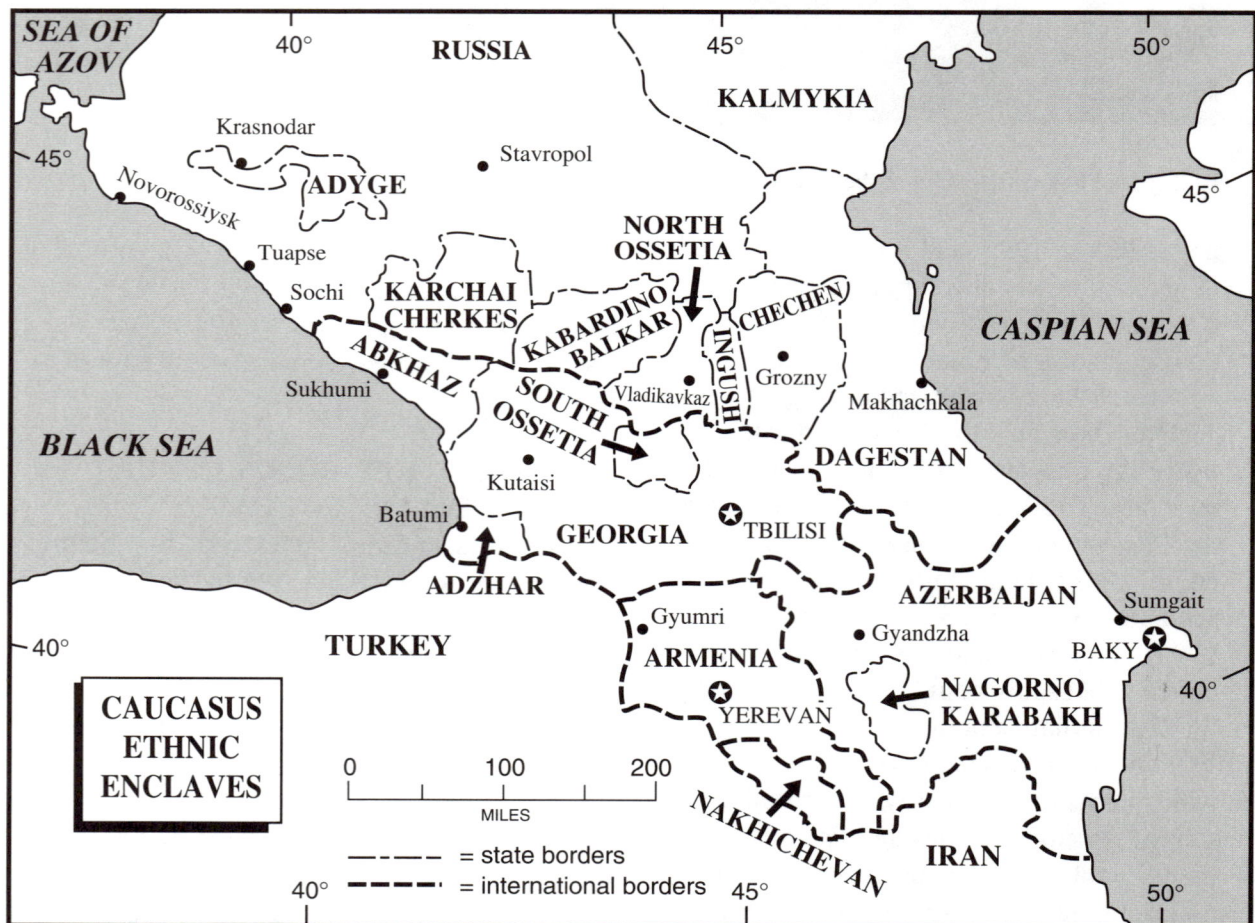

MAP 8 Caucasus Ethnic Enclaves

76

name Circassian has been incorrectly applied to all Caucasus mountain people. Circassians are also in the Crimea Originally Christian, they adopted Islam in the 17th century.

Journals and records report that Circassian women were extremely beautiful and many were sold into slavery in Turkey. This human trade continued into the early 20th century despite being outlawed.

Today, large numbers of Circassians are located in Jordan, Syria and Turkey as well as in the Russian Caucasus.

In 1943, Stalin feared the ethnics would aid the invading Germans so tens of thousands of them were deported to Siberia and Middle Asia. These included large groups of Chechens, Ingush, Karachay, Balkar and Tatars. For once, Stalin's fears were real for thousands of these people did join the German Army.

The **Adygey Republic (Adyge)**, at the foothills of the Greater Caucasus and near Krasnodar, is surrounded by the Krasnodar Territory. Maykop is its capital. Chief agriculture products are wheat, maize and rice. Cattle are raised along with sheep. Forests provide wood for a building material industry. Manufactured products include machine tools as well as wood products, including furniture. There is an oil refinery in Maykop.

Adygey who make up 22 percent of the population are related to other Circassians. Russians (68 %) are the dominant group. The Adyge are noted for their work in tapestries.

The capital city, **Maykop** (152,000), is in the center of an oil and natural gas field. It serves a pipeline to Krasnodar and the Black Sea port of Tuapse. Maykop is on one of the several small Belaya (white) rivers of Russia.

The **Chechen (Chechnya) Republic** is in the Greater Caucasus Mountains and extends north to the foothills. Grozny is its capital. The republic is rich in oil for its size. It also has natural gas, marl, quality limestone, alabaster and sulfur. Industries include oil refining, fruit canning, wine and cognac making and the production of chemicals. Its mineral waters are legendary and invite hardy tourists to a modest spa industry.

The Chechen are Sunni Muslim and speak a Caucasian language. They were anti-Czar and fought the Russians in a bloody but losing battle in 1859. However, rebellions continued.

In 1921 the Chechens were a part of the Mountain Peoples Republic which lasted until the Bolsheviks became organized and subdued them once again. Chechens were part of the group deported to Kazakhstan in 1943. Many of them returned in 1956. In 1991, ethnic Chechens made up fifty percent of the population and Russians twenty percent.

In 1991 Chechnya declared its independence. For three years it acted independent and set up a government and began making trade agreements using its oil as collateral. Russian President Boris Yeltsin sent troops to Chechnya on December 11, 1994. Russian attacks were met with guerrilla warfare and hostage taking. According to government reports, after 18 months of fighting the death toll reached 50,000, with about 100,000 wounded and 400,000 refugees.

In a speech Yeltsin likened himself to President Lincoln who fought a Civil War to prevent part of his country from breaking away.

The Chechnya capital city, **Grozny** (403,000), is the center of rich oil fields which are connected by pipeline to Tuapse on the Black Sea, Gorlovka in Ukraine and Makhachkala on the Caspian Sea. Grozny is one of the oldest oil producing regions of the world. Its first wells were drilled in 1893.

The **Daghestan (Dagestan) Republic** is on the middle Caspian Sea at the foothills of the Greater Caucasus. Its capital is Makhachkala. The land is naturally barren but farming is possible with irrigation. Wheat, maize, sunflowers, fruits and wine grapes are grown. Some forests in the west provide the basis for a limited wood industry.

Machines, textiles and wood products are the major industries. Most of the region obtains electric power from installations on small reservoirs of the Samur and Sulak Rivers.

There are at least thirty large ethnic groups in Dagestan including Avars, Darghins, Lezghians, Lakhs, Kalmyks, Tabasaran, Khaidag, Ingush, Chechens and Tats. Avartsy make up 27 % of the population, Dargintsy 16% and Russians 11%.

Makhachkala (318,000), the capital of Dagestan, is a port on the Caspian Sea. It has an oil refinery linked to the Grozny field. It produces small machines and textiles. The city was formerly known as Petrovsk.

The **Ingush Republic** was part of Chechnya at one time. When Chechnya declared its independence the Ingush asked for separation. The Ingush Republic is about fifty miles wide and eighty miles long, sandwiched between Chechen on its east and North Ossetia on its west.

The Ingush who first settled in the lowlands were considered Chechen. The two groups were forcibly joined into an autonomous district in 1934. Many Chechen and Ingush, dissatisfied by communist control, collaborated with the Germans in World War II. Several thousand were deported to the Far East and did not return to the area until 1956.

There are about a quarter million Ingush who make up about fifty percent of their republic. About thirty percent are Russian and the rest are mostly Chechen.

The **Kabardin - Balkar Republic** is located at the western end of the Russian Caucasus. It is a sparsely populated mountain wilderness with few roads. Nalchik is the capital. Balkars, Kabardins, Ukrainians and Russians live in the narrow gorges on tributaries of the Terek River. Mt. Elbrus (18,510 feet) is in this republic.

The Kabardins (50%) speak a Caucasian language, are pro-Russian and are Sunni Muslim in religion. The Balkars (10%) speak a Turkic language and are also Sunni Muslim. Russians make up about 30% of the population.

Sheep and poultry are raised in this region and wheat, maize, hemp and apples are grown. Industries are related to food processing and connected to small mineral deposits of chromium, gold, molybdenum, nickel and tungsten. Its position, centered between the Black Sea and the Caspian is strategic.

The capital city **Nalchick** (240,000), in the center of many mineral spas, is on a tourist route to Mt. Elbrus. The area around it is one of the remote wildernesses of the world. Russia had much difficulty subduing the mountain people who used this area as a base of operation.

The **Kalmyk Republic** borders on the Caspian Sea. Its capital is Elista which is about 150 miles northeast of Stavropol.

The republic is located in a great depression of the north Caspian Lowland. Mostly steppe and desert, it is dotted with salt lakes. There are no permanent waterways.

Kalmyk people live by stock raising which includes horses, sheep, cattle, camels and goats. Some Russians there raise hogs which are not eaten by Muslims. Farmers grow wheat, maize and fodder crops. Fishing in the Caspian is an important industry.

The people are mostly Kalmyk (45%) and Russian (37%). The former are descended from immigrants from Chinese Turkistan who came in the 17th century. Some still practice Buddhism. They became serfs under Catherine II. In 1771, about 300,000 Kalmyks decided to go back to Turkistan. They were met by cossacks who annihilated them. The name Kalmyk means "remnant", referring to those left behind.

During World War II the Kalmyks, like their neighbors, joined the Germans against the Soviets. As a result, they were deported to Siberia in 1943 and their autonomous district was dissolved. Nikita Khrushchev permitted the Kalmyks to return in 1958, and their autonomous region was reinstated. About six thousand returned to their old villages at that time and many more have since returned.

The **Karachevo - Cherkess Republic** is in the Greater Caucasus along the upper Kuban River. Caucasus foothills are in the south and steppe lowland in the north. The republic raises wheat and other grains, vegetables, fruits and livestock, mostly sheep and goats but some cattle. The metal resources include lead, zinc, copper and gold.

Russians make up 40 percent of the population, Karachay 30 percent and Cherkess 10 percent. The Karachay and Cherkess speak a Turkic language. They were original Circassians and members of the 1921 Mountain Peoples Republic.

The capital of the republic, **Cherkessk** (112,000), is on the Kuban River. It produces electrical equipment, footwear and food products.

The **North Ossetian Republic** is on the northern slope and in the middle of the Russian Caucasus. Its capital is Vladikavkaz. North Ossetia borders the South Ossetian Autonomous Republic in Georgia. They are connected by the Georgia Military Road.

Both sections of Ossetia have valleys that produce apples, peaches and grapes. Grain and cotton are also raised. Lumbering and sheep herding are found in the mountains. Goats and chickens are important backyard animals. Weaving of tapestries is an important cottage industry.

The republic has lead, zinc, silver, boron and some oil most of which is refined in the capital city. .

The North Ossetians are of Persian (Iranian) descent. The northern people are Sunni Muslim while the southerners are Eastern Orthodox. Ossetians are noted for their wood, silver and stone carvings. Today, the Ossetians are another group thinking independence. Ossetians make up 50 percent of the population, Russians 30 percent and Ingush 7 percent.

Vladikavkaz (305,000) formerly Ordzhonikdze, the capital of North Ossetia, is on the Terek River which flows into the Caspian Sea. Its population is Russian, Ossetian, Armenian and Georgian. The city is the northern starting point of the Georgian Military Road. It has several metal smelters and two oil refineries. Tractors, clothing, food products and chemicals are manufactured.

The **Terek River** rises in the Georgian Caucasus from glacier meltwater and flows 370 miles to the Caspian Sea. From its starting point on Mt. Kazbek it flows north past Vladikavkaz, then east past Grozny and northeast into the Caspian. Irrigation in the lower river course depletes much of its water before it meets the Caspian.. The Georgian Military Road parallels its valley in the upper reaches.

11. THE RUSSIAN PLAIN: EAST

The region from the middle Volga valley to the Urals was the jumping off point for settling the eastern frontier. Today it is the center of Russia's auto industry and the center for Russia's mercantile culture. Cities like Samara and Kazan are similar to Chicago.

The east central section of the Russian Plain is second in population to the Moscow region to its west. On the north is Vyatka on the Vyatka River and on the south is Samara on the Volga. The Volga is on the western margin and the Urals on the east.

This section of the Russian Plain is a highlands reaching westward from the Ural Mountains. As it approaches the Volga River it gets lower in elevation until south of Samara it is below sea level.

Samara and the area to the north receives 16 inches of precipitation which is enough for agriculture. The Saratov area to the south receives only 8 inches of precipitation, and requires irrigation.

The **Volga River** is actually a series of lakes created by many dams and hydroelectric facilities. Because the prevailing winds are from the southeast this "lake" water causes "lake effect" precipitation to the west. The lake evaporation, coupled with irrigation, has reduced the level of the Caspian Sea some thirty feet. Astrakhan, originally on the sea, is now thirty miles up the delta. By building dams and creating lakes much fertile land was inundated.

Winter freezing lasts five months in the north and three months in the south. The south has higher summer temperatures and can grow crops that require more heat such as maize. The Volga's western bank is a plateau with some higher hills; the eastern bank is a lowland subject to spring flooding.

The major tributary of the Volga flowing from the east is the Kama River which begins in the Urals around 60 degrees N. latitude and meets the Volga south of Kazan. Its main tributaries are the Belaya coming from the southeast and the Vyatka flowing from the north. These historic waterways were the new frontier after the Moscow region was settled. They have always been the home of non-Russian peoples.

Bulgars settled this area about the same time Muscovy was being settled by the Kievan Rus people. Bulgars were a Turkic people following Islam. Some Finnish groups had been in the area but the Bulgars became dominant. All of them were eventually subdued by the Golden Horde of Genghis Khan.

The Tatars of the Golden Horde settled along the middle Volga and set up the Khanate of Kazan. Their descendants are still there today. The early Tatars were nomadic herders who preferred the plains to forested areas. This attachment to the grassy plains probably saved Moscow from annihilation.

Ivan the Terrible, (Ivan IV), conquered the Tatars at Kazan in the middle of the 16th century. In a short period of time the entire Volga was dominated by Russians who founded such cities as Samara, Saratov and Volgograd.

Bashkirs settled on the Belaya River. They too were nomadic herders but the lush grazing lands of the region gave them reason to settle down. They too were subjugated by the new strong Russian armies who built a fort at Ufa in 1574.

Once the Bashkirs were subdued, it was only a matter of time until Russian trappers and fur traders crossed the Urals and opened up new territory claiming the land for the Czar. Although the Urals are not especially high mountains, they are still formidable. The lowest elevation of the Urals is just beyond the Bashkir lands. This is also a natural pass.

MAP 9   The Russian Plain: East

In order to win the region's loyalty, armies of Catherine the Great drove the Turks from the Crimea, thus preventing aid from the Ottoman Empire reaching the lower Volga. She further cemented the Russian hold on the lower Volga by resettling a new influx of immigrants from Germany, Poland and the Baltic Sea.

At the beginning of the 20th century, railroads began to appear in the region and the Trans-Siberian Railroad (TSR) was completed.

Many of the original settlers of the Volga took advantage of this new opportunity and moved eastward to settle along the rail line. New communities originated in many areas of southern Siberia.

Early industries were mostly **kustarny** or cottage industries such as weaving and leather tooling. There were small iron workings in the Ural foothills and in the German areas. Salt mining was at Perm. Most Kama region industry was connected with the forest.

The Bolshevik's put new emphasis on mineral exploration. Oil was discovered near

Perm. However, the bulk of Soviet oil still came from the Caspian region.

When World War II broke out, the Soviets began moving industry out of the Moscow area and relocating it further east. If it were not for World War II, it is doubtful this region would have been so heavily industrialized.

After World War II, oil production began to increase in the region. Coal, hauled across the Urals, was still the dominant fuel for industry. Caspian oil became less significant, and by 1980 two-thirds of Soviet oil production came from here. Natural gas discovered in the Saratov region, was piped to the industries and homes of Moscow. After World War II, emphasis was placed on taming the Volga and its tributaries. Two of the largest hydropower stations in the world were built at Samara and Volgograd. This was followed by many more stations along the Volga and the Kama system.

Samara, with its power station, oil and natural gas, is the central city along the Volga. It is the gateway to the east. Rail lines connect it to the TSR to the north.

Russians are relative newcomers to the region and many non-Russians still inhabit this large area. These include Chuvash, Tatars and Bashkirs who are of Mongol descent and Mordva, Udmurt, Mari and Permyak who speak a Finnish dialect. Most of these groups have their own "independent" districts.

EAST PLAIN REPUBLICS

The **Chuvash Republic** is in the middle Volga Valley with Cheboksary as its capital. The region is a wooded steppe with many bogs which supply peat.

Cheboksary (433,000) is on the Volga River near a large hydroelectric station. Its industries are related to agriculture. It has a state university and a 17th century cathedral.

The republic has deposits of limestone, dolomite, clay, sand and phosphate rock. The region produces wheat, barley, rye, potatoes, flax, apples, hemp and sugar beets.

Regional industries include natural gas, oil refining, food processing and flax processing. One third of the republic is forested and lumbering and woodworking are Chuvash specialties.

Chuvash make up 70 percent of the population and urban Russians about 25 percent. There are Mordvinian, Tatar and Ukrainian minorities.

The Chuvash are descended from the early Bulgars. They speak a Turkic language and follow the Orthodox religion.

The **Bashkir Republic** occupies the Belaya River Basin with its capital at Ufa. It is also listed as **Bashkortostan.** The TSR crosses its territory. The republic was a major battleground between the "red" and "white" armies during the 1917 Civil War.

Bashkir territory has natural gas, coal, salt, iron, gold, copper, zinc, manganese and bauxite. However, almost half the land is forested and its leading industries are sawmilling and the production of paper and plywood. Agricultural products are wheat, rye, oat and potatoes.

Russians are the majority (40 percent) while Bashkirs make up about 21 percent of the population. The Bashkirs are a mixture of the Finnish, Turkish and Mongol peoples who first settled here. They are Muslim and their common language is close to that of the Tatars. There are over 70 nationalities living in Bashkir.

In 1992 Bashkir's legislature declared the republic "independent" in foreign economic agreements and said it would no longer be regulated by Russian Federation law.

Bashkortostan and Tatarstan have effectively become states within a country. They are examples of independence

11-1 Landscape near Ufa, capital of Bashkortostan. Oil dominates the economy.

movements that threaten the future unity and stability of the Russian Federation.

Bashkir has railroads and pipelines which connect to European Russia as well as some European countries. In the favorable agreement made with the Russian Federation Bashkir can establish sports, economic and cultural events with foreign countries. They and only Tatarstan have this luxury.

In 1995, sixty percent of Bashkir industry had been privatized. This is managed by the State Property Management Committee. About half the stock shares of the privatized industries are owned by the actual workers. Most of the agriculture land has been privatized but farmers cannot sell or give away their property outside of their immediate families. Private farms usually have no machinery, electricity or telephones. There is a serious lack of roads connecting farms to markets.

Monetary policies for the republic are regulated by the National Bank of Baskortostan which is a branch of the Russian National Bank. There are forty commercial banks in the republic.

Russia still owes Bashkir industries and their workers payment for past products and labor, but it appears this money will not be forthcoming. Russian taxes on Bashkir profits were 85 percent in 1994, but the republic has refused to pay. Bashkir leaders of industry and commerce still retain a socialist agenda.

Baskir has the largest oil refining capacity of all the Russian republics. In 1995, oil production was 20 million tons, down from 50 million tons of 1970. Bashkir imports oil from other republics for refining.

Timber and lumber products account for 20 percent of the republic's income while oil and gas account for 50 percent. Machine tools and manufacturing account for 25 percent.

Bashkir is a major supplier of oil products including polyethylene synthetic rubber. Synthetic fibers and synthetic leather shoes are exported to England, Germany, India, United States, Hungary and Italy.

The **Belaya (White) River** is in the Bashkir Republic. Rising in the Urals, it flows 880 miles through oil fields before it joins the Kama River.

The **Mari Republic,** also **Marii el**, is in the middle Volga valley centered between the Vyatka and the Kama Rivers. Its capital is **Yoshkar-Ola** (242,000) which specializes in the manufacture of pharmaceuticals and agriculture machinery. The region is heavily wooded with coniferous forest. There is a large lumbering industry producing paper and pulp products.

Rye and some wheat are grown along with flax and hay which supports a small dairy industry. Like most dairy industries, milk and butter are sold in the cities.

The Mari speak a Finnish dialect. They were independent until conquered by the Golden Horde in the 13th century. Russia gained control of the area in 1552.

Mari make up 43 percent of the population while Russians are 47 percent. There are also Tatar, Chuvash and Udmurt minorities.

The **Mordovia Republic** is on the western side of the Volga and incorporates part of the Oka River and the headwaters of the Don. **Saransk** (315,000) is its capital. A sizable industry supports automobile manufacturing, furniture making, paper making, machine tools and the manufacturing of wooden utensils. There is also a modern wood chemical industry producing cellulose and rayon.

Cattle and sheep are raised. Farm products include wheat, hemp, flax, and potatoes. Beekeeping is a long established cottage industry.

About 60 percent of the population is Russian. Mordvinians make up about one third and Tatars five percent. Mordvinians speak a Finno-Ugric tongue and are Orthodox in religion. They were first mentioned in Greek literature in the 6th century. They have always had close association with the Slavic peoples of Muscovy.

Although most Mordvins are Christian, many still practice a form of nature worship. They will speak freely about the gods who watch over the streams and trees. Their chief divinity is Shkay, a sun god.

Mordvins have elaborate holidays and celebrate them by wearing richly embroidered native costumes.

The **Tatar Republic**, also **Tartarstan**, is found along the Volga and lower Kama River valleys. Its capital is Kazan, a leading riverport. The territory produces oil and natural gas, and has important deposits of lignite, limestone, gypsum, dolomite and marl. It is important in lumbering, textiles, leather processing and food preservation.

Farmlands produce wheat, hay, sugar beets, sunflowers and flax. The flax industry is not as important as it was before the days of abundant cotton. Much of the farm products are grown on irrigated lands.

Tatars make up about half the population, Russians about 40 percent. There are minorities of Chuvash, Udmurt, Mari and Mordvinian. The Tatars are Sunni Muslim and speak a Mongol-Turkic dialect. They are descendants of the Golden Horde who assimilated the Bulgars who originally inhabited the region.

The Tatars were the most powerful group of the Volga before their defeat by Ivan the Terrible in 1552. The Tatars have always had a good working relationship with Russians, but with the new cry for independence, there might be some future problems in this region. In 1992 the Tatar legislature declared itself an independent republic but would keep an associate membership with the Russian Federation.

Tatarstan has its own constitution, its own flag and national anthem. Its laws are supposedly above those of the Russian Federation. In May 1993, the president of Tatar signed a five year agreement with Hungary which will supply Hungary with 1.5 million tons of crude oil per year in exchange for industrial and agriculture products. Tatarstan is a major supplier to the Friendship Pipeline, an oil transport system to Europe.

When Tatarstan held a referendum in 1992, 82 percent of the adult population participated, many of them ethnic Russians, and 61 percent voted for sovereignty. Russia, under the guidance of Yegor Gaidar, made substantial concessions to Tatarstan. The most important allowed the republic to keep most of its hard (foreign) currency income. Another concession gave the republic control over its own natural resources.

Tartarstan may not have complete independence or true autonomy, but the republic does enjoy a large measure of freedom. More importantly, Russian concessions to Tatarstan may signal future relationships with the different republics.

The Udmurt Republic lies between the Kama and Vyatka rivers with Izhevsk as its capital. Railroads are the main form of transportation despite some navigable rivers and lakes. Although the soils are poor, rye, flax, sugar beets, peas and potatoes are raised. There is extensive exploitation of timber, peat and oil shale. Mineral deposits include quartz sand, clay, limestone and coal. Important industries are flax processing, steel rolling, and the manufacture of small machinery and parts.

Udmurts make up 40 percent of the population, but Russians are dominant at 55 percent. Mari and Tatars are the other minorities.

The Udmurts (a.k.a. Votyaks and Votiaks) speak a Finno-Ugrian dialect and are Orthodox in religion. Although their ancestors have been in this area since the 6th century many follow the oriental religion of ancestor worship. They are noted for their artistry in weaving, embroidery and wood carving.

Samara (1, 260,000), formerly Kuybyshev, is located on the east bank of the Volga and at the mouth of the 360 mile long Samara River. It is a major river and rail center connected to Moscow and Siberia.

Important industries produce automobiles, aircraft, locomotives, machinery, ball bearings, synthetic rubber, textiles, chemicals and oil products. A large British -American tobacco factory is a major employer. Grain and livestock are exported from the region.

One of the world's largest hydropower stations is located a few miles upstream (north) of the city. Samara also has easy access to coal, oil and natural gas which are produced in the vicinity.

Samara was founded in 1586 as a fortress for Russia's eastern frontier. The fort was attacked by Tatars in 1615 and Kalmyks in 1644.

During World War II, the central government of the Soviet Union was transferred to Samara and the city grew. Its name was changed to Kuybyshev in 1935, then returned to the original name in 1992.

Kazan (1,105,000) is located on the Middle Volga River where it is joined by the Kazanka. It is the capital of the Tatar Republic and a major historic, industrial and cultural center. Manufacturing includes small machines, chemicals, explosives, aircraft, electrical equipment, food products, building materials and furs. Kazan became the capital of a powerful khanate in the 15th century, the result of the dwindling Mongol Empire. Conquered by Ivan the Terrible in 1552, the city became an important outpost for further Russian expansion.

In 1774 a cossack revolt led by Yemelyn Pugachov was centered on Kazan. The city has a 16th century kremlin, a university, an academy of science as well as ancient cathedrals, monasteries and two 18th century mosques.

Kazan is the leading city in a movement to diminish federal power in Moscow. They are taking advantage of the present weak politcal situation in Russia to solidify their republic's economic future..

Ufa (1,105,000), the capital of the Bashkir Republic, is located on the western slopes of the Ural Mountains at the confluence of the Belaya and Ufa Rivers. The city was captured by Russia in 1574 and turned into a fortress. Ufa is an important stop on the Trans-Siberian Railroad.

Ufa industries include electrical apparatus, mining equipment and oil refineries. It is a crossroads and supplier for oil and gas pipelines.

Perm (1,100,000), located on the Kama River, is a transfer station for materials between the Volga and the Urals. Perm has oil refineries and a chemical industry based on timber and petroleum. A relatively new city, founded in 1780, Perm was named Molotov from 1940 to 1958. The city has a modern university and a technical institute.

Izhevsk (645,000), the capital of the Udmurt Republic, is a steel manufacturing city. It produces armaments, forest products and heavy machinery. There are many institutes dealing with agriculture and metallurgy. Several institutions are devoted to preserving Udmurt culture and language. Under the Soviets the city was named Ustinov.

Simbirsk, formerly Ulyanovsk (642,000), is an important rail crossing point on the Volga, where it is joined by the Svigaya, just south of the Trans-Siberian Railway. It is an industrial city in an excellent agricultural area. The city, founded in 1648, is noted for its products of beer, vodka and other hard liquor. Motor vehicles and flour milling are important industries.

Simbirsk is the birthplace of Vladimir Ilyich Ulyanov who came to be known as Vladimir Lenin, founder of the Soviet Union.

Tolyatti, also **Togliatti** (635,000) is situated about fifty miles upstream from Samara near the dam for a large hydroelectric station. The dam flooded much of the original city which was moved to higher ground. It has the largest automobile assembly plant in the world. The auto works was built in conjunction with the Italian Fiat company. There are two other large auto plants. The city also manufactures cement, artificial fibers, synthetic rubber and fertilizers. It is named after a famous Italian communist leader. It's original name was Novy Stavropol and it may be called that again.

Naberezhnye Chelny (505,000), on the Kama River, has the largest truck assembly plant in the world. It derives power from a large hydroelectric station on the lower Kama River. A nuclear station is planned for the future. The city was called Brezhnev from 1982 to 1988.

The 1260 mile **Kama River** originates in the foothills of the Urals and flows northwest, then east, then southwest before it empties into the Volga near the city of Kazan. The 800 mile long Vyatka River is the biggest tributary of the Kama.

Syzran (174,000) located near the junction of the Volga with the Syzran River is near large deposits of oil shale from which it makes oil products and asphalt. It also produces leather goods, glass, chemicals and wood products. It is the center of small limestone and slate industries.

12. WESTERN SIBERIAN LOWLAND

Siberia is the name given to the northern section of Asia. It is generally divided into three areas which are bordered by three great river systems. **The Western Siberian Lowland** extends west-east from the Ural Mountains to the Yenisey River and from Kazakhstan in the south, north to the Arctic Ocean. The center section, **The Central Siberian Plateau** extends from the Yenisey River east to the Lena River and Lake Baikal and from Kazakhstan in the south, north to the Arctic Ocean. The third section, **The Far East** extends from the Lena River to the Pacific Ocean and from China and Mongolia on the south, north to the Arctic Ocean.

The first Russian to enter and conquer parts of Siberia was Yermak Timofeyevich, a cossack leader in the employ of the Stroganov family who operated a salt works at Solvychegodsk near the headwaters of the Northern Dvina River.

The Stroganov's received permission from Czar Ivan the Terrible to exploit lands along the Kama and Chusovaya Rivers. The trading posts set up by the Stroganovs were often attacked by Tatar Siberians. Eventually, Ivan gave the Stroganov family authorization to invade Siberia.

Yermak (a.k.a. Ermak Timofeevich) led a force of 840 men up the Chusovaya River and across the Urals into Siberia. His men had firearms and the Siberian nomads had spears, bows and arrows. The central city of Siberia was Isker (Sibir) in the Khanate of Sibir located on the Irtysh River.

After many skirmishes with villages along the rivers, Yermak's forces conquered Isker in 1582. This victory firmly established the Russians in Siberia. A series of forts was quickly built across Siberia, and in less than 60 years Russians reached the Pacific Ocean.

The actual development of Siberia was slower due to the vast distances, the small numbers of Russians and the harsh climate. Only with the overpopulation of the Russian Plain in the 19th Century did the exodus to Siberia begin. The first big immigration began with the freeing of the Serfs in 1861. This was followed by the building of the Trans-Siberian Railroad in the 1890s and the practice of exiling criminals and political prisoners to Siberia by the last Czars and the Soviets.

The Western Siberian Lowland is bordered by the Ural Mountains on the west, the country of Kazakhstan on the south, the Yenisey River on the east and the Arctic Ocean on the north. The higher land in the south is the most developed, having the main highway and the most rail traffic. The region is so low that the Ob River, which drains most of the territory, only drops 300 feet from Novosibirsk to the sea.

The first non-military Russians to enter this region migrated across the northlands from St. Petersburg. These trappers and fur traders met little resistance from the widely scattered native peoples. The Russians did meet some resistance when they entered the southern lowlands where Kazakhs and other herders grazed livestock.

Today the southern lowlands of Western Siberia produces most of Russia's wheat. People complain that they provide Moscow with food and metal products but receive little in return. The area is a major producer of wheat, millet, sunflowers and the minor grains of rye, oats and barley.

Much dairy cattle is raised to provide milk for the growing cities. There is a surplus of butter and it is one of the leading exports of the region. Sheep are also abundant.

MAP 10   Western Siberian Lowland: Southern Region

Snow lies on the ground for five months of the year but in the summer temperatures rise high enough for fanning. Outside of the cities, farming is carried on in every available plot of ground south of the forest line. Precipitation averages 13 inches which is sufficient for most grain crops. If it falls below that, there is a crop failure. In some years the precipitation has been as low as eight inches. Today fanning ;n the southern high areas, though still risky, has been helped with the development of new crops through genetic engineering and experimental breeding.

Siberia is the taiga, the dark greenish blue forest that blankets the land. It is a mass of cedar, pine, spruce and larch interspersed with white of birch and aspen. It is a picture of color against a bright blue sky in all seasons of the year since there are few overcast days with rain. In winter the sun, though low in the sky, shines brightly.

Cities and villages are carved out of the taiga. In the north these are connected by thin roads. The southern section has good railroads and many excellent, though few, highways. Siberians of the taiga have a saying "We don't have roads, we have directions."

In the extreme south are the steppes and scattered throughout are hundreds of lakes, especially between the Irtysh and Ob Rivers. The lakes provide plenty of fish, especially carp, throughout the year. Lakes and their associated wetlands make up the Vasyuganye Swamp, the biggest swamp in the world.

Eighty percent of the region's coal is lignite which is widely used for electric generation even though it causes heavy air pollution.

The **Kuznetsk Basin** is east of Novosibirsk and the Ob River. It is the major supplier of high grade coal to all of Russia. Coal was first discovered here in 1721 but wasn't mined until a century later. The exploitation of this coal became heavy in the early 20th century when the Ural industrial complex needed high grade coal. An industrial region built around the coal deposits produces steel, zinc, aluminum and heavy mining machinery.

Despite the large industrial cities, the population remains half rural. Rural settlements follow the main railroad routes, especially the TSR.

The **Ural Mountains** are the traditional dividing line between Europe and Asia. For centuries they separated oriental people in the east from Caucasians of the west. Early in the 6th century, several Mongol groups made their way across the Urals and settled along the Middle and Lower Volga River.

The Urals are 1,500 miles long and extend from the Arctic Ocean to the Caspian Sea. They are low mountain ranges which appear more formidable due to the lowlands surrounding them.

Geographically, the Urals are divided into four sections. The Polar Urals are north of 64 degrees North. This area is a treeless tundra. The Ural Mountains extend into the Arctic Ocean and are manifested as the islands of Novaya Zemlya.

The Northern Urals extend from about 61 degrees to 64 degrees North. These are craggy, mostly treeless narrow ranges with an average elevation of 1300 feet. The Ural's highest peak, **Narodnaya**, is here at 6,214 feet.

The Middle Urals extend from about 59 degrees to 61 degrees North. These are covered with dense coniferous forests with very fertile valleys. This is the area of northern settlements including the aluminum city of Kraznoturinsk (240,000).

The Southern Urals extend from about 52 degrees to 55 degrees North and consist of three parallel mountain chains. There are plateaus with dense forests.

The Trans-Siberian Railway crosses the central Urals and the Samara-Tashkent Railroad bisects the southern Urals. The mountains are also criss-crossed by many oil and gas pipelines.

The Urals contain rich deposits of copper, manganese, gold, aluminum, potash, coal and iron ore. Oil deposits are on the western slopes. Mineral deposits also include emeralds, lead, silver, chromium, zinc, platinum, nickel, bauxite and tungsten.

The first iron works was established in the Urals in the 17th century. In the 18th and 19th centuries, the Urals had one of the world's largest steel complexes. Although steel is still produced here today, its relative importance is declining.

CITIES AND RIVERS

Yekaterinburg (1,370,000), formerly Sverdlovsk, is located at the eastern end of a good pass through the Urals formed by the Chusovaya River valley. The city was an important trade route and prospered before the advent of the railroads. On the Iset River, it is an important rail and air junction. A direct line connects the city with the TSR.

The city produces heavy machinery, building materials, electrical appliances and is known for gem cutting. It has copper, iron and platinum smelters. Gold and copper are mined in the vicinity.

Yekaterinburg, was originally named for Catherine I, wife of Peter the Great. Here Czar Nicholas II and his family were imprisoned and later executed by the Bolsheviks in 1918. The city was renamed Sverdlovsk in 1924 after Jocab Sverdlovsk, the Soviet military administrator who had ordered the murder of the Imperial family.

Several mining schools and one of the largest meteorological observation facilities in the world are part of the educational facilities. The city is also the birthplace of Boris Yeltsin, the first popularly elected president of Russia.

Chelyabinsk (1,149,000) is located just off the eastern slope of the Urals on a highland surrounded by lakes. It is on the TSR and originated in the 18th century as a Russian frontier city. The first steel plant was built in 1930. Today workers manufacture tractors, aircraft parts, chemicals, agriculture machinery as well as iron and steel.

Under Soviet rule Chelyabinsk became the center of a top-secret nuclear arms facility. A tragic nuclear accident in 1957 killed over two thousand people. Although this was not reported in the tightly controlled Soviet press, radiation detectors from around the world indicated something had happened. Today Chelyabinsk is thought to be the most radioactive spot on earth.

Orenburg (552,000) formerly Chkalov, was founded in 1737 as a fortress against the Kazakh nomads. It is located on the Ural River and is an important rail junction for goods traveling between Toshkent and Samara. Its agricultural region produces

wheat, sheep and dairy cattle. The city has extensive railroad repair shops and several oil refineries. There is a huge natural gas deposit southwest of the city which is a hub for most gas pipelines feeding Russia and Europe.

The city was originally further east, at the site of Orsk, on the bend in the Ural River. It was moved to its present location in 1743 on a natural crossing point between Russian trade and Kazakhstan.

Nizhni Tagil (445,000) is located north of Yekaterinburg on the Tagil River. Its heavy industrial base depends on deposits of iron, copper and gold in the immediate vicinity. Manufacturing includes railroad cars, heavy machinery and chemicals. It is a metallurgical center for research and development of the area's minerals.

Magnitogorsk (443,000) was built in 1929 under Stalin's First Five Year Plan. Located on the Ural River, it is the site of huge magnetite deposits and is near mount Magnitaya. Although it became a showplace for Soviet industrial propaganda, the city has horrible pollution problems. Coking coal is shipped into the city from Karaganda in Kazakhstan. The magnetite ore is depleted and ore must be imported from other regions to keep industry flourishing. There is also a sizable cement and glass industry.

The **Ob River** is 3,700 miles long if its longest tributary is included in its length.. Beginning in the Altai Mountains of Central Asia, it winds its way through the northern Urals before it empties into Obskaya Guba, an arm of the Arctic Ocean. The middle Ob flows through many miles of swamp before it is joined by the Irtysh River. The Irtysh has two great tributaries, the Tobol and Ishim, all three waters originate in the highlands of Kazakhstan.

The Ob is frozen in its upper reaches for five months of the year. Considerable year-

12-1 Magnitogorsk, one of the most polluted cities in the world.

round flooding is caused by ice blockage in the north. Principle cities along the Ob are Novosibirsk, Barnaul, Kamena and Mogochin. There is a large hydroelectric station at Novosibirsk. Tomsk, the oldest city in Siberia, is on the Tom River, a tributary of the Ob.

The Ob River and its tributaries have excellent fishing including sturgeon, salmon and carp. The rivers are navigable but because the outlet is to the Arctic Ocean river traffic is mostly local.

Several large Kazakhstan cities are on the **Irtysh River** , 2,560 miles long - Oskemen, Semey and Pavlodar. Where the river enters Russia the major city is Omsk.

The **Tobol River**, 1,050 miles long has Kustanay in Kazakhstan and Kurgan in Russia. Its valley contains important cottage weaving industries. The major city on the **Ishim River**, 1,130 miles long, is Petropavlov in Kazakhstan just south of where the TSR crosses the river.

Novosibirsk (1,444,000) formerly Novonkolayevsk, is located where the Trans-Siberian Railroad crosses the Ob River. It is the largest city in Siberia as well as one of the largest cities in Russia. It is the hub of rail, river and air transportation for Siberia.

The growth of the city was due to its location on the Ob River, the route of the TSR and the proximity of the rich mineral resources of the Kuznetsk Basin. Novosibirsk residents manufacture textiles, mining equipment, turbines, chemicals, heavy machinery, and they are heavily involved in metallurgy. There is a hydroelectric station on the river above the city.

12- 2 Novosibirsk, the largest city in Siberia

The area around the city and the steppe lands to the south mark the eastern point of the Russian agriculture triangle. The Black Sea and St. Petersburg are the other points.

The city received its current name in 1925. Its population grew during World War II when industry was shifted from the Russian Plain eastward.

Novosibirsk has a major university as well as an important scientific research center and opera and ballet companies.

Most major cities in Siberia have good airports and daily flights to Moscow as well as to other cities of Siberia.
Omsk (1,170,000) is located at the junction of the Irtysh and small Om River. The Trans-Siberian Railroad crosses here. Omsk is a major river port that produces agricultural machinery and railway equipment. It has grain processing, oil

refining, forest products and textiles. Omsk is the center of a major agricultural district.

The city was the headquarters for the White Army who opposed the Bolshevik Red Army after the Revolution. Omsk is about four hundred miles from Novosibirsk and about five hundred miles from Chelyabinsk.

Barnaul (610,000) is an important railroad junction on the Ob River, south of Novosibirsk. Five important rail lines meet here. They come from Aqmola, Semey, Kolchetav, the Kuzbas and one line that links up with the TSR.

The city is the administrative center of the Altai Territory and the major city in the rich agricultural Kulunda steppe. Its farms produce wheat, maize, oats and sugar beets. Industries produce cotton textiles, rayon fibers, automobile tires, forest products, refined silver and flour.

Novokuznetsk (602,000), formerly Stalinsk, is on the Tom River, a tributary of the Ob. Steel, iron alloys, aluminum, coke, chemicals and mining equipment are manufactured. "Old town" was founded by the Cossacks in 1617. A trading center until it was developed for industry in 1930, it was renamed in 1961.

12-3   A rayon factory in Barnaul.

Tomsk (508,000), located on the Tom River, was the largest city in Siberia before the construction of the TSR. It produces ball bearings, electric motors, machine tools, footwear and chemicals. A petrochemical complex producing a wide range of plastics is also here. The chemical industry is based on the development of the great gas and oil fields to the north. Tomsk has the oldest university in Siberia, founded in 1880.

The **Tom River**, 525 miles long, is navigable from Novokuznets to the Ob. It is an important transportation artery for the movement of coal, grains and sand dredged from the river bottom.

Kemerovo, Kemerowo, (525,000), another city on the crowded Tom River, is the center of coal mining in the Kuznetz Basin and has a sizable synthetic fiber industry. Like the region's other cities it manufactures textiles, forest products and produces chemicals.

Kemerovo was known as Shcheglovsk from 1925 to 1932.

Tyumen (484,000) was the first permanent Russian settlement in Siberia. The first fort was built here in 1586. Located 200 miles due east of Yekaterinburg, Tyumen is on a tributary of the Tobol River. Its location within the vast oil and gas fields of Western Siberia bodes well for the future.

Kurgan (360,000), located on the TSR and the Tobol River, is in the center of an agricultural district. It manufactures agriculture machinery and processed foods. Its name means "burial" after the many ancient burial mounds found here.

Surgut (350,000) located on the Ob River is one of the fastest growing cities in Siberia. Recent oil and gas development has made it a boom town. A former fishing and lumbering village connected to other towns by unpaved muddy roads, it now boasts a small but important air field.

Prokopyevsk (278,000) is another major coal center in the Kuznetsk Basin. It manufactures mining machinery and engages in food processing. In recent years there has been a population shift from Prokopyevsk to Kemerovo.

Biysk, Biisk (233,00), is an important town in the Kuznets Basin due to its flat terrain. It is located 80 miles southeast of Barnaul. A highway connects it to Mongolia and a railroad to Turkistan.

The manufacture of food processing equipment is a major industry in Biysk.

13. CENTRAL SIBERIAN PLATEAU

The **Central Siberian Plateau** is bordered by the Yenisey River on the west and by the Lena River on the east. To the north is the Arctic Ocean and to the south are high mountain ranges belonging to the Central Asian system.

The area between the Yenisey and Lena Rivers is a high plateau interspersed with some mountains. The highest peak (5,377 feet) is on the **Patom Plateau**, northeast of Lake Baikal. The central plateau is tundra where it borders the Arctic Ocean giving way to taiga all the way to the Central Mountains. In the south some areas can be classified as wooded steppe and a few others as steppe.

Most of the population live in the southern portion of the plateau. Only a few small villages, two small cities and one large city, **Norilsk**, are located in the north. Norilsk is situated just off the Yenisey River above the Arctic Circle. It is populated mostly by ethnic Russians while the surrounding tundra is inhabited by native Nentsy.

Other cities along the Yenisey above the Arctic Circle are **Igarka** (40,000) and **Dudinka** (25,000). The latter acts as the administrative center for the district.

Two great energy resources dominate the plateau's industries: the Kuznetsk coal deposit and a hydroelectric zone made possible by the Yenisey's headwaters. To the north of the Kuznetsk and west of the Yenisey is West Siberia's oil and gas fields with great promise for the future.

Plateaus are characterized by deep valleys making road and railroad construction across them difficult. The TSR spans many deep canyons as it rolls over a continuous string of bridges.

The southern mountains are eroded plateau about 7,000 feet above sea level with occasional peaks over 13,000 feet. The mountains over the border in Mongolia and China are much higher.

This is an area of heavy seismic activity, much like southern California. Hot sulfur springs emerge from deep beneath the earth, and the fault in Lake Baikal is over a mile deep. Lake Baikal is a seismic trench which is slowly widening.

Because the Central Siberian Plateau is in the continental interior, it has some of the coldest temperatures on earth. The average January temperature at Yakutsk is 46 degrees Fahrenheit below zero. Permafrost exists throughout the region except for the southern portion.

Lake Baikal, " The Blue Pearl of Siberia", does not freeze over until January. Temperatures along its immediate shore are fifteen degrees warmer than temperatures only forty miles away. The water is so deep that the fish population and the seals which feed upon them can swim to great depths for protection. About 300 rivers empty into the lake.

Ice fishing on Lake Baikal is done with huge nets that are slipped through the ice. The nets are then pulled by horses along narrow slits in the ice to large holes where they are extracted. Winter ice fishing on the lake is a profitable enterprise.

The lake is home to eight thousand seals called **Nerpa** which are an important tourist attraction. Over 1,400 species of plants and animals are unique to Lake Baikal and a delight to naturalists.

The lake has a dozen small towns along its shore. About 3,000 people live on Olkhon Island, one of 27 islands in the lake.

Lake Baikal contains more fresh water than any other lake in the world. It is 50

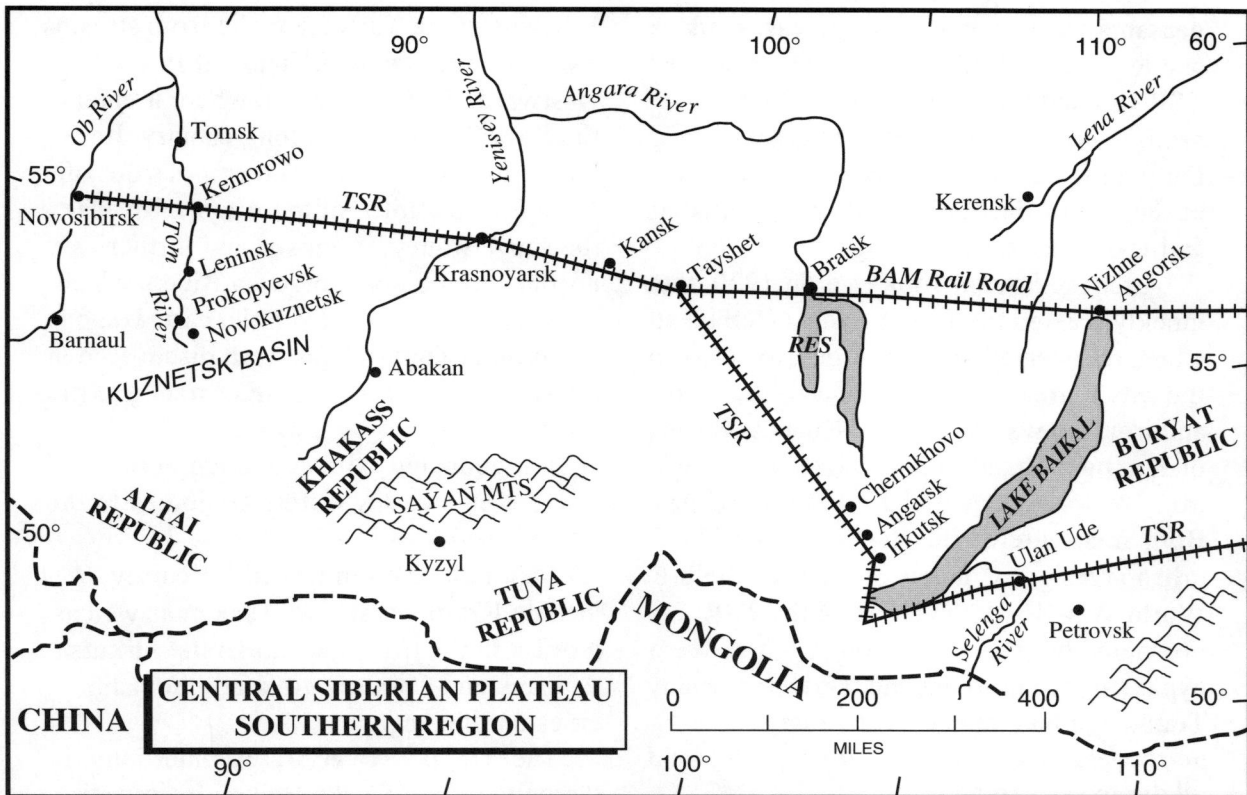

MAP 11   Central Siberian Plateau: Southern Region

miles wide and 395 miles long. Its greatest depth was measured at 5,714 feet, more than a mile. The lake has many feeder streams but the Angara River is its only outlet. A hydropower station at Irkutsk is used in the aluminum industry. Many of the beautiful hills surrounding the lake are denuded of timber and the lake is an avenue for timber movement in the summer. The TSR passes south of the lake.

The taiga here is pine, birch, cedar, fir and larch. The Altay and Sayan ranges receive over fifty inches of precipitation a year allowing the growth of extensive forests. It also fills up the many streams flowing from the mountains.

This area was first settled by the Yakut, an Eskimo-like group who were herders and foresters. Then came invasions by Mongol Buryats from the south who pushed the Yakuts up the Lena River to the north.

China once ruled the Altai and Sayan Ranges as well as lands in present day Mongolia and Tuva. After Chinese influence declined, Russia laid claim. However, the present borders are not surveyed and remain in dispute.

Russia established hegemony by building trading posts across the southern plateau. In the l7th century there were forts and trading posts along all the major rivers, and from Lake Baikal to the headwaters of the Amur River. W;th the discovery of lead, copper, coal and silver, Russian settlement accelerated. The new villages were protected by cossacks volunteers.

95

After serfdom was abolished in 1861 peasants were permitted to go eastward and lease lands from the Czar. When the TSR reached the Ob River in 1896 it brought with it a wave of immigrants. During the next twelve years, the railroad pushed on to the Pacific and carried Russian and Ukrainian settlers along.

After the Soviets took over in 1920, they quickly created the Ural-Kuznets Combinat which transferred coal and iron ore between those two areas. Coal was sent to the Urals and iron ore was sent to the Kuznets Basin or **Kuzbas**. This changed somewhat when iron ore was discovered around the Kuzbas. Both areas entered the steel age. Today's urban areas grew mostly in the years before World War II. All the cities on the TSR prospered but those like Tomsk which were bypassed, began to decline. However, today Tomsk is a bustling city with a large petrochemical industry based on the gas and oil discoveries to its north.

The plateau is a treasure trove of water power, and much of it was developed during the hectic industrializing days of Stalin. Since then, few attempts have been made to complete the great programs discussed and projected for the region. One such project was to dam up the headwaters of many of the streams, the Lena River in particular, and force the water to run into the dry steppe lands now in Kazakhstan.

A large hydropower station at Bratsk backed up a huge lake, and began producing power in 1961. Many small hydroelectric stations were also built in the region but nothing as grand as the Bratsk station.

Branch lines of the TSR connect Turkistan, China and Mongolia to Russia. There is also a direct line to Beijing. A branch line to the warm water at Port Arthur in China was once a main avenue of trade for Russia but its importance has declined over the years.

The **Yenisey River** is 2,500 miles long. It begins in the Tuva Republic from streams rising in the Altay Mountains. It flows westward, then turns north where it enters the Kara Sea through a long estuary. Its main tributary, the Angara, empties out of Lake Baikal. North of the Angara River is the small Stoney Tunguska and further north is the Lower Tunguska Rivers which also join the Yenisey from the east. Huge reservoirs of natural gas were discovered in the region, increasing the importance of the rivers.

Sturgeon and salmon abound in the rivers. The Yenisey waters are joined to the Ob by a series of canals.

Major cities on or near the Yenisey include Krasnoyarsk and Abakan as well as Norilsk in the frozen north. Bratsk, Irkutsk, Angarsk and Cheremkhovo are the main cities on the Angara.

The **Angara River**, 1,150 miles long, is the only outlet of Lake Baikal. It flows from the southwest end of the lake. There are three dams on the river, the largest is at Bratsk.

The largest city on the Yenisey is Krasnoyarsk located where the TSR crosses the river. It is halfway between Moscow and Vladivostok. The double track railroad crosses the river on two four thousand foot bridges. The city is a flour milling center and its products are shipped out by water, rail and air. In winter, ski planes land on the river.

There is a mud road paralleling the river for most of its length. This road connects small villages scattered every thirty to fifty miles. Turukhansk, located at the junction of the Lower Tunguska with the Yenisey, is considered a big town yet it only has around eight thousand inhabitants. These people make a living by lumbering and trapping in the long winter and fishing in the short summer.

13-1 Laying track for the Trans-Siberian Railroad.

The road passing through these small villages is usually a mass of mud and the best time to use them is when they are frozen solid which is at least eight months of the year. Many villages have put logs on the road inside the village. These are topped with sawn lumber. There is a constant struggle to keep the ends of the boards from coming loose.

Igarka (80,000), one of the largest towns above the Arctic Circle is located on a hundred foot terrace above the river. Although it is 400 miles from the ocean it is considered an ocean port; ocean going vessels come in warm weather to deliver materials and pick up sawn lumber. Traveling from Krasnoyarsk to Igarka, a thousand mile journey, takes about one month because the rutted road makes driving hazardous. Getting enough gasoline is also a problem. The same trip by boat takes two weeks and by seaplane, one day.

Rafts of timber are floated to Igarka from all points upstream. These rafts interfere with river traffic. When they reach Igarka they are set aside and eventually sawn into boards. About half the adult population of the city works in the sawmill when it is in operation. In recent years the sawmill has experienced long periods of idleness.

The major cities of Igarka and Norilsk have city water which is transported in pipes set in trenches in the permafrost. The water pipes have a steam pipe running next to them and both pipes are surrounded by sawdust. Many of the area's log houses are also banked with sawdust and the first floors are usually underlain with sawdust.

Food consumed in the villages is procured by hunting and fishing. The larger cities receive food shipments from upstream. Elaborate greenhouses near Igarka and Norilsk raise tomatoes, radishes, cauliflower, lettuce and the Russian favorite cucumbers. Cabbages and potatoes are grown during the short growing season along with strawberries and raspberries.

The **ALTAI REPUBLIC** borders on Mongolia and incorporates most of the Altai Mountains. About 200,000 people live here, mostly Russians with about 45,000 Altaians including Oirots, Temuts, Shors, Tilengets and Kumands. These are Turkic speaking of Mongolian descent.

The Altai Republic has gold, mercury and manganese deposits. Most of the people are engaged in livestock raising and lumbering.

The **KHAKASSIA REPUBLIC** is an area drained by the upper reaches of the Yenisey River. It is bounded on the south by the Sayan Mountains and its lowlands are in a black earth steppe region. Steep slopes provide abundant hydroelectric power.

Khakassia is rich in mineral deposits: gold, coal, iron ore, barite, copper, lead, molybdenum and gypsum. Limestone and marble are also mined.

The lowland steppe provides grain and hay for livestock. Peaches and apples are grown on the slopes. Logs are floated down the Abakan River to the city of Abakan where they are processed into lumber products.

Russians make up about 60 percent of the population with Khakass at 35 percent. The latter are a Turkic speaking people and Orthodox Christian in religion.

The capital city **Abakan** (190,000) engages in trade with the mountain peoples to the south and the industrial peoples to the north. Minerals from the mountains and lumber products make up the bulk of the trade.

The **TUVA REPUBLIC** was one of the few enclaves that willingly joined the Russian Empire. But today, the republic is talking independence. It is located on the Mongolian border south of Krasnoyarsk. Its capital is Kyzyl on the headwaters of one of the Ob's feeder rivers. The area has many glacial lakes.

The Tuva, which make up 65 percent of the population, are a Mongol Turkic-speaking people who follow the Buddhist Religion. Russians are 30 percent. Tuvians are herders who raise cattle, horses, reindeer, goats, camels and sheep. They also engage in auto repairing, woodworking, leather tooling and are known for their artistry with stone, wood, bronze and silver.

The people have a colorful folklore, and a unique style of singing called "throat singing."

Tannu-Tuva, as it was known, belonged to the Chinese Empire from 1757 to 1911. During the 1911 revolution in China, Imperial Russia encouraged Tuva to seek independence. The district was independent off-and-on until 1944 when it was formally annexed by Russia.

Kyzyl (84,000) is the capital of Tuva. The city is on the headwaters of the Yenisey River. The main Buddhist Temple is located here. Bricks, furniture and processed food are produced here. A culture institute preserves Tuva language and customs.

MAJOR CITIES

Krasnoyarsk (924,000), located on the Yenisey River where the TSR crosses, is a major river and rail port. Its industries include shipbuilding, railroad and heavy equipment, farm machinery, aluminum, textiles and cement.

Krasnoyarsk was founded by cossacks as an outpost for the Czar in 1628. It has an Institute of Forestry and one of the world's largest hydroelectric stations.

Irkutsk (640,000), located at the confluence of the Irkut and Angara Rivers, is considered to be on the shores of Lake Baikal although it is forty miles away. The city manufactures aircraft, automobiles, machine tools, textiles, food products and chemicals. Its large aluminum industry is

13-2 Norilsk, located north of the Arctic Circle, is the northernmost city of Russia.

responsible for much of the pollution in Lake Baikal.

Bratsk (280,000) is located on one of the world's largest dams and reservoirs. Its hydroelectric station supplies power to the upper Angara River cities. The Oka River (not to be confused with the Oka of the Moscow Region) was a 600 mile long tributary of the Angara. Much of its valley was flooded by the reservoir and thus the reservoir appears to have two arms.

Angarsk (268,000) is in the Irkutsk industrial circle, just north of Irkutsk. Angarsk processes petroleum into various chemical products including synthetic fibers, plastics and fertilizers. Abundant electricity powers its industries. Just north of Angarsk is the city of **Chermkhovo** (130,000).

Nizhne Vartovsk (245,000), near Lake Samotlor, had a population of less than 25,000 in 1965. When oil was discovered, the village became a boom town.

Norilsk (174,000), north of the Arctic Circle, was a center for forced labor until the glasnost era. It once had a population of 201,000, mainly prisoners, former prisoners, camp commanders and guards. Today. the city is at the hub of an active mining region producing copper, cobalt, nickel, coal and platinum. It utilizes natural gas piped up from the Tyumen field. There is an excellent road from Norilsk to Dudinka on the Yenisey River. An airport also serves the region.

14. THE RUSSIAN FAR EAST

The long winding **Amur River** symbolizes the Russian Far East. The Amur begins in the mountains southeast of Lake Baikal then flows eastward to the Tatar Strait and the Sea of Japan. The Far East begins in the valley of the Lena River. To the north and east of the Lena is one of the largest expanse of mountain ranges in the world. The steep mountains go straight down to the sea.

At the eastern tip of the mountainous northeast, Russia stretches out to within thirty miles of Alaska. Here, thousands of years ago, during the last Ice Age, the first Mongol people crossed the frozen Bering Strait to begin settling North America. These were the ancestors of the people who later would be called American Indians.

The Russian Far East is Russia's Pacific Gateway, and is similar to the states of Washington and Alaska. People here are adventurous and independent in spirit. They live so far away from the rest of Russia they refer to a trip back west as "visiting the continent." (Garreau 1994) This attitude is similar to Alaskans who call the rest of the United States the "lower 48".

Alaskan businesses are hoping to cash in as the Russian Far East market opens up. Bering Air runs a charter service between Nome, Alaska and Provideniya, only 252 miles away. Russians can use their relatively worthless rubles to buy VCRs, vodka, cassette tapes, tobacco and volleyballs in Nome. Nome businesses accept the rubles hoping to foster good relations.

The Nome Chamber of Commerce hopes someday to see Russians arriving with 72 hour visas. Nome wants an open border based on tourism. (Cutler 1994:120) Of course, open borders and tourism work both ways and American tourists departing from Alaska could someday transform the Russian Far East.

Winter sports are popular in Siberia. Snowmobiles, ice skates and skis are for sale in every city. Large cities have nearby ski slopes with traditional ski lifts.

Siberian cities have access to the world's goods and fresh fruits and vegetables. Bananas are available throughout the year in most cities. In February, bananas are cheaper than potatoes.

To many Siberians, Moscow is in another world. They want as little contact with western Russia as possible. They see little economic return for the taxes sent west. To many Siberians, they are a colony today, much as their ancestors were two hundred years ago.

Rivers in the northeast flow north to the Arctic Ocean or east to the Bering Sea. Most rivers are frozen six months of the year. During brief summers, when the Arctic Ocean is unfrozen, a Russian supply ship makes its way through the slush to bring supplies from Murmansk and Archangel to Vladivostok.

From the northeastern extremity the **Kamchatka Peninsula** reaches south to separate the Sea of Okhotsk from the Pacific Ocean. It covers ten degrees of latitude: from 51 degrees North to 61 degrees North. Many streams and lakes dot this 750 mile long stretch of land. There are at least 30 active volcanoes. (The entire earth has about 850 active volcanoes). The Kamchatka is traversed by two active volcanic mountain ranges trending northwest to southeast. The central area is wide and level.

Klyucheuskaya Sopka, a volcano in the eastern range, is the highest peak at 15,585 feet. The eastern Pacific Coast is mostly steep cliffs.

Kamchatka is cold and moist. In the

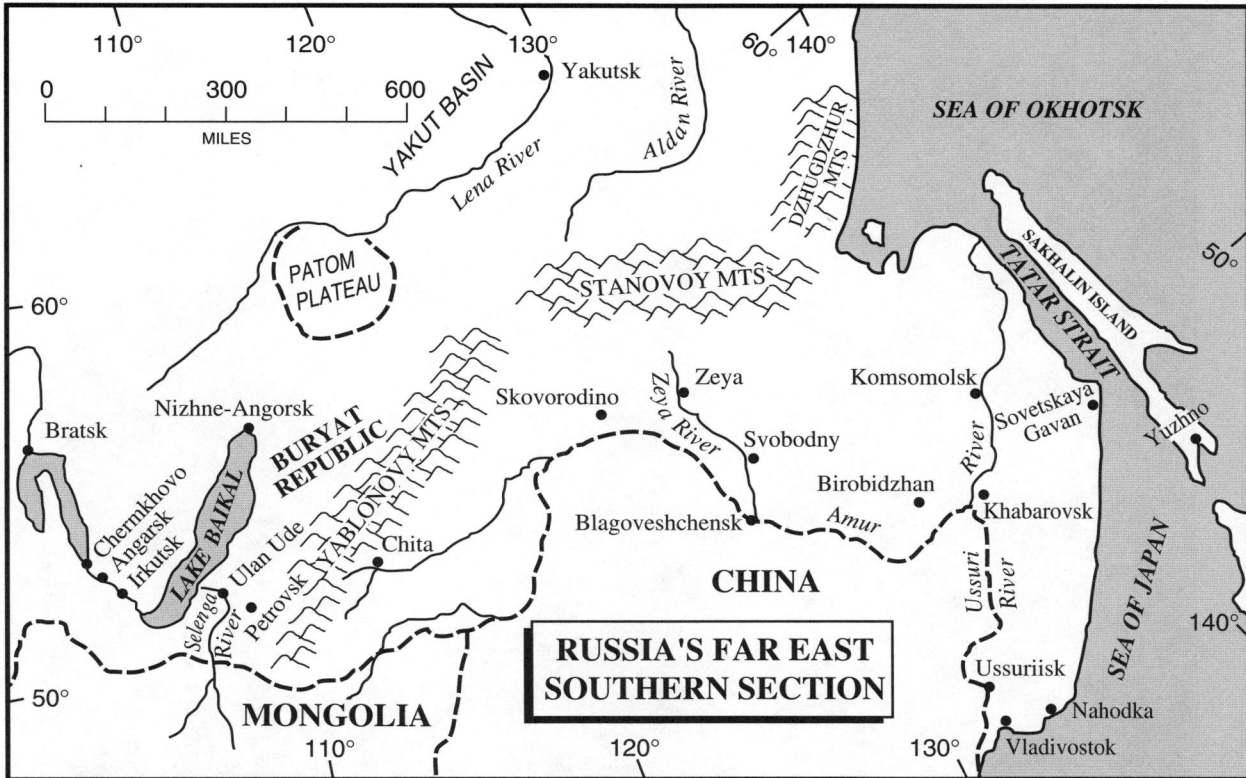

MAP 12 Russia's Far East: Southern Section

south some rye, oats, barley and potatoes can be grown. Fishing, herding, lumbering and hunting are the main occupations. Reindeer are the dominant grazing animal. Wild animals include bear, seal, deer, sable and mountain sheep.

Mineral resources include gold, copper, oil, coal, mica, pyrites, sulfur and tufa, a rock formed from the deposits left behind when water from hot springs evaporates. Most of these minerals are exported.

The Kamchatka Peninsula is the center of a valuable fishing industry. Crabs, the main product, are sold in international trade. There is also a sizable seal harvest each year as well as herring from the Sea of Okhotsk and whales from the Bering Sea.

Native people include Tungus, Koryaks and Kamchadals. They are mainly hunters, trappers and fishers as they've been for

centuries. Immigrants: Russians, Chinese and Koreans, work mostly in heavy industry and mining.

Petropavlovsk (270,000) is the capital of Kamchatka. It is an important port on the Northern Sea Route connecting Vladivostok to Archangel. Due to its location on the southeastern shore of the peninsula, it is free from ice for seven months of the year. Petropavlovsk is a naval base as well as home to a large fishing fleet.

The famed Siberian Tiger lives across the Sea of Okhotsk from Kamchatka. Poachers have decimated their population and in 1994, less than 300 animals were believed to be left in the wild. These are the largest cats on earth and have a territory of over one hundred square miles. International efforts are being made to preserve these magnificent animals.

101

14-1 Buryat herdsmen bring in the sheep.

The **Chukchi (Chukotskoye) Peninsula** is the northeastern extremity of Asia. It is an extension of the **Anadyr Mountain Range.** The area is sparsely settled mostly by Russians with native Chukchi, Yakut, Eveny, Koryak and Inuit. These people make their living by coastal fishing and semi-nomadic hunting. **Anadyr** (40,000) is the region capital.

The **Buryatia Republic.** located just east of Lake Baikal, extends to the Yablonovy Mountains. Its capital is Ulan Ude. The land is mountainous and heavily forested. Rivers, which provide hydroelectric power, are loaded with fish. This is one of Russia's most prosperous districts.

The Buryats are woodsmen and foresters. Their mineral wealth includes coal, iron ore, tungsten, molybdenum, gold, wolfram, nickel, bauxite and manganese. Farmers raise wheat and fodder crops for reindeer and cattle.

People here manufacture railroad equipment, locomotives, pulp, paper and textiles. They also have extensive fish canning enterprises.

Buryats speak a Mongol language and are descended from Mongols, Huns and Turks. Most are Buddhists whose religion is governed from across the border in Mongolia.

Only about one fifth of the population are Buryat. Russians make up the majority at 70 percent with Tatars, Tuva and Ukrainians forming a considerable minority.

The capital city **Ulan Ude** (358,000), formerly Verkhne-Udinsk, is on the Selenga

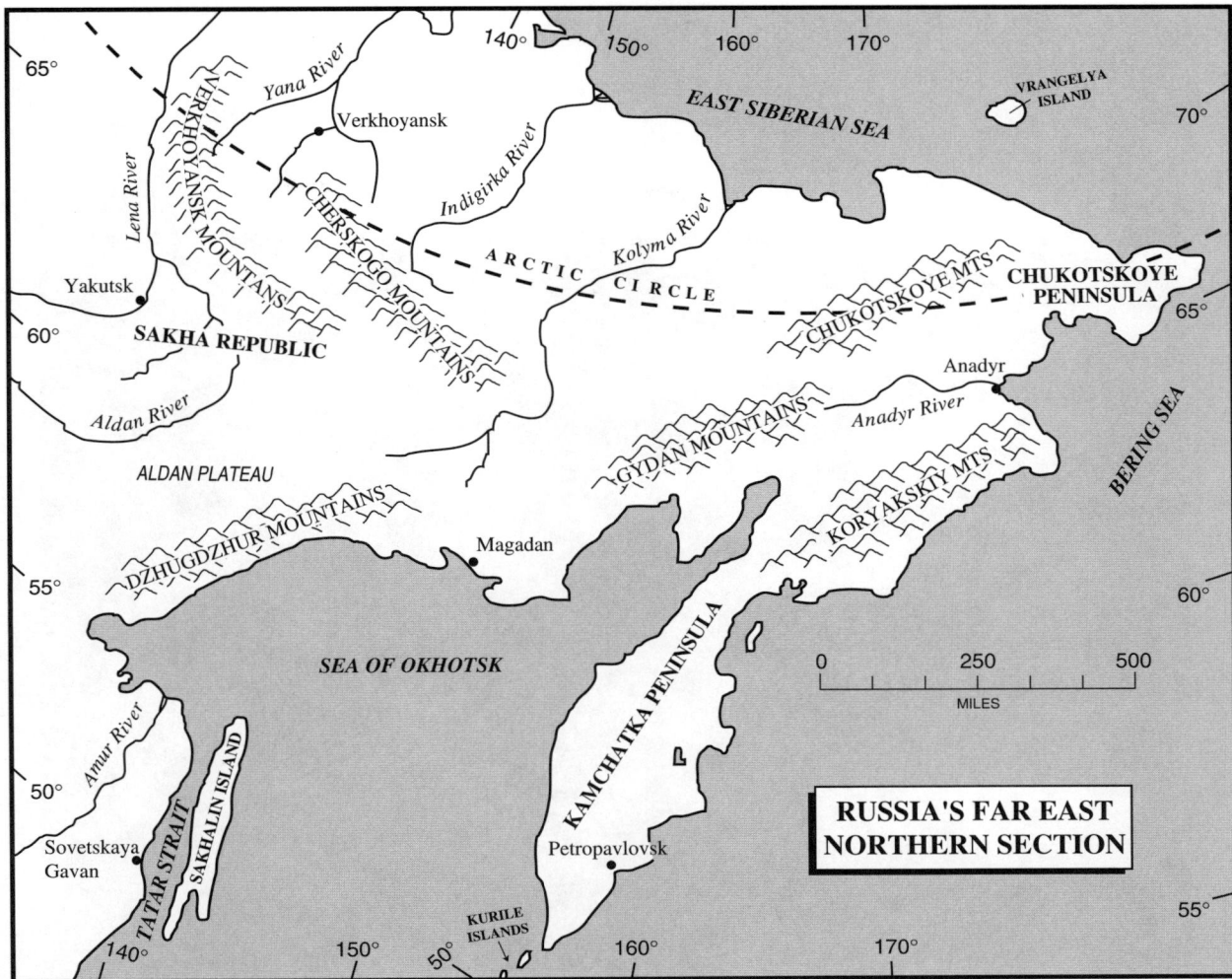

MAP 13   Russia's Far East: Northern Section

River, near a confluence with the Uda. It is on the TSR with a branch line to Beijing, China. The city was founded in 1689 as a cossack fortress. It was a stop on the route from Lake Baikal, up the Selenga and on to China.

Like most cities on the TSR, Ulan Ude manufactures railroad equipment. It also is engaged in food processing, tanning, sawmilling and the manufacture of glass and bricks.

The next largest city on the way to the east is **Chita** (372,000) at the confluence of the Chita and Ingoda Rivers. It too owes its size to its location on the TSR. It has a large locomotive repair center and produces textiles.

Chita is about 250 miles east of Ulan Ude. Chita was founded as a fort in 1653. It later became the place of exile for some of the Decemberist Rebels, a group of political dissenters who rose against Czar Nicholas I in 1825. Formed after the Napoleonic Wars, the Decemberists were ex-army officers who had been influenced by western democratic ideals. Their leaders were executed and the others exiled.

Right next to China, the most populous country in the world, are the lonely outposts of Far Eastern Russia, five thousand miles from Moscow. Here is a land of long winters and cool summers where the temperature seldom reaches 70 degrees Fahrenheit.

14-2 Housing development at Mirniy at the headwaters of the Vilyuy River, a tributary of the Lena. Mirniy is the center of diamond mining in Sakha Republic. Russia produces more diamonds than any other place on earth. In 1995, Russian diamond sales brought $500 million. Russia's stockpile of diamonds is worth more than $4 billion.

Note the wooden plank sidewalks between buildings and the rutted main street. Mirniy has one of three airports in all of Sakha Republic . The city is 500 miles north of Lake Baikal and 500 miles west of Yakutsk. These are the former barracks of convict and slave labor.

The **Lena River** , 2,670 miles long, begins in the highlands north of Lake Baikal and flows northeast on the eastern side of the Siberian Central Plateau. It is navigable for 2,135 miles and is ice free at Yakutsk from June to October.

Other than Yakutsk, there are no large settlements on the Lena. Deposits of gold, diamonds, coal and oil along the Lena support many small mining towns.

The **SAKHA (YAKUT) REPUBLIC** is the largest Russian administrative unit outside of Russia itself. It encompasses

most of the territory traversed by the Lena River. **Yakutsk** (225,000) is its capital. More than 40 percent of the republic lies above the Arctic Circle.

A highway connects Yakutsk to Skovorodino just north of the China border. The town is also connected to Siberia and the Pacific Ocean by roads and a railroad.

The minerals mentioned for the Lena River are also found in this republic. Lumbering, fishing, hunting and trapping are other enterprises.

Yakut produces lumber and leather

products. It also has a large brick manufacturing industry.

The Yakut people are Mongolian but speak a Turkic language. Many Yakut became Orthodox Christian during the Russian colonization period of the 17th century. Others still follow a primitive religion led by shamans.

Verkhoyansk (2,500), 425 miles northeast of Yakutsk, has recorded temperatures of minus 90 degrees Fahrenheit. The average January temperature is below 0 degrees F. Permafrost exists in all but the southern portion of the region.

The **Verkhoyansk Mountains** form along the east banks of the Lena and Aldan Rivers. They are 8,150 feet at their highest, and have important reserves of gold, silver, lead, zinc and coal.

Siberian winter air is cold but calm. People can live comfortably in insulated houses. Outside they dress in layered clothing and wear coats that reach to the ground. There is little snow and the air is still so there is no wind-chill factor. However, people must walk very slowly in extremely cold weather because the act of walking causes a wind-chill that can freeze one's face.

Verkhoyansk has recorded the most extreme temperatures in the world - plus 90 degrees in summer and minus 90 degrees in winter. It is on the Yana River which is frozen for nine months.

The area around Verkhoyansk has wild horses, moose, reindeer, elk and rabbits. Hunters dig a hole under their houses and deep-freeze the meat in permafrost.

Beginning in 1887, this area was used as a place of exile by the Czars. The Soviets made it a part of the gulag. Today Verkhoyansk has a police station with the only telephone in town. There are no churches, trains, buses, hotels, restaurants or newspapers.

Nothing can grow here and everything is brought in by truck from Yakutsk, 400 miles away. Once a year a supply boat comes up the Yana River. Local mines closed after the gulags were abolished.

The **Kolyma River**, in the northeast of Siberia, rises in the Kolyma Range and flows 1,500 miles to the Arctic Ocean. It is ice free from June to October. Its upper course is swift while its lower course meanders into swamps. One of the world's richest gold fields is in its upper tributaries.

Under Stalin, male and female prisoners were sent to Magadan on the Sea of Okhotsk. From there, they would march to the goldfields where they lived and worked under pitiful conditions. Almost all of them died. Soviet records indicate at least 400,000 prisoners died working the gold deposits.

Magadan (150,000) is the biggest port on the Sea of Okhotsk with shipyards, fish canning and a highway to the goldfields. It also has a large airport.

Magadan is the infamous city that was once the "capital" of the Kolyma Region of the Soviet gulag archipelago. As late as 1988 the city was still closed to foreigners. During the 1930s slave laborers came in every few days from Vladivostok, making the city a "gulag boomtown", the "gateway to hell" (Remnick 1993:121).

Magadan was the creation of the Kremlin leadership and NKVD (later the KGB), an administrative center for slave labor and mass murder. The Kolyma region, an area six times larger than France, contained 100 camps. Between 1936 and 1953 three million people died in the camps.

"In Magadan the dead are everywhere, in the abandoned mine shafts, under the taiga, under the seabed. One of the roads to the northern camps was built on a bed of bones. Eighty percent of the standing structures in Magadan were once barracks for prisoners or headquarters for police administration or shooting halls." (Ibid): 424).

In the tundra occasional sudden winds, called **buran** or **purga**, seem to rise out of nowhere. These are dangerous to humans and animals caught in them. In most of northern Russia warm spells, called **ottepeli**, occur in winter and thaw the ground causing swamps and river flooding. Ottepeli do not last long but are dangerous when they occur.

For the entire country, the big thaw occurs in April and is called **rasputitsa**. At this time nearly all of Russia is a sea of mud and water.

The Russian Far East depends heavily on imports of food and machinery. Recently introduced steel operations have given the people the ability to make their own machinery. In this far eastern territory there is little farmland as forest covers the land.

The **Amur River** holds the population together although its valley is narrow and villages of any size are few. But the river does flow for 2,900 miles and brings a coherence to the region.

For more than a thousand miles the Amur flows southeast and forms a border between Russia and China. As it reaches the east, it makes a dramatic turn to the northeast and empties into the Tatar Strait which separates the mainland from Sakhalin Island. The Amur is navigable for its entire length. It is ice free from May to November.

The region is in the path of the cold winter monsoon air which flows southeast out of Siberia and keeps the temperatures below freezing for five months. Summer temperatures are cool.

Russians first became serious about expanding into this territory in the early 19th century. The area was then claimed by China but was mostly uninhabited. Neighboring Manchuria was an empty land crossed now and then by traders.

Russian fur traders had crossed the Bering Strait and built the first village on the Alaskan coast in 1784. Sitka was founded in 1799 but was destroyed by Indians in 1802. Russians reached the northern shores of California in 1812. But European Russians were engaged in the Napoleonic Wars at the time and paid little attention.

Russian interest in Alaska gradually declined, and after the Crimean War Russia needed money. Alaska was sold to the United States in 1867 for $7,200,000. The entire deal was negotiated by U.S. Secretary of State William H. Seward. For a time it was called "Seward's Icebox".

When the TSR reached the Amur River China was too preoccupied with her own problems to worry about Russian expansion. Therefore Russia was able to run the TSR through part of northern China and knock off 300 miles of proposed line north of the Amur. An extension of the line proceeded to Port Arthur in China on the Yellow Sea. This gave Russia an excellent warm water outlet to the Pacific Ocean.

By the beginning of the 20th century Japan had become a major naval power. Conflict with Russia over territorial waters resulted in a Japanese attack on Vladivostok in 1905. Japan won the short war and ownership of Sakhalin Island.

After the war Japan became the major player in Manchuria, Korea and on Sakhalin Island. This forced Russia to reconsider the railroad though Manchuria. A northern line along the Amur completely inside Russian territory was completed in 1916, just before the Bolsheviks came to power.

Japan eventually left the Soviet Far East and concentrated on Manchuria and Korea. The Japanese moved out of the northern section of Sakhalin Island but kept the south because of the large numbers of Japanese immigrants who had settled there.

The Soviets expanded the fisheries. A

new steel mill was built at Komsomolsk. Chinese and Korean immigrants, fleeing the Japanese, settled in the valleys. Their descendants are still there today.

On May 28, 1995 a 7.5 earthquake occurred at the town of Neftegorsk on the northern end of Sakhalin. Of the 3,000 inhabitants, over 2,000 of them were killed. There were 19 five story prefabricated apartment buildings in the town and all of them collapsed. Rescuers were dispatched from Moscow and Kurgan. The injured were taken to the closest hospital which was in Vladivostok.

An attempt was made to create a Jewish autonomous state at Birobidzhan, which is in the middle of a great swamp on a southern elbow of the Amur where the Biro and Bidzhan Rivers meet. About 40,000 Russians of Jewish origin settled here but more than half of them later moved elsewhere. Today, Birobidzhan city publishes a Yiddish newspaper and has a Yiddish radio station.

The region has gold, tin, iron ore and graphite. Limited agriculture is practiced in the river valleys.

Sakhalin Island is 600 miles long from north to south and one hundred miles wide at its greatest width. The Japanese call it *Karafuto*. Resource exploitation includes fishing, lumbering, mining, oil and coal. In 1855 Japan and Russia had joint ownership but Japan gave up its share for the Kurile Islands. It was divided again after the War of 1905.

By 1940 about 500,000 Japanese lived on Sakhalin. After the Japanese bombed Pearl Harbor and the United States entered World War II, relations between Russia and Japan still remained peaceful. Russia was busy on its western front and didn't declare war on Japan until World War II was nearly over. However, at the end of the war Stalin insisted on the return of the entire Sakhalin Island to the USSR. The Soviets also took over the Kurile Islands.

The **Kurile Islands** form an arc from Japan to Kamchatka creating the Sea of Okhotsk. Russia controls the Sea which provides abundant crabs, seals and fish.

There are no products manufactured in the Russian Far East that are essential to western Russia. In order to be a part of the Russian economy, the Far East had to expand its timber and fish resources. Russia's position as the world's number two fishing nation is probably due to increases in Far Eastern fishing. Most of the catch is quick frozen or canned because main markets are so far away.

Due to the distances between Moscow and the Far East, autonomous regions and individual cities are making separate economic deals with China, the Koreas and Japan. Vehicles manufactured in Khabarovsk are in demand in China. Most businesses in Khabarovsk are owned by South Koreans. Soybeans were introduced by Koreans as a major cash crop.

Forest resources have been slowly taken over by Japanese companies who have penetrated all the way to Lake Baikal. They have several working timber treaties with the autonomous Buryat people.

The majority of the Far Eastern population lives within fifty miles of the TSR. People are mainly Russians with Korean, Chinese and Jewish minorities. Today, there are about 400,000 Koreans, 30,000 Chinese and 15,000 Jews in the Amur region.

FAR EASTERN CITIES

Vladivostok (645,000) is situated on a prominent rock outcrop in the southernmost portion of Russia's eastern territory. Its peninsula extends to two bays; the most famous is the Golden Horn Bay also known as Peter-the-Great Bay. Vladivostok is at the terminus of the TSR and is the Far East's most important sea port. The railroad reached Vladivostok in 1905, just in time for the bombardment by Japanese forces in the short Russo-Japanese War. After the Japanese victory, the city was occupied by Japanese, American, British, Italian and French troops. It took the new Soviet government until 1922 to drive out all the foreign forces.

Although the city is mostly Russian, it has a large Ukrainian minority. There are many universities and trade schools. The name Vladivostok means "Ruler of the East".

The city's economy is based upon shipbuilding, forest products, food processing (mostly fish), and the smelting of zinc and copper.

Khabarovsk (610,000) is about the same size as Vladivostok. Khabarovsk is located on a great bend in the Amur River at its junction with the Ussuri. It is a major point on the TSR. Industries include oil refineries, iron and steel working, shipyards, farm machinery, trucks, aircraft, diesel engines and machine tools. Khabarovsk was a small trading post when the TSR arrived it 1905.

The city boasts a modern medical school and a teachers college. It has several museums and a theater.

The Khabarovsk region which contains 1.6 million people is beginning to integrate itself into the economies of Asia -- Japan, China and South Korea. South Koreans are the region's fastest growing employers with a new Gold Star television factory, restaurants and several more manufacturing plants planned. Although the Japanese were the first to arrive, American companies, particularly western mineral and timber concerns, have started showing up. Chinese peddlers are the most populous with their cheap clothing, instant noodles and inexpensive toys. Khabarovsk's international

airport has flights to Anchorage, Seoul, Harbin, China and Niigata, Japan. Many people in the region believe their future lies more with the Far East countries rather than with Russia.

Komsomolsk (315,000) was built by young communist volunteers in 1932 as an example of the power of the people. It is on the Amur River, halfway between Khabarovsk and the sea. Komsomolsk-na-Amure (to separate it from other cities named Komsomolsk) has a modern steel plant, shipyards, oil refineries, paper and pulp industries, chemical industries, fish processing, lumber industries and a canning factory. It was a major manufacturer of submarines under the Soviets. There is tin mining nearby in the town of Solnechy. The Baikal-Amur Mainline (BAM) traverses the Amur at Komsomolsk by a 1240 feet bridge.

Completion of the BAM to this point was extremely expensive. It had to cross seven major mountain ranges. More than 4,000 bridges were built. Many of the small towns created during its construction are now ghost towns.

After the break-up of the Soviet Union in 1991, more than 40,000 people left the city for the Moscow region. To stop this emigration the Russian government placed everyone in the city on a pension.

The Baikal-Amur-Mainline continues from Komsomolsk to the twin cities of Vanino and Gavan.

Blagoveshchensk (210,000), on the junction of the Zeya River and the Amur, was originally a cossack fort. Its main industries involve food processing. On the TSR, it is in the center of a small agriculture district. It supplies materials from the TSR to the goldfields on the Zeya uplands.

The **Zeya River** rises in the Stanovoy Range and flows 800 miles to join the Amur. It has a large dam which provides hydroelectricty to the region which

108

14-3 Nahodka harbor in Russia's Far East.

produces, not only gold, but significant amounts of graphite and lignite.

Nahodka (210,000) is a good sea port just north of Vladivostok and should grow in the future. It has a better harbor than Vladivostok and it is ice free.

Ussuriisk (165,000) is a center of agriculture on the Usurri River just north of Vladivostok. The **Ussuri River**, 365 miles long, is used mostly for floating logs from the highlands to its junction with the Amur.

The **Ussuri River** is an important international boundary, separating China from Russia. It rises in the Sikhote-Alin Range and flows north to join the Amur. Arguments over the river meanders and borders erupted in fighting between Soviet and Chinese troops in 1972. The river has excellent fishing and is used to transport logs. Most of the region around the river and to the north are part of a newly created **Maritime Province**.

Today, there are many foreign countries interested in Siberia. There is a scramble to get its oil, timber and mineral wealth. It resembles the mad dash to develop Alaska's resources.

Most of Russia's 85 *zapovedniks* (nature preserves) are in Siberia. Because Russia no Environmental Protection Agency, the nature preserves are in jeopardy. Recently there has been some talk about combining part of the Far East and northeast Alaska into one huge Arctic Reserve.

15. THE BALTIC REGION

The Baltic countries are Belarus, Estonia, Latvia and Lithuania. This region was covered with ice sheets during the last glaciation. Terminal moraines from the last phase of glaciation are found in Belarus. The area north of it is ground moraine with drumlins, low hills, many swamps and meandering streams.

The four Baltic countries and the Kaliningrad Region have much in common. Their soils are gray **podzolic** which in Russian means "**ashen earth**". These soils have been created by a combination of factors. Podzols originate in areas of cool climate which have trees for the dominant vegetation. Conifer needles and deciduous leaves form highly acidic soils. Not only do these soils need fertilizer but they need sweetening with lime or some other material to counteract the acid nature.

Agriculture patterns are also similar. They all raise flax, potatoes and cool climate grains such as rye, oats and barley. Hay or pasturage is a mainstay of each country and all have a sizable dairy cattle industry. Raising dairy cattle is a common activity in cool climate, glaciated regions around the world.

Over the centuries agriculture has been the main economic activity. Even today one third of the population is still engaged in farming.

Because this Baltic region is a crossroads, it has been at different times invaded and overrun by Germany, Sweden, Poland and Russia. The conquerors have always treated the Baltic people as inferiors which has left a lasting bitterness, especially toward Russia who exploited them unmercifully.

In 1558 Czar Ivan IV of Russia invaded the region and partitioned it between Russia, Poland and Sweden. This gave Poland authority over Lithuania, Sweden over

Latvia and Estonia and Russia over Belarus. These influences persist to this day.

During this same period the Hanseatic League appeared, dominated by Germany. It was an economic league which selected certain European towns as trade centers. While Riga and Novgorod prospered under this system, the general population remained subservient. The Hanseatic League established German culture and dominance all along the Baltic coast..

Napoleon marched through this area on his way to conquer Moscow in 1812. The retreating Russians laid waste to the land. Then when Napoleon's army retreated they destroyed what was left.

By World War I all these lands were bound to the Russian Empire. Serfdom had been declared illegal, but the general population was still impoverished peasants. Railways connected Riga with St. Petersburg and Minsk. The forest industry employed about one third of the people. Coastal cities like Liepaja had a higher population before World War I than they do today. German influence remained in many of the Baltic coastal cities.

After World War I the Baltic region was left to the victorious Allies. Countries were formed according to ethnic populations. By 1920 the independent countries of Estonia, Latvia and Lithuania had been created.

Also by the 1920s Lenin had consolidated his power. The Bolsheviks controlled Russia. Belarus, which contained strong Bolshevik elements, remained in the Russian sphere.

Estonia, Latvia and Lithuania remained independent until 1939 when a secret pact between Hitler and Stalin gave the Soviets control of the Baltics. Nevertheless, the Baltic states never forgot their brief period of independence.

Despite the Nazi-Soviet pact, Germany

MAP 14   The Baltic Region

111

invaded and conquered the region. Heavy fighting and bombing decimated the countries before the Soviets regained control. All four countries suffered terribly. Belarus was completely destroyed as an economic unit. Its capital city of Minsk was leveled.

After World War II, Stalin effected an understanding with the rest of the Allied countries that gave Russia de facto control over the area. But the Baltics resisted and many guerrilla movements continued sporadically until the Soviets took firm control in 1950. Rigged elections were held to legitimize this hegemony. Nationalist flags like Estonia's blue, black and white pennants were banned.

The Soviets began an industrialization drive in the 1960s and 1970s that severely damaged the environment, causing much

15-1 Women harvesting flax. Belarus.

lasting bitterness. During this period, eight ministries in Moscow controlled industries that polluted the Baltic Sea as well as rivers and lakes. Russians were encouraged to move into the Baltics and this created ethnic tension. The Estonian population became one third Russian. Russian became the official language and speaking the native language became a form of protest.

The Baltics came to rely on Russia for their energy needs, and as their main trading partner. The Russians also spent a great deal of money on post-war reconstruction in the region.

When Gorbachev began his program of openness, the communist leaders of the three republics began moves toward independence. They were more loyal to their republics than to the Soviet Union. In one momentous event, they organized "Baltic Way" which was held on August 23, 1989. A human chain of hand holding was formed which stretched from Tallinn to Riga to Vilnius. Two million people participated, almost half of the entire non-Russian population in the region. This passionate, fervent anti-Soviet protest stunned Gorbachev and other Kremlin leaders.

When the four republics became independent in 1991, they found themselves still tied to Moscow. Extricating themselves will not be easy, but Lithuania took a major step in January 1994 when it applied for NATO partnership.

Except for timber and peat, the four republics have few natural resources. Half the region is forest, swamp or both. Most of the farmland needs drainage as well as fertilizer and lime to be productive. The best farmland is in central Belarus and southern Lithuania.

Flax is the main cash crop. Its fibers are used in making a fine linen for which the region is noted. Flax seeds are pressed to produce linseed oil.

There is a traditional hemp growing region in Belarus but the demand for its fibers has been declining due to widespread use of artificial fibers and plastics. However, Belarus was able to develop one of the largest synthetic fiber industries in the world.

Fodder crops are important to the dairy industry and butter is a major export. Much of the land is in hay.

Tourism is already emerging as a major industry and source of hard currency. Tallinn, Estonia's capital, is an old historical town and many tours to Russia and Finland begin there.

The region has many small hydroelectric stations which provide cheap electricity. Oil shale, mined in Estonia, is also used to produce electricity. Peat and timber remain important resources. Lithuania has two nuclear power plants producing electricity but they rely on Russia for nuclear fuel.

The **Kaliningrad Region** is a territory in the Russian Federation. With the Baltic Sea on its west, it is hemmed in by Poland on the south and Lithuania on its north and east. It is cut off from Russia by Lithuania.

The capital **Kaliningrad** (406,000) is an ice free Baltic Sea port and naval base. It has world class botanical and zoological gardens. The population is almost entirely Russian.

Under German rule, Kaliningrad was known as **Konigsberg** and was part of East Prussia. The city is located on the small Pregolya River which empties into the Gulf of Kaliningrad in the Baltic Sea. Its ice-free harbor makes it an important Russian seaport and naval base. Kaliningrad is an industrial and commercial center which produces ships, small machinery, automobile parts and textiles.

Konigsberg was founded in 1255 as a fortress of the Teutonic Knights. It became a member of the Hanseatic League in 1340 and enjoyed many privileges. It was the residence of the Dukes of Prussia from 1525 until 1618. Prussian kings were also crowned here. The name means "city of kings".

The University of Konigsberg had Immanuel Kant, who was born here, as one of its celebrated professors. Much of the city, including the university, was destroyed during World War II.

Along with the northern part of East Prussia, the city was transferred to the Soviet Union after World War II. It was renamed Kaliningrad after Mikhail Kalinin, a Russian revolutionary who had sided with the Bolsheviks.

Most of the Germans are now gone, having been replaced by Russians. There are no natural resources in the region and farming is poor. Its only asset is its location on the Baltic Sea.

ESTONIA
(pop. 1,630,000 - 17,413 sq. mi.)

Estonia is the northernmost country of the Baltic states. Encompassing 17,413 square miles, it is about the size of New Hampshire and Vermont combined. The Baltic Sea lies on its west and the Gulf of Finland on its north. To the south Estonia borders on Latvia. To the east it borders on Russia. Tallinn is its capital city.

Since much of Estonia is surrounded by water, it enjoys a mild climate compared to most northern European countries. It is a lowland with many lakes and swamps. Lake Chudskoye (Peipus) is the largest, and it is an important source of fish. Rivers include the Narva, Parnu, Ema and Kasari. These are navigable for a short distance but not important for river trade.

Lake Peipus at 1,300 square miles is a large source of fresh water for Estonia as well as Russia. It is the center of a fishing industry and is drained by the 50 mile long Narva River which empties into the Gulf of

15-2 The ancient city of Tallinn is surrounded by the modern city.

Finland. The lower section is known as Lake Pskov.

In 1242, forces led by Alexander Nevsky defeated a force of Livonian Knights on the frozen lake. He was named after the Neva River because of his victory.

There are over 1400 islands in the Baltic Sea which are claimed by Estonia. The largest of these is **Saarema** at the entrance to the Gulf of Riga with an area of 1,050 square miles. Its inhabitants were first conquered by the German Brothers of the Sword in 1227. Today its people are mainly engaged in cattle raising. **Hiiumaa Island** is the second largest of the Estonian islands in the Baltic Sea. It is north of Saarema and encompasses 960 square miles. Most of the people are of Swedish descent who engage in fishing.

Oil shale is an important product for the Estonian economy. Other raw materials include peat, limestone, marl, clay, timber, dolomite, sand and phosphorite. Manufactured products include glass, ceramics, fertilizer, cellulose, paper, bricks, plywood, chemicals and oil. Shoes, ships, furniture, radio and electrical apparatus, and processed fish are also produced.

Dairy farming is important. Pigs are raised in great numbers. Cattle and sheep are also valuable meat sources. Agriculture products include flax, potatoes and sugar beets. Flax is the basis of an important cottage linen industry. Textiles are also made from imported cotton and from local sheep wool.

Ethnic Estonians make up 65 percent of the population. A large Russian minority, 30 percent, lives mostly in the cities. Other groups include Finns, Ukrainians, Jews and Belorussians.

Most people follow the Evangelical Lutheran religion. Christianity came to the country through the Danes who founded Tallinn in 1219. Later invasions and subsequent settlement by Germans and Swedes cemented Protestant worship.

Estonian language is now the official language but Russian is widely spoken. Estonian language is a variation on Finnish with many of the same root words. During the period of Soviet domination, using the Estonian language became a symbol of dissent and nationalism. Estonians had to learn the Russian language during the Soviet years. Today, in order to qualify for Estonian citizenship one must be a descendent of Estonians who were in the country between the two world wars. If this qualification is not met then one must be proficient in the Estonian language. This has upset the Russians who make up thirty percent of the population.

In the middle 19th century, Estonians began to clamor for independence. Czars countered with a Russification program. Official business had to be carried on in Russian and the Russian language was used in schools. This caused a mass emigration from the country. Many Estonians fled to the United States and Canada. During the Stalin era tens of thousands of Estonians were accused of opposing Soviet rule and deported to Siberia.

When the Soviet Union began to breakup in 1990, the Estonian parliament declared itself occupied territory and voted for independence. Soviet leadership officially recognized Estonian independence in 1991. The first free elections were held in Estonia in 1992.

Tallinn (540,000), the capital city, is located 35 miles directly opposite from Helsinki, Finland. It is a major port and railroad junction as well as a crossroads of highways, and the home of extensive naval operations. It is also a jumping off point for an emerging tourist industry. Tallinn boasts shipbuilding as a major industry, along with cement, paper-making, furniture, textiles, metalworking, electrical appliances, radios, and fish processing.

The city was destroyed by the Danes at the beginning of the 13th century and a fort was built on the site. It changed hands with the changing rule of the country, but was always the most important city in the area.

The old historical city consists of a medieval cathedral and a section of town dating back to the 13th century. There is a medieval wall with massive towers. Its most famous landmark is the 13th century Danish Toompea Castle which is still used for government offices today. There is also a 13th century church, the Church of St. Olai and a 14th century city hall.

Tartu (120,000) is Estonia's second largest city and an important rail junction and cultural center. It has a splendid university that was founded in 1632 by King Gustavus II of Sweden. Tartu's leading industry is the manufacture of agriculture implements. The city also engages in food processing, lumber products, shoemaking, publishing and printing. Tartu winds around a hill topped by an old castle fort and a 13th century cathedral.

There are 33 towns in Estonia. Seventy two percent of the population lives in towns and cities. **Narva** (84,000), located on the Narva River, is a leading textile center that produces cotton, jute and flax products. It is an important supplier of electricity for the country. Electricity is produced from a dam on the Narva River and from oil shales.

Parnu (60,000) on the Gulf of Riga is a seaport exporting timber and flax. It has a well publicized beach and health resort.

LATVIA
(pop. 2,764,000 - 24,900 sq. mi.)

Latvia, on the Baltic Sea, is slightly smaller than South Carolina. The Baltic Sea and the Gulf of Riga make up its western boundary. On the south is Lithuania and on the north is Estonia. Russia is to its east and Belarus to its southeast. Riga, the capital city, has about a third of the population.

Latvia is a lowland plain drained mostly by the Daugava (Western Dvina) River and the lesser rivers of Venta, Gauja and Lielupe. There are many lakes and moraine hills left behind by glaciers from the Ice Age. The highest elevation of the country is at 1020 feet.

The 635 mile long **Daugava (Western Dvina) River** originates in Russia, flows through Belarus and then to Latvia. It has two hydroelectric dams and is connected to the smaller Berezina River by canals.

About 27 percent of the land is arable and potatoes, oats, rye and barley are the main crops. There is a sizable cattle industry, mostly dairy cattle. Butter is a major export .

Timber is the most valuable natural resource of Latvia. Forests occupy one fourth of the land. The main tree species are typical northern climate of pine, spruce, boxwood, linden, birch and aspen. The forests are home to deer and wild boar.

Latvia's manufactured products include electrical appliances, small machines, paper and textiles. Alcohol distillation and shipbuilding are also noteworthy. The manufacture of electric railway passenger cars has increased in production to become the major economic enterprise.

Latvians make up 52 percent of the population. Russians are a large minority at 34 percent. There are also Belorussians, Poles, Lithuanians and Jews. Latvians are of two groups - the Letts and Latgalians which are almost indistinguishable. Prior to World War II, Latvians made up 75 percent of the population.

The Letts were Christianized by the Livonian Brothers of the Sword in the 13th century. Today their religion is mainly Evangelical Lutheran which was introduced to the region by German settlers and invaders.

Latvians enjoy a rather high standard of living compared to most emerging industrial nations. The bulk of the labor force (41%) is engaged in forestry and its products. About 16 percent are engaged in agriculture.

Latvia is very dependent on outside sources for coal, oil and natural gas. In 1992, Latvia doubled Russia's fee to operate the pipelines across its territory. Russia retaliated by cutting back on energy to Latvia which forced its factories to close and its cities to ration electricity. In 1993, Russia cut off all natural gas deliveries to Latvia which desperately needs the fuel.

Latvia did not join the Commonwealth of Independent States. In 1994 it issued new currency called the **let**.

Riga (920,000) is the capital city located on the Gulf of Riga where the Daugava River empties. It is a major Baltic port, a rail junction and a military base. Riga's industries include woodworking, food processing and the manufacture of diesel engines, streetcars, pharmaceuticals, buses, tractors, electric appliances, television and telephones.

The port of Riga exports timber, flax, wooden materials and dairy products. It imports sugar, industrial equipment, coal and fertilizer.

The monk Meinhard built a monastery at Riga near the end of the 12th century. Riga's acceptance of the Reformation in 1522 ended the power of the Roman and Orthodox Churches there.

Riga has a 13th century Lutheran cathedral, 15th century Hanseatic House and the Church of St. Peter with a 412 foot high steeple. There is also a medieval "old town" with winding streets, gabled dwellings and old storehouses.

Riga enjoys a warm seaside summer with temperatures in July averaging 62 degrees F. It has a famous seaside resort, the Riga Yurmala. The city has a symphony orchestra, several theaters, several museums and a zoological garden.

Daugavpils (130,000) is a rapidly developing city and a railroad crossroads on the Daugava River. It produces building materials, iron products, foods, electrical equipment, leather goods and textiles.

Liepaya (118,000), an ice free port on the Baltic Sea, is located on a narrow isthmus which separates the Baltic from Lake Liepaja. Metallurgy is its leading industry. It manufactures wood products and canned foods. There is a sizable export trade through its port. The town has a former residence of Peter the Great and the 18th century Church of the Trinity.

Yelgava , Jelgava (65,000) on the Lielupe River is a major trade center for grain and lumber. The city grew around a fort built by the Livonian Knights. It manufactures linen, leather and metal products and has a 16th century Trinity Church and an 18th century ducal palace.

There are 56 towns in Latvia and 27 of them are considered urban in nature. The official language is Latvian although German and Russian are spoken by more than half the population.

LITHUANIA
(pop. 3,800,000 -area 25,170 sq. mi.)

Lithuania is about the size of West Virginia. It has the Baltic Sea for its eastern border and Latvia to the north. On the east it shares a border with Belarus. To its south lie Poland and the Russian territory of Kaliningrad. Its capital is Vilnius.

Lithuania is a flatland drained by the Nemen River. Highest elevations are less than 700 feet. Part of a glaciated region, much of the land is wet and swampy.

Timber is the main resource of the country. Agriculture includes dairy farming and growing of grains, flax, sugar beets, potatoes and vegetables. Livestock includes a large number of pigs and cattle.

In the last one hundred years the country has developed industries which now produce textiles, electrical equipment, metal products and chemicals. Most of the raw materials for these products are imported.

Lithuania has ample supplies of gypsum, peat and clay. Small deposits of oil were recently found off the coast but these are not enough to satisfy even basic energy needs. Electricty is produced along the Nemen River and there are two nuclear power plants which are closed frequently due to radiation leaks.

Considering its latitude the country enjoys a mild climate. Inland the average July temperature is 62 degrees F. and the average January temperature is 17 degrees F. The coastal region has an average July temperature of 66 degrees and an average January temperature of 19 degrees.

Lithuanians make up 80 percent of the population. Russians are a minority when compared to their numbers in Latvia and Estonia. Here they make up only 9 percent of the population. Poles account for about 7 percent. There are also Belorussians, Letts and Jews.

Roman Catholicism is the dominant religion of Lithuania. Despite severe reprisals against the Catholics by the Soviets, the people clung to their faith. Religion was a focal point for resistance and nationalism, as it was in Poland.

The Lithuanian language is the official language. It belongs to the Baltic sub-family of Indo-European languages and is

15-3 A religious festival.
Silute, Lithuania.

considered the most ancient of the Indo-European language family and closest to the language from which all the Indo-European languages are believed to have evolved.

The largest part of the labor force, 29 percent, is engaged in agriculture with 25 percent in industry. Fishing is an important enterprise. Forested areas contain wild boar, deer, fox and wolves.

After the Soviet break-up, employment dropped 25 percent. Lithuania did not join the Commonwealth of Independent States. New currency, the **litas**, was issued in 1994.

Vilnius (595,000) on the Neris (Viliya) River, is the capital city. It is a rail and highway junction intimately connected with Minsk, Belarus. Vilnius was officially founded in 1323 when the Lithuanian prince Gediminas built his castle there. With the destruction of Kiev by the Mongols in the 13th century, Vilnius became the major city of a Lithuanian principality that stretched into Belarus and most of Ukraine.

Present-day Vilnius shows the strong influence of its history. Poles, Russians, Jews, Germans as well as Lithuanians all contributed to the cultural mix.

A tourist and religious attraction in the old part of town is the Ausros Vartai or Pointed Gate, the last remnant of what was once the city wall. Above the gate is a shrine containing an image of the Virgin, an object of worship and pilgrimage. Ruins of the 14th century castle built by Gediminas still exist.

The city has a university founded in 1579. It also boasts an academy of science, several theaters, museums and a research institute.

Kaunas (435,000), the second largest city in Lithuania, is the rival of the capital. Its population is 85 percent Lithuanian. It is at the junction of the Nemen and Neris Rivers. Industries include iron and steel, chemicals, plastics, synthetic fibers, electrical goods, flour milling, meat packing and textiles.

Kaunas was a medieval trading center which passed back-and-forth between Russia and Poland over the centuries.

Prior to World War II, Jews made up about thirty percent of the city population. Almost all of the Jews were exterminated during the Nazi occupation (1941-44). Many other citizens emigrated.

The city has a 16th century town hall, ruins of a 14th century castle, the 15th century Vytautus church and a famous 17th century monastery. It also boasts a university, a polytechnical institute and a medical institute as well as several museums.

Klaipeda (210,000) is the major Lithuanian port on the Baltic Sea. It has shipyards and industries producing fertilizers and timber products. A large fishing fleet is berthed here. Under German rule the town was called **Memel**. It was here Frederick William III of Prussia signed the edict emancipating the serfs in his kingdom. Since World War II the large German population has been replaced by Russians.

After a slow start, Lithuania has adjusted well to independence. Trade with Poland and the west has kept unemployment low.

BELARUS
(pop. 10,437,000 - 80,134 sq.mi.)
BELORUSSIA, BYELRUSSIA

Belarus is about the size of Idaho. Its capital is Minsk. It borders on Poland to the west, Ukraine to the south, Russia to the east and Latvia and Estonia on the northwest.

Most of Belarus is lowland with occasional hills deposited by the last glaciation. The country's highest point is less than a thousand feet above sea level. A terminal moraine separates drainage which flows north and west to the Baltic Sea from drainage flowing south to the Black Sea.

Belarus is drained by the rivers Dnieper to the south, and Western Dvina, Western Bug and Nemen to the west. None of these streams are navigable to large ships in Belarus.

Belarus has a moderate humid continental climate with warm summers and cold winters. Northern temperatures average 17 degrees Fahrenheit in January and 62 degrees F. in July. In the south, the January average is 25 degrees F. and the July average is 66 degrees F.

About a third of the land is covered with peat and swampy soils. The Pripyat Marshes of the south are shared with Ukraine. Peat is the republic's most valuable mineral resource. It is used for fuel and fertilizer and as a base for a moderate chemical industry.

The **Pripyat Marshes** are swampy areas along the 500 mile long Pripyat River. A large portion of it is forested. Because the marshes are remnants of a large glacial lake the soils are sandy and bog-like when drained. The marsh extends from Mahilyow on the north to Brest in the west and to Kiev, Ukraine.

A dense network of canals, lakes and streams connects the Pripyat waterways to the Western Bug River which leads into the Vistula in Poland. Other canals are connected to the Nemen and Dnieper Rivers. Draining the marsh began in 1870. Since then, a third of the land has been restored to cattle grazing and potatoes.

Another third of the land is forested with pine, fir and birch in the north and elm, oak and white beech in the south. Lumbering is a major industry in Belarus.

15-4 Belarus pipers in concert.

Another third is suitable for agriculture. Potatoes, flax, hemp, sugar beets, buckwheat, rye, oats, barley and wheat are the main agricultural crops. The cattle herd has been steady at about six million head, mostly dairy cattle and single cows owned by families. Pigs and chickens are raised by most rural families.

Besides peat, Belarus has deposits of clay, sand, chalk, dolomite, phosphorite and limestone. These form the basis of a cement, fertilizer and chemical industry. Agriculture machinery is a prominent manufactured product. Belarus also manufactures motor vehicles, television sets, timepieces, bicycles, textiles and electrical equipment.

Hemp is used to make rope and backing material for rugs and furniture. Production of this material has fallen off since the invention of artificial fibers. However, Belarus has entered the synthetic fiber industry which has become its major export. The country is also expanding its linen, woolen and cotton textile industry.

Belarus has a good system of highways and railways connecting its major cities. Along with small boat river traffic, this makes goods easily available throughout the country.

Belorussians make up 80 percent of the population, Russians 13 percent. There are also a sizable number of Poles, Ukrainians, Jews and Lithuanians. The word "belo" in Slavic means "white". Hence the people are known as White Russians as opposed to the ethnic Great Russians originating in the

Moscow region. The country went from 30 percent urban after World War II to 65 percent urban in 1995.

Belorussian is the official language. However, most people also speak and write Russian. Eastern Orthodox is the major religion, but there are also a large number of Roman Catholics.

Belarus has been a historic battlefield between invading armies and Russia. It was a World War I battlefield and was completely devastated during World War II.

Of all the republics separated from Russia after the collapse of the Soviet Union, Belarus is the one most likely to rejoin Russia, either as an actual Russian republic or at least in a closely knit economic union. In 1994 Belarus voted to accept the Russian ruble as its unit of currency.

Serious economic problems developed after the dissolution of the Soviet Union. Russia increased its price of oil and natural gas to world market levels and ten percent of the Belarus industry had to close. Inflation was out of control and only recently reduced to acceptable levels. Unemployment has been high.

In 1996, Belarus and Russia agreed to a pact which practically guarantees Russia control over the economic future of Belarus.

Minsk also **Mensk** (1,620,000) is a noted cultural and industrial center on the Suisloch River. About one-fifth of the entire Belarus population lives in and around Minsk. Workers here make automobiles, trucks, motorcycles, machine tools, refrigerators, radios and tractors. There are also food processing factories and textile mills.

Minsk began as an outpost and supply area on the road between Lithuania and Moscow. It was part of Poland in the 16th century.

During the Middle Ages Minsk had one of the largest Jewish populations in Eastern Europe. Before World War II its Jewish population was 40 percent (1938). Most of these people were exterminated by the Nazis who occupied the city from 1941 to 1943.

Despite the extreme devastation during World War II, several ancient structures remain. These include Ekaterin Cathedral and a Bernardine convent dating back to the 17th century. The city also has a well known university and the Lenin State Library. It has an opera and ballet company, a music conservatory and several theaters and museums.

Minsk is the headquarters of the Commonwealth of Independent States.

Gomel, (Homyel), also Homel (510,000) is on the Sozh River, a tributary of the Dnieper. It is in the center of a large agriculture district. Industries include manufacturing of building materials, food processing, and textile making. Gomel also produces timber products and fertilizers. It has the famous Petropavlovsk Cathedral built in 1819. It also has a university.

Like Minsk, about 40 percent of the population was Jewish until they were killed during the Nazi occupation.

Vitebsk, Vitsyebsk, (355,000) Located on the Western Dvina (Daugava) River, Vitebsk is closely tied with Lithuania. Like most of the larger cities in Belarus, it processes food and manufactures building materials and textiles. Vitebsk, also like other cities on the small rivers, was more important in earlier times when river transportation was the method of moving heavy cargo great distances.

Mahilyow, also Mogilev (363,000), is a railroad and highway junction on the Dnieper River. It produces artificial fibers, small machines, food products and chemicals. The city grew around a castle built in 1267 by princes of Smolensk. Mahilyow was on the direct trade route between Scandinavia and Russia it was alternately governed by Swedes, Poles and Russians during its long history. A tower built by Tatar invaders in the 13th century still stands.

Bobruisk, also Bobruysk (235,000), is a railway junction on the Berezina River. It is the only tire manufacturing city in Belarus. Industries also include wood products, chemicals and machine manufacturing.

Grodno (275,000), located on the Nemunas (Nemen) River near the Polish border, is also a railway center producing small machines, synthetic fibers, electrical appliances, textiles. Its newest factory produces heavy duty trucks. and food. It also has a tobacco processing factory. Its culture and heritage are Polish. It was part of Poland in 1920. In 1939 it became part of the Soviet Union. Grodno has a 12th century Eastern Orthodox Church, a 16th century palace and a 16th century Bernardine Church. Its 13th century ruins of a ducal residence is one of the oldest brick architectural remains in Europe.

The 580 mile long **Nemen River** originates in Belarus and flows to the Baltic Sea. It forms part of the border between Lithuania and Kaliningrad Region. An important meeting between Napoleon and Czar Alexander I took place on a raft in the middle of the river in 1807. They signed the Treaty of Tilset.

Brest, also Brest-Litovsk (265,000), is a fast growing city on the junction of the Western Bug and Mukhavets Rivers near the Polish border. It is the main border crossing point between Belarus and Poland. During its history it was alternately held by Russia and Poland. Oil and gas pipelines pass through Brest on their way from Russia to the west. Manufacturing includes food processing, textiles and light machinery.

A treaty between Lenin and Germany was signed here in 1918 ending Russian participation in World War I

A forest north of Brest extending into Poland is home to the last remaining herd of European Bison. The animals are protected but a permit is given to hunt one animal per year. In 1996, the price of that one license was $100,000. The money is used for habitat enhancement.

The **Western Bug River** is 470 miles long and forms the border with Poland in the southwestern corner of Belarus. It is a tributary of the Vistula, a major river in Poland. A canal connects the Bug to the Dnieper.

Baranovich (162,000) is a major railway junction with metal working and textile industries. It was in Poland from 1920 to 1939 when it was annexed by the Soviet Union according to the Molotov-Ribbentrop Pact which split Poland and gave the Baltic States to Russia. The inhabitants of this territory were never consulted..

Chornobyl Legacy

Of all the areas affected by the 1986 Chornobyl disaster, Belarus suffered the most, especially in the southeast. The fire which burned out of control spread more than 50 tons of radioactive fallout, most of it in Belarus.

Normal life for cities such as Gomel ceases to exist. People are afraid to have children. Blood diseases are five times higher than in similar non-radiated areas.

When the Soviet Union dissolved, the country was left alone to handle immense social problems created by the explosion. From Gomel to the Ukraine border, thousands of acres of radioactive farmlands and forests are restricted areas and no one is legally permitted to live there.

16. LANDS OF THE COSSACKS

UKRAINE   UKRAYINA

(POP. 52,200,000 - 233,100 sq.mi.)

Ukraine, slightly smaller than Texas, is one of the largest countries in Europe. Ukraine borders on Belarus in the north, Poland in the northwest, on Slovakia, Hungary, Romania and Moldova in the west and southwest, on Russia in the east and the Black Sea and the Sea of Azov on the south.

The country is a vast flat plain, mostly below 1000 feet. A small section of the Carpathian Mountains reach into the western part of the country. The highest point is Mt. Hoverla at 6,762 feet. There are also mountains on the Crimean Peninsula.

The country can be divided into its vegetation units: mixed forest in the north, forest steppe in the center and steppe in the south. Much of the forest has been cut and the land put into crops. The remaining northwoods houses deer, beaver and marten. Rare birds in the country include the Eurasian black vulture, steppe eagle and the grey heron.

The land is drained mostly by the central Dnieper River and its tributaries, mainly the Berezina, Pripyat and Ingulets. To the west is the Dnestre and the Southern Bug Rivers. The Danube is in the far south. The large Pripyat Marshes are found in the northwest. The Donets is the main river in the east.

The **Dnieper River (Dnepre)** begins in Russia, southwest of Moscow, flows into Belarus and then through Ukraine to the Black Sea. The Dnieper is 1430 miles long and is frozen in its northern reaches for four months. Rapids near Zaporizhzhya were eliminated with the construction of the Dneproges Dam.

Canals link the Dnieper to the Southern Bug, Berezina, Pripyat, Daugava and Nemunas Rivers. The Dnieper is the main link in a waterway from the Black Sea to the Baltic Sea.

The **Donets River** flows for 650 miles through one of the most industrialized regions of the world. It transports coal and raw materials despite being frozen from December to March. Its tributaries are the Aydar, Luhan and Oskol.

Ukrainan soils are gray podzolic in the north and northwest and chernozem in the south. The north and northwest is wooded and the south is steppe. The term *steppe* originated here. The climate is moderated by the Black Sea.

North and northwest Ukraine receive slightly more than twenty inches of precipitation annually and the south and southeast receives slightly less than twenty inches. This is adequate for growing grain.

In northern Ukraine the average January temperature is 18 degrees Fahrenheit and the average July temperature is 68 degrees F. In the south, the average January temperature is 23 degrees F. and the average July temperature is 73 degrees F. Relative humidity is as low as 40 percent at noon in July and August.

The country is relatively dry and winter snow often melts before the regular spring thaws. Northern Ukraine receives only ten inches of snow annually while the drier south receives only five inches.

The northeast is an extension of the Russian Plateau. The Dnieper River basin forms a distinct lowland where it makes a large bend as it flows along the eastern edge of the Dnieper Plateau. In the southeast, just north of the Sea of Azov, is the Azov and Donets Plateaus, a series of dissected hills rich in mineral wealth. The Crimean Peninsula, jutting into the Black Sea is

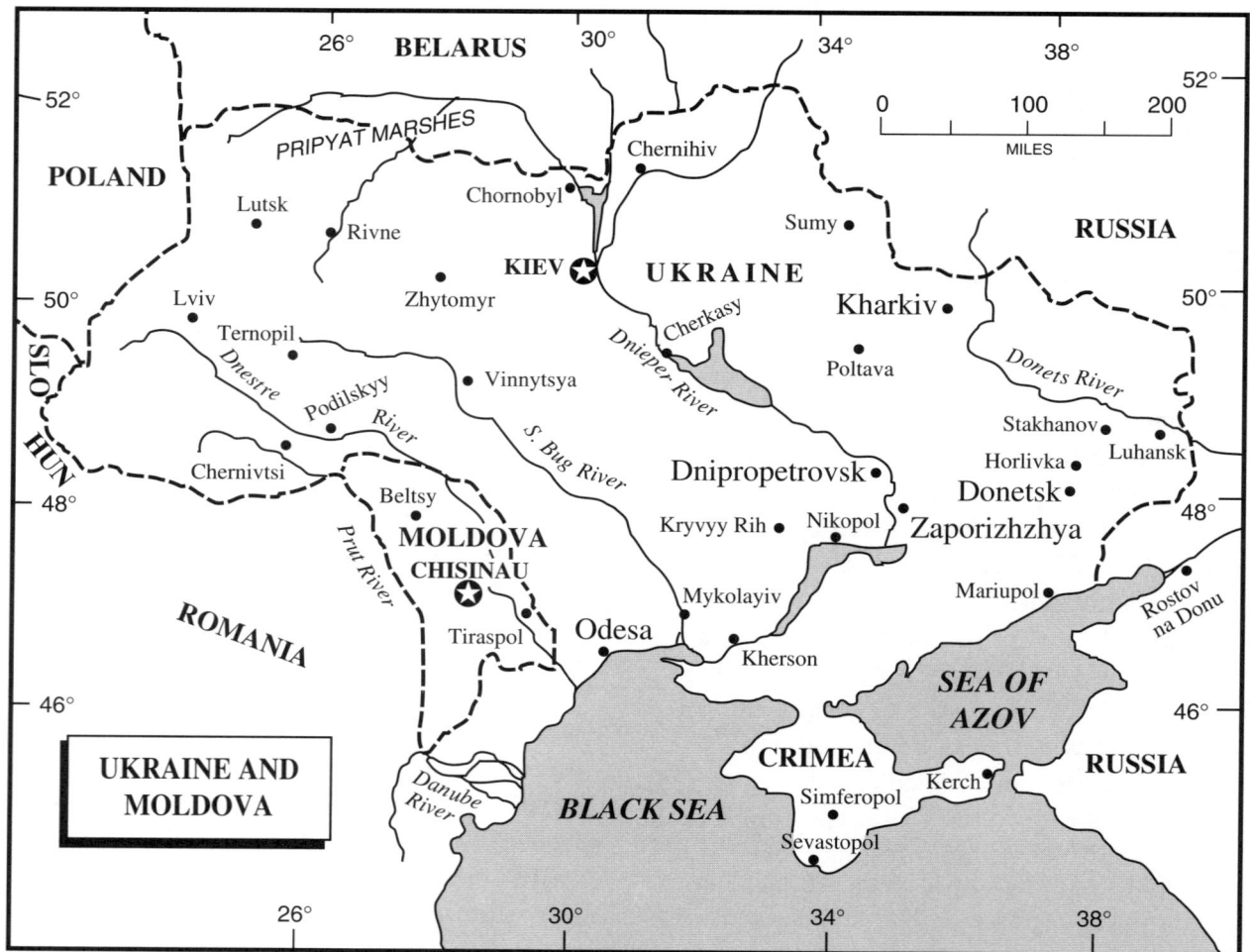

MAP 15   Ukraine and Moldova

mountainous with slight indentations and lowlands at the edge of the sea.

Ukraine, one of the best wheat growing regions in the world, can aptly be described as a "bread basket". However, wheat shares the land with maize. Together they occupy two thirds of the arable land. Other crops, mostly grown in the north, include potatoes, sunflowers, rye and barley. Southern crops include melons, sugar beets and flax.

Industries related to agriculture include meat packing, sugar refining and flour milling. Sugar production is the main agriculture industry.

Compared to other European countries, Ukraine is rich in mineral resources. The region east of the Dnieper River has one of the largest concentrations of industry in the world. The region's metallurgical, chemical and machine building industries are based on the anthracite and bituminous coal of the Donets lowlands, the manganese of Nikopol and the iron ore mines of Kryvyy Rih. Some iron ore is imported from Kerch on the Crimean Peninsula.

A large dam at Dneproges powers one of the world's largest hydroelectric stations. The dam backs up the Dnieper River to make it navigable throughout its course in Ukraine. The lower Dnieper is a chain of lakes created by dams.

Metal resources include bauxite and aluminum, zinc, mercury, chromium, copper, titanium and nickel. Small deposits

16-1 A grocery store in Ukraine

of oil and natural gas are also exploited. Most of the oil used in the country is imported from the Caspian region of Baky. The natural gas comes from Siberia and Turkmenistan.

Industrial products of Ukraine include machinery, steel, cast iron, cement, fertilizers, glass, paper, plywood, pottery, furniture, textiles, clothing, shoes and refined metals.

Cattle and hogs are raised in large numbers. There is also a sizable forest industry in the northwest.

Ukrainians make up 73 percent of the population. Russians account for 22 percent, Jews two percent, and minor groups of Poles, Belorussians, Hungarians and Moldovians.

The Ukrainian Orthodox Church claims 78 percent of the people while the Ukrainian (Roman) Catholic accounts for 14 percent. Muslims, found mostly in the southeast and on the Crimean Peninsula, are a significant religious minority. Others practice Judaism and there are some Protestant groups. The Ukrainian Catholic Church was officially banned by the Soviets.

There are seven major universities in Ukraine. The literacy rate is close to one hundred percent.

About 20 percent of the people are engaged in agriculture, 49 percent in industry and 28 percent in service type industries. The country is classified as 68 percent urban.

The Ukrainian language is recognized as a separate language from Russian. It is part of the large group of Slavic languages.

In Czarist times the Ukrainian language was outlawed and was used only as a spoken dialect. After the Bolshevik Revolution began an army of Ukrainian nationalists, led by Simon V. Petlura and Yevhen Konovalets, began fighting the Red Army. This war was extremely brutal,whole villages were destroyed and over a million people were killed. (Sudoplatov 1994:9).

Nationalist groups had been fighting for independence from Russia since "Sitch", an independent fiefdom, had been incorporated into Russia as the Ukraine. During World War II the Ukrainian nationalists sided with Hitler hoping the German Army would liberate them from Russia. When this didn't happen, the nationalists continued a guerrilla war that lasted virtually until 1991. Russians referred to these nationalists as "the Ukrainian nationalist gangsters". (Ibid) Throughout the period of Soviet rule there was a Ukrainian government-in-exile based in Paris.

The worst nuclear accident in history occurred at Chornobyl (**Chernobyl** in Russian) located in northern Ukraine. On April 26, 1986, the protective roof blew off one of the four reactor containment buildings of the nuclear power station. Radioactive gas and moisture escaped. The Soviet penchant for secrecy kept the news of the accident from the world for about a week before intense radioactivity was detected in Poland and the Scandinavian countries. Eventually, the Soviets asked for western help in containing the radioactivity.

About 200,000 people were evacuated from the immediate area. The land within a hundred mile radius of the accident will be contaminated for several thousand years. Even though the area is highly radioactive, many people are illegally returning to their homes and drinking contaminated water and raising contaminated vegetables. Since the accident, an estimated ten thousand people

have died as a result of exposure to radiation. Cracks in the sarcophagus on the defective reactor have developed and these pose a distinct danger for the future. The G-7 nations have agreed to give Ukraine money in exchange for its cooperation in giving up nuclear weapons and the dangerous nuclear power plants such as the three remaining reactors at Choronobyl. The G-7 nations include the United States, Great Britain, Germany, France, Canada, Japan and Italy.

So far the three surviving reactors are still operating. Ukraine needs the electricity and cannot afford to either remodel Chornobyl or develop alternative energy sources.

"For us," Lenin wrote, "to lose the Ukraine would be to lose our head." Nonetheless, Ukrainian nationalists believed that one day their republic of over 50 million people would drive for independence and destroy the Soviet Union. Ukrainians believe that the Soviet Union collapsed "practically and metaphorically" on April 26, 1986 at 1:23 a.m., the moment of the Chernobyl nuclear accident, an accident which "embodied every curse of the Soviet system". (Remnick 1993:244).

During the days of serfdom, many Ukrainians fled to lands south and east of Kiev which were still under the influence of the Turks. These newcomers were referred to by the Turkish term "kazak" which later became **cossack**. Eventually the cossacks threw off Polish domination and sided with the Russians of Muscovy. The cossacks, mounted on horseback, became the frontier troops of the Czars.

Crimea, an autonomous republic under the Soviets, was incorporated into Ukraine territory in 1954. Bessarabia and Eastern Galicia which included Lviv also became part of Ukraine. Later Moldova was created from Bessarabia and stretched to the Black

Sea. However, the Ukrainians had some influence on the Soviet parliament and the section of Moldova bordering on the Black Sea and the Danube River was given to Ukraine.

Independence was restored to Ukraine on December 26, 1991 but Ukraine remains tied, both politically and economically, to Russia. Many communists are still in power.

During the 1994 elections, the country seemed to split into two factions: the heavily pro-Russian east in the industrial regions and the anti-Russian west centered in Lviv.

Tensions were eased between Russia and Ukraine when an agreement was reached concerning the disbursement of the powerful Black Sea Naval fleet based in Odesa and ports of the Crimea. Many important political persons in Russia have stated that the borders concerning the Crimea need to be redrawn.

Ukraine, which means "The Borderland", was the Soviet Union's breadbasket. Before the communist takeover, Ukrainian farmers helped feed Europe. They may do so again.

Like other former republics who were forcibly incorporated into the Soviet Union, Ukraine is emerging as a nation in its own right. On December 1, 1991 over 90 percent of the population voted for independence. In March 1994 President Leonid Kravchuk met with President Bill Clinton in Washington, D.C.

Ukraine has joined in a partnership with NATO which could lead to full membership in the future. Russia is not happy about this possibility. Geopolitical experts believe Ukraine is pivotal to the stability of Europe and Russia.

After independence in 1991, industrial production declined 30 percent. Russia cut off supplies of oil and natural gas when Ukraine defaulted on payments. Unemployment was high and Ukraine decided to postpone privatization. As of 1995, 95 percent of agriculture, industry

16-2 An Ukrainian family portrait.

and property was still owned by the state.

Crimea and the Crimean Peninsula is a serious point of contention between Russia and Ukraine. It passed to Ukraine in 1954 when Nikita Khrushchev decided to reward Ukraine for its unity and cooperation with Russia. The name comes from the Russian term **Krym** which is derived from the Tatar Kirim, meaning fort.

Russians make up two-thirds of the Crimean population of 2.7 million and Ukrainians are 25 percent. Its capital is Simferopol. It was considered the "Soviet Riviera" and thousands of Soviet bureaucrats vacationed there over the years. This was where Mikhail Gorbachev was vacationing when the coup was attempted in August 1991.

People have lived on the peninsula since recorded history. Tatars arrived in the Middle Ages. In 1944 Stalin expelled the Tatars to other regions, mainly to Central Asia. Since the dissolution of the Soviet Union the Tatars have slowly returned and have found their homes and lands occupied by Russians. About 250,000 Tatars have returned with another contingent of the same number waiting to return. Today Tatars make up ten percent of the Crimean population.

The Tatars are united with the Ukrainians who are holding their breath to see if the Crimeans will attempt to break away and unite with Russia. The Crimean legislature, made up mostly of Russians, did vote for independence from Ukraine. The agreements of the Commonwealth of Independent States call for recognition of the borders that were established before the break-up of the Soviet Union. Russia has agreed to honor those commitments.

The major Crimean port is Kerch located on the Kerch Strait where the Black Sea and the Sea of Azov meet. Kerch gives handy access to the Donbas.

Crimean farms produce wheat, barley, sunflowers and grapes. Much of the land is irrigated with water drained from the Dnieper River.

MAJOR UKRAINE CITIES

Kiev (Kyyiv) (2,630,000), capital of Ukraine, is a port city on the Dnieper River and a leading industrial, commercial and cultural center. Kiev is the center of the sugar beet processing industry. Other industries include metal refining, machinery, aircraft, motorcycles, river boats, leather shoes, electronic calculators, machine tools, chemicals, building products and textiles.

One of the oldest cities in Europe, Kiev has been called the "Mother of Russian Cities" because it was here that Russians first emerged as a coherent, powerful ethnic group.

The city became the capital of Kievan Rus, the first Russian state. It was one of the principle cities on the Scandinavia, Novgorod and Constantinople (Istanbul) trade route. Kiev was the most powerful city in the region until 1240 when it was captured by invading Mongols. It was forced to pay tribute for the next 200 years.

Kiev has a modern subway, an academy of sciences, several museums, a research institute, a gallery of Russian Art and a large sport stadium. Its 11th century Cave Monastery with extensive catacombs is a major tourist attraction.

Kharkiv (Kharkov) (1,625,000) is located in the upper Donets valley at the confluence of the Kharkiv, Lopan and Udy Rivers. Ukraine's main rail junction, it is the focal point for eight railroads. Kharkiv is close to the iron mines of Kryvyy Rih and Donets Basin coal. A leader in steel making and heavy metal engineering, it also produces tobacco products, locomotives, tractors, aircraft, turbines, motorcycles, farm implements, bicycles, printing and the

16-3 The Dnieper River as it flows through Kiev.

manufacture of chemicals.

The city was an important fortification for the Ukrainian Cossacks who were loyal to the Czar who rewarded them with an autonomous district - the Kharkiv Oblast.

The annexation of the Crimea in 1783 followed by colonization of the steppes increased Kharkiv's fortunes. The University of Kharkiv, which includes many scientific institutes, was founded in 1805. It also has an academy of sciences and several research institutes.

Kharkiv suffered heavy damage during World War II but most of the city has been rebuilt.

Donetsk (1,140,000), located on the Kalmius River in the Donets Basin, is one of Ukraines largest industrial centers. It has coal and iron and chemical industries. Both bituminous and anthracite coal are mined in the Donets region.

The city was founded in 1870 as Yuzovkan in honor of a Scottish financier named Hughes (Yuz). It was called Stalino from 1924 to 1961, There are many mine tunnels under the city and subsidence is a problem.

The area around the **Donets Basin** has one of the densest industrial concentrations in the world. Referred to as "the **Donbas**," its development was due to its proximity to European markets. Other important cities in the Donbas include **Luhansk,** formerly **Voroshilovgrad** (499,000), at the confluence of the Luhan and Olkhov Rivers produces locomotives, wool processing, chemicals, steel pipes, mining equipment, machine tools, textiles and food.

16-4 A worker's rally in the Donbas.

Makiyivka (570,000), **Horlivka** (350,000) and **Kramatorsk** (200,000) are centers for the coal industry as well as the production of steel, machinery and transportation equipment. Each has some type of chemical industry with coal as the raw material. Horlivka is noted for huge slag and mine waste piles which are scattered around the city.

Odesa, also Odessa (1,120,000), is Ukraine's main port on the Black Sea and a major resort center. It exports include grain, sugar, coal, machinery, petroleum, cement, jute and timber. Industries include shipbuilding, metal working, food processing, engineering instruments, industrial acids, fertilizers, movie equipment, clothing and products made from silk, cotton, wood and jute. The jute is used mostly for rug and stuffed furniture backing.

Odesa is the port of entry for western goods. The city administrators want Ukraine to give the city a "free port" status which they claim will aid foreign trade. The city is hampered by Ukraine's shaky economy and wavering legislation as well as its sluggish approach to privatization. Odesa is the beginning and the end of Ukraine's transportation grid.

Odesa has one of the biggest naval bases in the world and is home to a part of the famed Black Sea Fleet. It is the home port of a major Antarctic whaling fleet. Many other fishing fleets also call Odesa home.

Throughout much of history, Turkey and Turkish culture have influenced Odesa. It was Turkey's chief port and launch pad for Ottoman invasions into mainland Europe. The Ottoman Turks ruled the northern Black Sea area for more than two centuries.

Odesa once had a large Jewish population, but it was decimated by the German occupation during World War II. Approximately 200,000 Odesian Jews lost their lives.

Odesa is a great cultural center, boasting a university, an opera and a ballet, an historical museum, a large library, an astronomical observatory and a world class art gallery.

Dnipropetrovsk (1,200,0000) is the second largest city on the Dnieper River. The hub of both water and rail transportation, it is located on the great bend in the river. It has developed because of its proximity to the iron ore of Kryvyy Rih, Donbas coal, Nikopol manganese, hydroelectric power from the Dneproges Dam and natural gas from Shebelinka.

This city also has a huge iron and steel industry and produces heavy machinery, locomotives, railroad cars, bridge girders, vehicle tires, chemicals and food products.

Dnipropetrovsk was the site of an old cossack village on the big bend in the Dnieper River. It was named Ekaterinoslav for Catherine II (Catherine the Great).

Population and industry both increased in 1932 with the construction of the dam and hydropower station. Its many museums are the basis of a sizable tourist industry.

Zaporizhzhya (Zaporozhye) (890,000) is at the site of the first dam on the Dnieper. It had one of the first aluminum smelters in the world, and is also known for its premium alloy steel. Access to cheap electricity has made the city a center for electroplating as well as the specialty smelting of ores. The city also produces coking coal, magnesium and electrical transformers.

The **Dneproges Dam** on the Dnieper River near Zaporizhzhya is a major hydroelectric station. It supplies power to the industrial centers of Dnipropetrovsk, Kryvyy Rih and Zaporizhzhya. The dam is more than one half mile long and 600 feet high. It raises the Dnieper River level 123 feet. The dam was destroyed by the German army in 1942, then rebuilt from 1944 to 1949.

Lviv (Lvov) (865,000) at the watershed of the Western Bug and Dnestr rivers is a major rail and highway junction as well as an industrial and commercial center. Oil is refined here and forms the basis of a pharmaceutical industry. Motor cars, radios, television sets and other electrical apparatus are manufactured here.

Lviv is an educational center and houses the Ukrainian Academy of Sciences created in 1256 by Prince Daniel of Galich. The city was a major trade route between Vienna and Kiev. It has a 16th century Polish palace and two 14th century Roman Catholic cathedrals.

The city used to be in Poland before the Nazi-Soviet Pact changed the borders. Today Lviv is a major trade center between Poland and Ukraine.

Kryvyy Rih (Krivoy Rog) (713,000), on a tributary of the Dnieper, in the center of a great iron mining region. It gets its name which means "Crooked Horn" from the shape of the iron deposits and from the ancient mines within them.

Mykolayiv (Nikolayev) (514,000), at the mouth of the Bug River, is a major shipbuilding center and naval base.

Mariupol formerly **Zhadov** (420,000) is a seaport where the Kalmius River joins the Sea of Azov. It too produces iron and steel as well as chemicals. In its role as a seaport for the Donbas it exports coal, salt and grain and iron and steel.

Vinnytsya (376,000) is the major city on the upper Southern Bug River. It is an important railroad junction involved in sugar beet processing as well as other foods.

Kherson (357,000), near the mouth of the Dnieper River as it empties into the Black Sea, is a railroad, sea and river port. It ships grain, timber and manganese ore and manufactures cotton textiles and ships. Oil refining and food processing are also here.

Poltava (318,000), on the main highway between Kiev and Kharkiv, is on the Vorskla River, a tributary of the Dnieper. It is located in the black earth agriculture region. Tobacco is a major crop and food processing is the main industry.

Stakhanov (300,000), in the Donets Basin, was named after Aleksey Grigorevich Stakhanov, a local coal miner. His team cut over one thousand tons of coal in one sixteen hour shift. He was given the Soviet Hero of the People award and promoted to manager of the mine as well as a coveted five room apartment.

Chernihiv (298,000), in northern Ukraine, is on the Desna River. It has excellent highway, air, river and rail connections. The city manufactures tires, wood products and processes wool and food. One of the oldest cities in Ukraine, it was an important city in Kievan Rus. Several structures from the 10th century still exist. Within the city limits there is a complete 11th Century church and monastery.

Sumy (297,000), in northeast Ukraine, is a sugar refining center which also makes furniture and shoes. It is 150 miles north of Kharkiv and 125 miles southwest of Kursk in Russia.

Cherkassy (294,000) is a city which should grow in importance because of its location on the large Kremenchug Reservoir in central Ukraine. Its major industries are food processing, synthetic fibers and fertilizers.

Kirovohrad (272,000), on the Ingul River, is in the center of a rich agriculture district. It manufactures agricultural machinery and has food processing.

Cherovitsi (258,000) in on the Prut River in the Carpathian foothills just north of Romania. It has 15th Century architecture. The city lies in an area of extensive beech forest. Food processing, textiles and the manufacture of small machines are done here. It was once the capital of Romanian Bukovina until it was taken over by the Soviets in 1940.

Ternopil (210,000) on the Seret River, a tributary to the Dnestre is noted for its porcelain products. It also manufactures building materials and processes food.

Crimean Cities

Sevastopol (355,000), on the southwest tip of the Crimean Peninsula, is the chief naval base in the Black Sea and shares the Black Sea Fleet with Odesa. **Simferopol** (344,000) is the capital of the Crimea Republic. **Kerch** (174,000), the leading commercial port of the Crimean Peninsula, has a strategic location on the strait separating the Sea of Azov from the Black Sea. **Yalta** (89,000) is the leading Crimean tourist city. Soviet **dachas** and summer homes are here. The Yalta Conference between Stalin, Roosevelt and Churchill was held here in February 1945.

16-5 Kharkiv, the second city of Ukraine.

MOLDOVA (MOLDAVIA)
(pop. 4,500,000 - 13,012 sq. mi.)

Moldova is a landlocked country slightly larger than Maryland. Bordering Romania on the west, it is separated from that country by the Prut River. Ukraine surrounds the rest of Moldova. Its northern and eastern border is formed by the Dnestr River. The capital city is Chisinau. Historically, the territory occupied by Moldova, between the Prut and Dnestr Rivers, was known as **Bessarabia**.

The **Prut River** rises in the Carpathian Mountains and flows 530 miles to meet the Danube near the Black Sea. It forms most of the Moldova/Romania border.

Moldovian topography is a hilly plain yet there are many cliffs and steep slopes. Because Moldova is close to the Black Sea, it enjoys a mild climate. At Chisinau the average July temperature is 72 degrees Fahrenheit and the average January temperature is 25 degrees F.

Moldova's soils are gray-brown in the north and chernozem or black earth in the south. These fertile soils produce a variety of crops including maize, wheat, corn, barley, sugar beets, soybeans, tobacco and sunflowers. Fruit orchards produce apples, pears, plums and cherries. Walnut trees abound as well as grape vineyards. Wine from grapes and plums are two major exports. Thin shelled walnuts are also exported.

Moldovian wines are considered world class and Spanish wine interests have invested heavily in vineyards and bottling plants.

Beekeeping and silk production are unique Moldavian enterprises. Honey from this area was a major trade item over a thousand years ago. Other important agriculture exports are the perfume essences of rose and lavender.

There are over one million head of cattle, sheep and pigs. Food is not a problem in Moldova as it is in many other parts of the former Soviet Union.

Lignite and gypsum form the country's basic mineral wealth. These are used locally as well as exported. A sizable metal working industry uses imported materials. Manufacturing is confined to small machinery, refrigerators and mostly agricultural implements. Food processing, the main industry, includes canning, wine making and meat packing.

The extensive forests which once covered the country are now limited to the central portion. Trees include beech, oak and hornbeam. Deer, wolves, badgers and martens are major forest animals.

Two thirds of the population is Moldavian, 14 percent is Ukrainian and 13 percent Russian. There are also Bulgarian, Gagauz and Jewish minorities. Gagauz are a Turkish group that migrated into Bessarabia

16-6   Grape harvest in Moldova.

16-7 Landscape of Upland Moldova.

from the Balkans in the 15th century.

Moldavians belong to the Romanian ethnic group. Their language is Romanian and they use the Latin Alphabet. After Moldova was forcibly absorbed by the Soviet Union, a Soviet "scientist" declared that Moldavians and Romanians were separate peoples. An intensive Russification program followed. Russian became the official language, Russian had to be taught in schools, the Cyrillic Alphabet had to be used and Moldavians had to pledge loyalty to the Soviet Union.

After the Soviet Union's dissolution, Moldova immediately declared its independence. Moldovians insisted they were Romanian and they returned to using the Latin Alphabet. Sometime in the next century Moldova will likely reunite with Romania. However, in 1995, the country overwhelmingly voted not to join with Romania.

Many Moldovians also speak Ukrainian because Ukraine is Moldova's biggest trading partner. Russian is also widely spoken. Eastern Orthodox is the main religion. Ninety-eight percent of the people declare themselves to be members of that church.

The Dnestr River, flowing east of the Carpathian Mountains and south into the Black Sea, was a natural transportation route from northern Europe to the wealth of the Arab and oriental world. This historic passageway between Europe and Asia was also the frequent scene of invasion and war.

The **Dnestr (Dnister)**, 850 miles long, forms part of the border between Ukraine and Moldova. It rises in the Carpathians and flows through Tiraspol before it empties into the Black Sea southwest of Odesa.

Moldova was independent until it came under Ottoman Turkish rule in the 16th century. Turkey fortified the region and many battles between Turkey and Russia took place here.

Russia first acquired part of the territory in 1791 then the entire region in 1812. Romania took over Bessarabia during the Russian Revolution in 1918. Once the new Soviet government became stabilized, it refused to recognize Romania's claim and the region came under Soviet rule. Romania officially transferred the territory to the Soviet Union in 1940. However during World War II Romania, fighting on the side of the Germans, recaptured Moldova which they then had to give back at the end of the war.

Moldova once stretched to the Black Sea, but in 1956 the Soviet leadership permitted Ukraine's annexation of the area between the Black Sea and along the Danube River. Moldova became an independent country with the dissolution of the Soviet Empire in 1991.

The area on the east bank of the Dnestr (Trans-Dnestr) is settled by Russians. In 1992, this area declared itself independent of Moldova. Since the Russian 14th Army was stationed there the Moldova government wisely declined to challenge them.

Since this area is not bordered by Russia there seems little likelihood that it could be annexed once again by Russia. The stalemate in its relationship to Moldova will continue for many years. The Gagauz in the south have asked for and received autonomous status.

Moldova is a member of the CIS. In 1993, it issued a new currency, the **leu**. Moldovian agriculture and its modest industry are so successful that the leu is accepted exchange currency worldwide.

Chisinau, also Kishinev (676,000), the capital city, is located on the Byk River, a tributary of the Dnestr. Its major industries are food processing, wine making, tobacco, leather working and metal. It also makes artificial rubber and plastics as well as producing textiles.

Chisinau was founded in the 15th century as a monastery town which recruited students from most of southeastern Europe.

Today it has a modern university and an academy of science.

Tiraspol (185,000), on the Dnestr River, was founded in the late 18th century as a Russian fortress. Its location in the southeast makes it the "Gateway to the Black Sea." It is a major food processing center. The city is occupied by a contingent of the Russian army and it appears they will be there for years to come.

Bel'tsy (165,000), on a northern tributary of the Dnestr, is a railroad junction as well as a local center for food processing.

Tighina (162,000), also Bendery, is a rapidly expanding city, near to, but not in the Trans-Dnestr. Since Tiraspol is the center of the Trans-Dnestr "rebellion" the Moldova government has transferred many offices and funding here rather than to Tiraspol. It should soon become the second city of Moldova.

Its main industries center around timber, fruits, tobacco, footwear, textiles and electrical appliances.

Rybnitsa (110,00) in the northeast Trans-Dnestr and **Kagul** (90,000) in the southeast near the Romanian borders are important agriculture centers.

17. THE CAUCASUS COUNTRIES

The Caucasus Mountain Ranges extend from the Black Sea to the Caspian Sea. Three historic countries are found in the mountains - Armenia, Azerbaijan and Georgia. The mountains trend northwest-southeast and contain three peaks over 16,000 feet above sea level. The highest is Mt.Elbrus at 18,841 feet, off the Georgian border just inside Russia.

This region was formerly known as Circaucasia. In Russian it is the Kavkaz. The city of Vladikavkaz can be translated as "Ruler of the Caucasus" or "Gateway to the Caucasus". The southern Caucasus is referred to as Transcaucasus.

The Caucasus Region has three distinct areas of relief. On the north is the Greater Caucasus with the highest elevations. On the south is the Lesser Caucasus which border Turkey and Iran. Between the two mountain chains are low hills connecting them. This area, the Suram Uplands, acts as a divide, causing rivers to flow in different directions. The Rioni River flows west into the Black Sea and the Kura River flows east into the Caspian.

As the Rioni River flows west to the Black Sea it forms a low alluvial plain, the Kohkhida and Mingrelia Lowlands. On the other side of the divide the Kura River creates the Lenkoran Lowlands as it winds its way to the Caspian Sea.

The Caucasus are crossed by several passes which contain highways called Military Roads. Two in particular are the Ossetian Military Road and the Georgian Military Road.

This area was settled early and many sites have been dated to the 8th century B.C. During all this history the area has been a continuous crossroads between Eastern Europe and Asia.

Lowland climates are mild and enjoyable.

The summer average temperature on the Kolkhida Lowlands is 72 degrees Fahrenheit while winter temperatures average 40 degrees F. Precipitation is high on the Kohkhida with 78 inches annually. This warm and rainy climate allows a variety of crops to be grown: lemons, oranges, tangerines, grapefruit, ginger, bamboo, tobacco and mulberry trees for the silkworm. Slopes are covered with vineyards.

The Lenkoran Lowland in Azerbaijan has a subtropical climate with 50 inches of precipitation annually in the upper valleys. However, at sea level there is almost no precipitation for this is an extension of the desert areas found on the other side of the Caspian Sea.

The Rioni and Kura river valleys have been the historic thoroughfares throughout the mountains. Today three railroads traverse the region. An oil pipeline runs from the Caspian Sea oilfields to the Black Sea.

Major deposits of copper, alunite and manganese and minor deposits of coal, iron ore and molybdenum are found here. The Apsheron Peninsula on the Black Sea is a center for oil production. Baky, located on the peninsula, supplied more than half the world's oil in 1900. The major oil fields are at Baky and at Grozny and Maykop in Russia. Although production is still good, the region does not have the importance it once enjoyed.

Power is provided by several large hydroelectric installations on the fast moving streams. The largest is located at Inguri, Georgia. Each of the three republics have at least one large thermal power plant. Armenia has a nuclear power installation with two generators.

Persians, Khazars, Arabs, Huns, Turks,

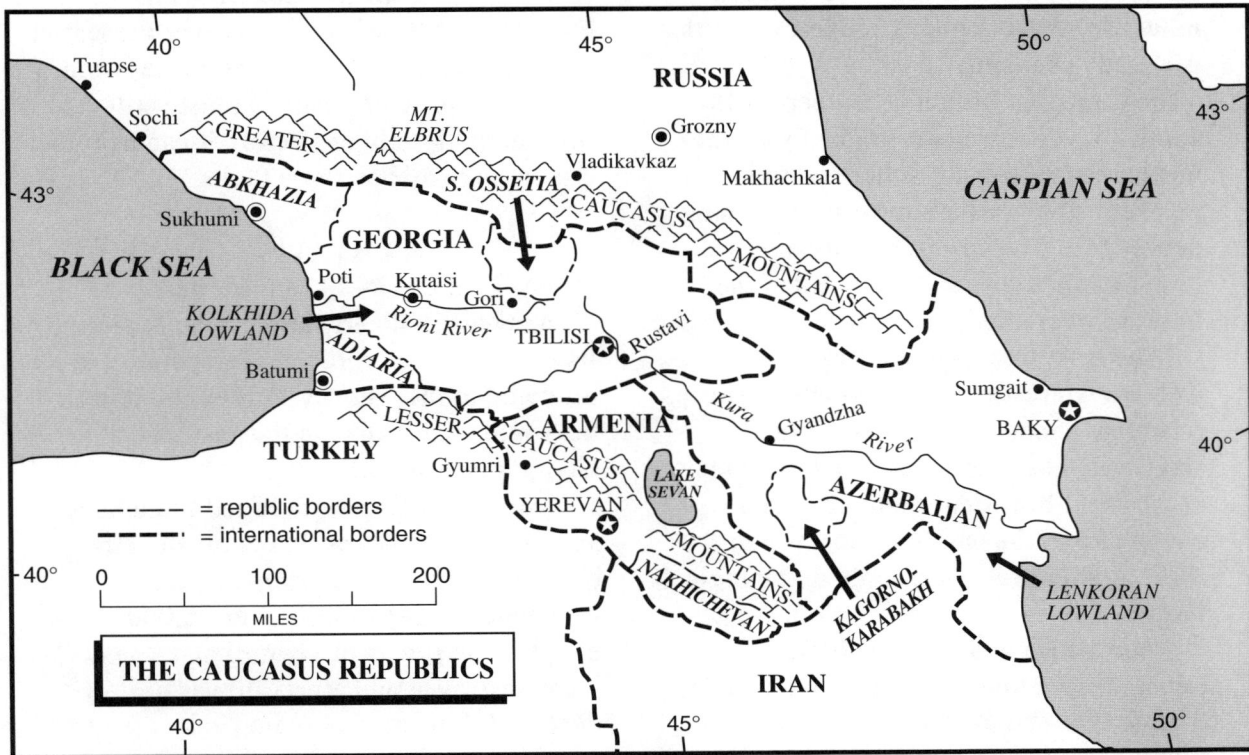

MAP 16 The Caucasus Republics

Mongols and Russians have each taken turns invading the area. Russians are simply the latest to claim the territory. There are over 50 different languages spoken in the Caucasus along with a myriad number of ethnic groups. The dominant ethnic groups are Azeris, Georgians and Armenians which have their own countries. The northern Caucasus is inside Russia.

The Russian Caucasus consists of Krasnodar Region, Adygey, Stavropol Region, Kabardino, Balkar, Karachay, Cherkess, North Ossetia, Dagestan, Chechna and Ingush. The Southern Caucasus consists of the three major countries and five autonomous areas. Abkhazia, Adjaria, and South Ossetia are in Georgia, and Nakichevan and Nagorno-Karabakh are in Azerbaijan.

Orthodox Christianity is the main religion although there are large numbers of Muslims in Azerbaijan. Each territory in the republics has its own version of the Orthodox Religion.

The Soviet Union with its Russification programs had helped consolidate the diverse region. Russian, as the official language, helped to unify the 40 or so different speakers before the breakup of the Soviet Union. Today, as these republics assert their independence and autonomy, languages are emerging as a nationalist issue.

The ethnic grouping of the Caucasus have ancient roots. Many of them developed

137

their isolated valleys over thousands of years. Russians, although only 6 percent of the total population, still have a strong influence on the region's economy, but this is already changing.

The Caucasus Mountains, steep on the southern slopes, retreat gradually on the northern slopes and it is here on the northern slopes where most of the mountain people live. The largest populations are found on the two sea coasts and in the lowland river valleys.

The frost free, sunny Black Sea coast is a well known resort area although it remains relatively undeveloped by western standards. High, snow covered mountains and ancient historical landmarks also contribute to the budding tourist industry that could figure significantly in the region's future.

Azerbaijan and Georgia balked at joining the Commonwealth of Independent States. War and civil uprisings, aided by rogue Russian army units, caused economic blackmail by Russia and forced the two to join the CIS.

Abkhazia and South Ossetia recently claimed independence from Georgia. This was met by armed intervention by the Georgian army. South Ossetia has asked to join North Ossetia in Russia. Adjaria for all practical purposes is independent. Georgian refugees from the fighting in Sukhumi were not treated well when they sought sanctuary in Tbilisi. Most of them went across the border to North Ossetia.

Except for a few skirmishes fighting between Armenia and Azerbaijan has settled into a tenuous peace. However, after a slow start Armenia controls about a third of the territory of Azerbaijan. This will have to be resolved.

Western oil interests have begun developing the oil fields of the Aspheron Peninsula. This has upset Russia who looks to future influence in the entire Caucasus region. Georgia has agreed to let Russia establish three army bases within its borders. The Russian army is ever present in the Baky region. The three countries need Russia but presently Russia must settle its own internal problems before it can help the Caucasus republics settle theirs.

ARMENIA
(pop. 3,565,000 - 11,306 sq. mi.)

Armenia is slightly larger than Maryland. Its capital city is Yerevan. The country is bordered in the west by Turkey, by Iran to the south, Azerbaijan in the east and Georgia on the north.

Armenia is a land of rugged mountains and extinct volcanoes. It sits on an active earthquake zone: an earthquake on December 7, 1988 killed over 55,000 people. The towns of Gyumri and Spitak were destroyed and Yerevan was heavily damaged. Several mountain peaks are over 10,000 feet with the highest snowcapped peak being Mt. Aragats at 13,432 feet.

Major rivers are the Araks and the Razdan which provide water for irrigation as well as hydroelectricity. A large lake, Lake Sevan, provides fishing and recreation as well as hydropower.

Lake Sevan covers an area of 540 square miles and its greatest depth is 330 feet. Its average altitude is 6,280 feet above sea level. The largest lake in the Caucasus, Sevan is fed by 30 streams. The Razdan River which is ice free in winter is its only outlet. When the lake level was lowered by a tunnel built to feed water to a hydro - electric plant, manipulating the feeder streams restored the water level.

A monastery was built on a small island in the lake. Sevan Island, in the northwest corner, is used today as a rehabilitation center and rest home.

Only about ten percent of Armenia is

17-1 Armenia's Lake Sevan is the largest lake in the Caucasus.

arable but the rugged mountains provide good pasture for sheep and goats. The lowlands are very productive with wheat, barley, sugar beets and potatoes. Figs are one of the more important fruits of the region. Grapes, peaches and apricots are also grown. Irrigated cotton is grown in the lowlands.

The southeastern and northwestern portions of the country are forested with oak and beech. Several rare animals can be found here including boars, jackals, lynx and the Syrian Bear.

Armenia has a continental climate with cold dry winters and very hot summers. Lake Sevan helps to moderate the local temperature.

Several mineral resources form the basis for Armenian industry: copper, chromite, molybdenum, zinc, lead, iron pyrites, manganese, gold and mercury. Some salt lakes have spawned a spa resort industry.

Wines and cognac are famous Armenian exports. Other industries include textiles, automobiles, food processing and nonferrous metallurgy. Stalin began to industrialize Armenia in the 1930s and Moscow built the republic into a leading chemical producer. One result is chronic air pollution.

Ninety-three percent of the population is Armenian. Three percent are Azeri with minor groups of Russians and Kurds. The official language is Armenian which is a

17-2 An Armenian family enjoys afternoon tea.

direct descendent of the ancient Phrygian tongue. It is also the liturgical language of the Armenian Church. Armenia became Christian in the 3rd century.

The Church resembles other Eastern Orthodox religions: priests may marry and communion is bread and wine.

Armenia is 70 percent urban. Cities are centers for manufacturing and processing of raw materials.

Present day Armenia only makes up a fraction of the original territory of Armenians. As many ethnic Armenians live outside the borders of the country as within. Armenians suffered terrible persecutions in the past and many Armenians have fled to different countries around the world including the United States. In 1915, during World War I, more than one million Armenians were massacred by Turks. To this day Turkey continues to persecute its

Armenian minority. In 1986 a rally for autonomy in the Armenian region of Turkey resulted in over 200,000 Armenian deaths.

There are two autonomous regions of Azerbaijan which contain large Armenian populations, Nakhichevan and Nagorno-Karabakh. The former is surrounded by Armenia and the latter is entirely in Azerbaijan. Nagorno-Karabakh was given to Azerbaijan by Stalin in 1923, reportedly in exchange for favorable oil deals.

As soon as the Soviet Union unraveled Azeris systematically slaughtered Armenians living in Baky and in Nagorno Karabakh. When a civil war broke out, arms were supplied to Muslim Azerbaijan from Iran, but no one stepped in to help Christian Armenia. The bloody conflict started in 1987 with riots in the Azerbaijan city of Sumgait. The violent clash between Armenians and Azeris in Sumgait left 32 dead and 400 wounded and was the worst ethnic clash in Soviet history. The fighting continued throughout the dissolution of the Soviet Union until 1994 when a tenuous cease-fire was imposed by Russian troops. The ongoing conflict between these two ethnic groups is just one example of the many local ethnic wars that is plaguing many regions of the old Soviet Union. Unfortunately, these conflicts will likely persist well into the 21st century.

Armenia became part of Russia in 1921 when it sought protection from the Turks. Today they still rely on Russia for that protection. Armenia is a loyal member of the CIS. Its currency is the **dram**, but the Russian ruble is also legal tender.

Armenia, which showed early signs of democratic reforms, banned several newspapers and news gathering organizations in 1995. Political assassinations continue in Armenia and throughout the Caucasus. None of the Caucasus republics seem ready for democracy. The mayor of Yerevan was killed outside his home on December 17, 1994.

Yerevan (1,210,000), located on the Razdan River, is one of the oldest cities in the world with archeological sites dating from the 8th century B.C. The city is 2,700 feet above sea level and in view of Mount Aragats and Mount Ararat both over 12,000 feet. Mount Ararat is in Turkey.

An important rail junction, Yerevan is also a leading industrial, cultural and scientific center. It produces chemicals, machine tools, turbines, lamps and generators, plastics and synthetic rubber. It also smelts aluminum ore and produces footwear, food products, wines and wood products.

Yerevan has a university, academy of sciences, several museums, theaters, an opera company, a music conservatory and botanical and zoological gardens.

Hydropower is supplied from several near-by stations. Electricity from thermal units uses oil and natural gas from Azerbaijan. Despite the hostilities between the two countries, these supplies have not been curtailed. A nuclear power plant near Yerevan produces electricity.

Yerevan was the capital of old Armenia under Persian rule in the 7th century A.D. It has been a constant battleground between Turks and Persians (now Iranians).

Yerevan was an important crossroads on the old caravan routes between Europe and Asia. Ancient ruins are everywhere and could form the nucleus of a tourist industry if the country ever stabilizes.

Gyumri, also Kumayri and formerly Leninakan (130,000), is near the Turkish border. It has textile, meat packing , rug making and metal industries. Gyumri is famous for the old craft of rug making. It was originally founded as Alexsandropol on the site of the Turkish Fort Gumri. It has been renamed several times. Before the earthquake of 1988 its population was 210,000.

AZERBAIJAN
(pop. 7,790,000 - 33,400 sq. mi.)

Azerbaijan is about the same size as South Carolina. It is bordered on the west by Armenia, on the south by Iran, by Russia on the north and the Capian Sea on the east. Baky, its capital, is located on the Caspian Sea.

Azerbaijan is in the eastern Caucasus Mountains. High western mountains are separated from the mountains in the east by a wide valley created by the meandering Kura River. The Aras (or Araks) River in the south forms the boundary with Iran's Azerbaijan Province.

Fertile river valleys produce wheat, barley, maize, and potatoes as well as tobacco. Apples, peaches, apricots and wine grapes are found on the mountain slopes. Cotton and rice are grown with irrigation. Mulberry orchards provide food for silkworms and a silk industry.

The **Kura River** begins in Turkey, flows to Georgia and then through Azerbaijan. At 950 miles, it is the longest river in Transcaucasia. There is a hydroelectric station on it near Tbilisi. It is joined by the Aras (Araks) River before it empties into the Caspian Sea south of Baky. A canal leading from a reservoir on the Kura to the Aras shortcuts the trip for boats.

There is a sizable cattle herd in the country. Goats and sheep graze on the highland slopes. There is one goat or sheep for every Azeri.

The **Apsheron Peninsula**, with Baky at its center, was one of the richest oil producing regions in the world. It once produced half the world's oil. It still produces oil today, but its importance has declined. Its oil fortunes should improve in the future. A contract between the government and several foreign oil companies will bring important capital and technology into the economy. The oil industry around Baky is developing with the aid of Amoco, British Petroleum, Pennzoil, Unocal, Statoil of Norway, Turkish Petroleum and Lukoil of Russia.

Other mineral resources include an abundance of natural gas as well as deposits of copper, lead, zinc, limestone, pyrites, cobalt, alunite and iron. Salty water from several springs have created a health spa industry.

Chief manufactured products include cement, building materials, steel, aluminum, chemicals, textiles, small machinery and electrical appliances.

Sheep and goats provide hair for the cottage weaving industry. Long staple cotton is grown in the Kura Valley. Azerbaijan rugs fetch a high price on the international market.

Azerbaijanis make up 82 percent of the population. Russians are six percent and Armenians another six percent. However, since the bloody fighting between Azerbaijan and Armenia, it is difficult to calculate the exact number of Armenians still living in the country.

Azeri and Turkish are the dominant languages. The Azeri tongue is an offshoot of Turkic. Azeris are Shiite Muslim, closely tied to the old Persian culture and to modern day Iran.

Azerbaijan is equally rural and urban. The largest urban area is Baky and its suburbs with one fourth of the population. .

Shortly after the dissolution of the Soviet Union, fighting between Muslim Azeris and Christian Armenians broke out in the autonomous province of Nagorno-Karabakh. Azeris hoped to force the resident Armenians to evacuate the territory and then settle it with ethnic Azeris. After many setbacks, the Armenians were able to regroup and defend themselves. A shaky cease fire is in effect with Russian "peace" keepers.

The **Nakhichevan Region** is separated from Azerbaijan by Armenian territory. It borders on both Iran and Turkey. The population includes Azeri and Turks with Russian and Armenian minorities.

Irrigated lowlands produce cotton, tobacco, rice, wheat and peaches. Resources include salt, molybdenum, lead and zinc deposits.

The **Nagorno - Karabakh Region** is located between the Caucasus and the Karabakh ranges. It's population was 75 percent Armenian in 1992. The entire area is within the Azerbaijan Republic and continues to be a source of antagonism

17-3 Baky, Azerbaijan

between Armenians and Azeris. Russian, Kurdish and Azeri minorities also live here and further complicates the situation.

The region has many mineral springs as well as deposits of marble, limestone, and copper. Farming and grazing are important economic activities.

The Karabakh conflict began in 1988 when Armenians tried to separate the region from Azerbaijan. The war that followed claimed 15,000 lives and produced a half million refugees. Russia wants to maintain influence over the region and is a major player in all conferences and negotiations.

Azerbaijan should be one of the wealthiest countries in the world. It has oil reserves that could makes its seven million citizens individually rich. But they don't seem to have the will nor the political leadership to stabilize their society and economy. They have been defeated by Armenia yet they outnumber them two to one. Foreign investors, especially oil interests, seem more committed to the country's future than its own government.

Armenians took over most of the land in western Azerbaijan and created over a million Azeri refugees. Most of these have settled in Sumgait where a quarter million people are homeless and sleep in the streets. Others have fled to join their Azeri relatives in Iran. About four million Azeris now live in Iran.

There are rich people in the country who drive the most luxurious cars. They seem to be oblivious to the plight of most of the people. Old Russian imperialism is always present in the minds of the Azeris who

143

identify most strongly with Iran. However, the Azeris are more inclined to trust the Russians than the Turks who are increasing their influence over the entire Caucasus.

Baky, (Baku) (1,785,000), located on the Caspian Sea, takes up the entire Apsheron peninsula. The city is the country's leading industrial and cultural center, dominating the economy. Until World War II, Baky was the Soviet Union's biggest supplier of oil. The major economic activity of Baky and its environs is still oil. Other industries include shipbuilding, meat-packing, engineering, cotton textiles, leather, flour milling, wood products and tobacco processing.

Baky and its suburbs is a complex of oil derricks, refineries, pipelines and industries dealing with petroleum. Oil wells are drilled from platforms in the Caspian Sea. The pipelines which lead to shore have been made into causeways containing shops and entertainment facilities.

The city receives much of its water from a canal which brings water from the Samur River (north) directly to the city.

Baky has a 13th century fort and a 17th century palace built by the khans who were vassals of the Persian shahs. A mosque (Synyk-Kala) dates back to the 11th century. There is also a 12th century tower (the Maiden's Tower). Most of the Russians in Azerbaijan live in Baky.

The city has a modern subway system as well as cultural and social institutions found in a large modern city.

Gyandzha (279,000), also Ganza and formerly Kirovabad, is the second largest city after Baky. It produces cotton and silk textiles plus cottonseed oil, carpets and farm implements. It is becoming an important producer of aluminum. Its history goes back to the 6th century. The city was devastated by an earthquake in 1139 and by the Mongols in 1231. Tourist highlights are the tomb of the 12th century poet Nizami

Gandzhevi (city's namesake) and a 17th century mosque.

Sumgait (234,000), founded in 1948 by Russians on the Sumgait River north of Baky, is a major industrial center. It has a pipe-rolling mill and aluminum and synthetic rubber factories. Its pipes are used in the oil industry. Oil forms the basis for its petrochemical industry. An influx of refugees from the ethnic fighting has nearly doubled the city's official population. In 1987 Sumgait was the site of a violent ethnic clash between Azeris and Armenians.

GEORGIA (Sakartvelos)
(pop. 5,730,000 - 26,911 sq. mi.)

Georgia is slightly larger than West Virginia. The citizens call their country Sakartvelos. Its capital is Tbilisi. Georgia is bordered on the west by the Black Sea, on Turkey and Armenia in the south, on Azerbaijan in the east and by Russia on the north.

Georgia has the dubious distinction of being the birthplace of Soviet dictator Josef Stalin.

Georgia includes three large autonomous regions: Abkhaz in the northwest, Adzhar in the southwest and The South Ossetian Region in the central area. South Ossetia borders on the North Ossetian district in Russia.

On the southern slopes of the Greater Caucasus and the Lesser Caucasus, Georgia is a mountainous country except for the Black Sea coast and a small western valley created by the drainage of the Rioni River. The headwaters of the Kura River flow through eastern Georgia before entering Azerbaijan.

In the mountains the highest peak, Mt. Kazbek, rises to 16,541 feet. It is perpetually snowcapped and a reliable source of water for the valleys below.

In the lowland, known as Mingrelia, the

climate is humid subtropical. The highlands are alpine and the dry areas around the Kura are steppe.

Agriculture products include citrus fruits and tea in the subtropical areas as well as tobacco. Wine grapes and mulberry trees, for the silk industry, abound in the subtropical areas bordering the Black Sea.

Wheat is grown in the upland areas as well as in the lowland. Maize, barley and oats are also grown. Grazing animals remain constant at two million sheep and one and a half million cattle. Almost every rural family raises at least one pig and dozens of chickens.

Manganese is the biggest ore resource but there are also sizable deposits of bituminous and lignite coal, barite, iron, molybdenum, oil and peat. Marble, dolomite, talc and clay are also mined and form the basis for a large construction industry. Timber related industries employ the most non-agriculture people.

The country manufactures railroad and mining equipment, chemicals, machine tools, iron and steel. There is an abundance of hydroelectric energy.

Russian enterprise endowed Georgia with some spectacular road and railway construction. There is a railroad line connecting the Black Sea at Batumi with Tbilisi and Baky. The Georgian Military Road, through steep mountain passes, was a great engineering achievement as was the Ossetian Military Road.

The **Georgian Military Road** is a 135 mile highway that was begun in 1799 and completed in 1863. It skirts the high Mt. Kazbek and crosses the rugged Caucasus at an altitude of 7,815 feet. It begins in the north at Vladikavkaz, Russia and ends at Tbilisi.

The **Ossetian Military Road** is 170 miles long and crosses the Caucasus, linking Kutaisi on the central plains with Alagir. It passes the village of Mamison.

The Georgian Black Sea coast has always been a tourist attraction. Even the ancient Greeks wrote about it, and thought it a desirable tourist destination. Later, high level Soviets built dachas here.

Ethnic Georgians make up two thirds of the population with Adzhar and Abkhazian minorities. The Adzhars are dominant in the southwest around the city of Batumi. The Abkhazians are in the northwest around the city of Sukhumi.

There are also large minorities of Ossetians, Azerbaijanis, Russians and Armenians. The Ossetians speak a Persian dialect. Other Georgian groups speak a tongue related to the Ibero-Caucasus family. About half the population can communicate in Russian which was the official language during the Soviet regime.

Georgian Orthodox is the main religion and Russian Orthodox is second. To an outsider, they appear to be the same religion but to the adherents there are strong emotional differences. The Georgian Church is one of the oldest Orthodox religions. The Northern Ossetians of Russia are Muslims while the Southern Ossetians of Georgia are Orthodox Christian. However, they speak the same language.

There are at least one hundred recognizable ethnic groups in Georgia. Twenty of them have more than 20,000 members. There are some rivalries among them. The Meskhetians were expelled to Central Asia by Stalin during World War II. When the Soviet Union dissolved, many of them tried to return to reclaim their former homes and lands in Georgia. In one confrontation in 1992, they were met at the border by other Georgian groups who turned them back.

Strong nationalist feelings erupted in Georgia in 1989. Soviet troops attacked demonstrators in April, killing 20 people. This only caused nationalist feelings to increase,

17-4 Harvesting tea in Georgia.

and in 1991 Georgia declared independence which was assured when the Soviet Union dissolved.

In 1992 the Abkhazians decided they wanted their independence and fighting broke out in their province. Heavy fighting in Sukhumi ended with a temporary victory for the Abkhazians. The Georgian president, Eduard Shrevardnadze, accused the Russians of aiding the enemy.

Since Georgians outnumbered Abkhazians, the Georgians eventually prevailed. The civil war ended in 1993 with the Abkhaz Region still part of Georgia. After this brief war Georgia took a second look at its relationship with Russia and President Shrevardnadze agreed to be a working partner with the Commonwealth of Independent States even though Georgia did

not seek membership.

Georgia signed an agreement to let Russia establish three military bases on their territory thus giving Russia a highly visible presence in the Caucasus.

Georgia is emerging as a player in international affairs. In March 1994, President Shrevardnadze traveled to Washington D.C. and met with President Bill Clinton. Georgia, like other recently independent republics, is trying to become independent of Moscow.

Like south Florida in the U.S., Georgia is a land of warm weather, nice beaches, tourist attractions, smugglers and drug runners. A successful, more developed tourism industry will likely figure prominently in the country's economic future.

Despite the ethnic wars in Georgia the trains still run on a regular schedule between

Baky to Yerevan to Tbilisi to Iran and Turkey. There are regular airline flights from Tbilisi to Frankfort, Germany.

The European Union is an unofficial economic and commercial advisor to the Caucasus Republics. All three are desperately seeking economic aid from the west. In 1994, Georgian inflation was 10,000 percent. In 1993, its coupon currency was valued at 687 to the U.S. dollar. In 1995, the value was 1.5 million to the dollar.

Foreign companies have invested in Georgia's tobacco, dairy and aerospace industries, but the political and military situation creates a nervous uncertain atmosphere. Georgia has excellent mineral deposits but no capital to exploit them

The **Adzhar (Adjar) Region** is located on the Black Sea and borders Turkey on the south. Its capital is Batumi. The district is mountainous and forested. A subtropical climate permits many health resorts as well as the growing of tobacco, tea, lemons, oranges, tangerines and avocados. Livestock raising and copper mining are large industries.

The Adzhars are Muslims who belong to the South Caucasian linguistic family. Other groups in the district are Georgians, Greeks, Armenians and Russians.

Adzharia is virtually independent. In 1996 it paid no taxes to Tbilisi and conducted business without consulting the federal government.

The **Abkhazia Region** is located between the Black Sea and the Greater Caucasus Mountains. Sukhumi is its capital. Despite some spectacular snow capped peaks the region is mostly subtropical. Tobacco is the leading crop and many American tobacco companies have bought up large land parcels here.

Peach and citrus orchards are common and tea is raised on the highland slopes. Industries include sawmilling, tanning leather and food processing. Coal is the main mineral resource.

Abkhazians are a mixture of Orthodox Christian and Muslim religions. Other peoples in the region include Georgians, Russians and Armenians. Abkhazia was made an autonomous republic in 1921 then became part of Georgia in 1930.

Abkhazia declared its independence from Georgia in 1992. Civil War broke out and Georgians who were living in Abkhazia fled the territory. This was **ethnic cleansing** in the extreme sense. With clandestine help from Russia the Abkhazians have managed to control their region which is separated from the rest of Georgia by the Inquiri River. Georgian president Eduard Shevardnadze asked the United Nations to come in as peacekeepers but the Abkhazian leader, Vladislav Ardzinba, wants the U.N. under different conditions, mainly to keep out the Georgians. The capital city of Sukhumi lies in ruins and it will take many years to restore it.

The **South Ossetia Region** is in the north central portion of Georgia. It borders the North Ossetian Republic of Russia. Its capital is Tskhinvali. The population numbers about a hundred thousand.

The valleys produce fruit, wine, grain and cotton. Lumbering and livestock raising are important in the mountains.

In 1992 South Ossetia demanded either independence from Georgia or incorporation into the North Ossetian Republic of Russia. The Georgian government sent in troops which shelled the capital city of Tskhinvali. Ossetian territory was divided into two districts under the Russian philosophy of divide-and-rule. South Ossetia said the borders were artificially drawn by the Soviets and now they can be redrawn.

Tskhinvali (36,000), the capital city of South Ossetia, produces lumber products and small electric appliances. During the Stalin years it was known as Staliniri. Georgian

17-5 Georgian folk dancers.

troops first shelled and then occupied the town in 1992.

Tbilisi (1,265,000), the capital city, is located on the Kura River. The Transcaucasian Railroad connects it with the rest of the Caucasus. It is at the southern end of the Georgian Military Road.

Industries include film making, printing, food processing, leather tanning, silk weaving, the production of locomotives and plastics. Vineyards and orchards abound in the suburbs.

Archeological evidence indicates the city was settled as far back as the 4th century B.C. It was ruled alternately by Arabs, Turks, Persians and Mongols before coming under Russian control. Each left a mark on the character of the city and its people.

Ruins of churches and other buildings go back to the 6th century A.D. There are many seminaries and a university as well as an Academy of Science. One of Georgia's native sons, Josef Stalin, studied at the city's Orthodox seminary. During the Bolshevik Revolution, he worked with communist underground groups in Tbilisi.

The city has a university, an academy of arts and an academy of sciences. It also has museums and theaters.

Kutaisi (238,000) is located in the Kholkida Lowland on the upper reaches of the Rioni River. It was Georgia's ancient capital. Today it is the center of the important subtropical agricultural region. Some coal is mined nearby and this provides heat and thermal energy for the city. Its main industries are silk textiles, mining equipment, chemicals, food processing and motor truck assembly. It

17-6 Tangerine harvest in Georgia.

receives electricity from a hydrostation on the Rioni River.

Rustavi (163,000) is in east Georgia on the Kura River just south of Tbilisi. It is founded in 1948 near the site of the ancient city of Rustavi which was destroyed around 1400 by Tamerlane's army.

Rutavi is an iron and steel city as well as the center of a small chemical industry.

Batumi (139,000) is the capital of the Adzhar Region. It is the western terminus of the Trans-Caucasus Railroad with Baky on the eastern end. Batumi has oil refineries and receives oil from a pipeline that begins in Baky. There are also shipyards and food processing factories. Besides oil, tea is an important export.

Sukhumi , also Sokhumi (123,000), on the Black Sea, is the capital of the Abkhazian Region. Sulfur baths here were first visited by the ancient Romans. They are still a major tourist attraction.

Sukhumi was the site of a Greek colony in the 6th century B.C. Under Rome, it was known as Sebastopolis. The Sukhumi Military Road crosses the Caucasus at Klukhori Pass (9,235 feet) and continues to the city. Its length is 120 miles.

Gori (64,000), in central Georgia, was known in the 7th century as Tontio. It was later named after a fort, Gori, which passed to Russia in 1801. Josef Stalin was born Josef Vissarinonovich Dzhugashvili in this city in 1879. Attempts at getting a memorial museum dedicated to Stalin have met with resistance from the federal government.

Poti (57,000), on the Black Sea at the mouth of the Rioni River, is a port from which wine, manganese, maize and lumber are shipped. The city is surrounded by swamps belonging to the Colchis Lowland.

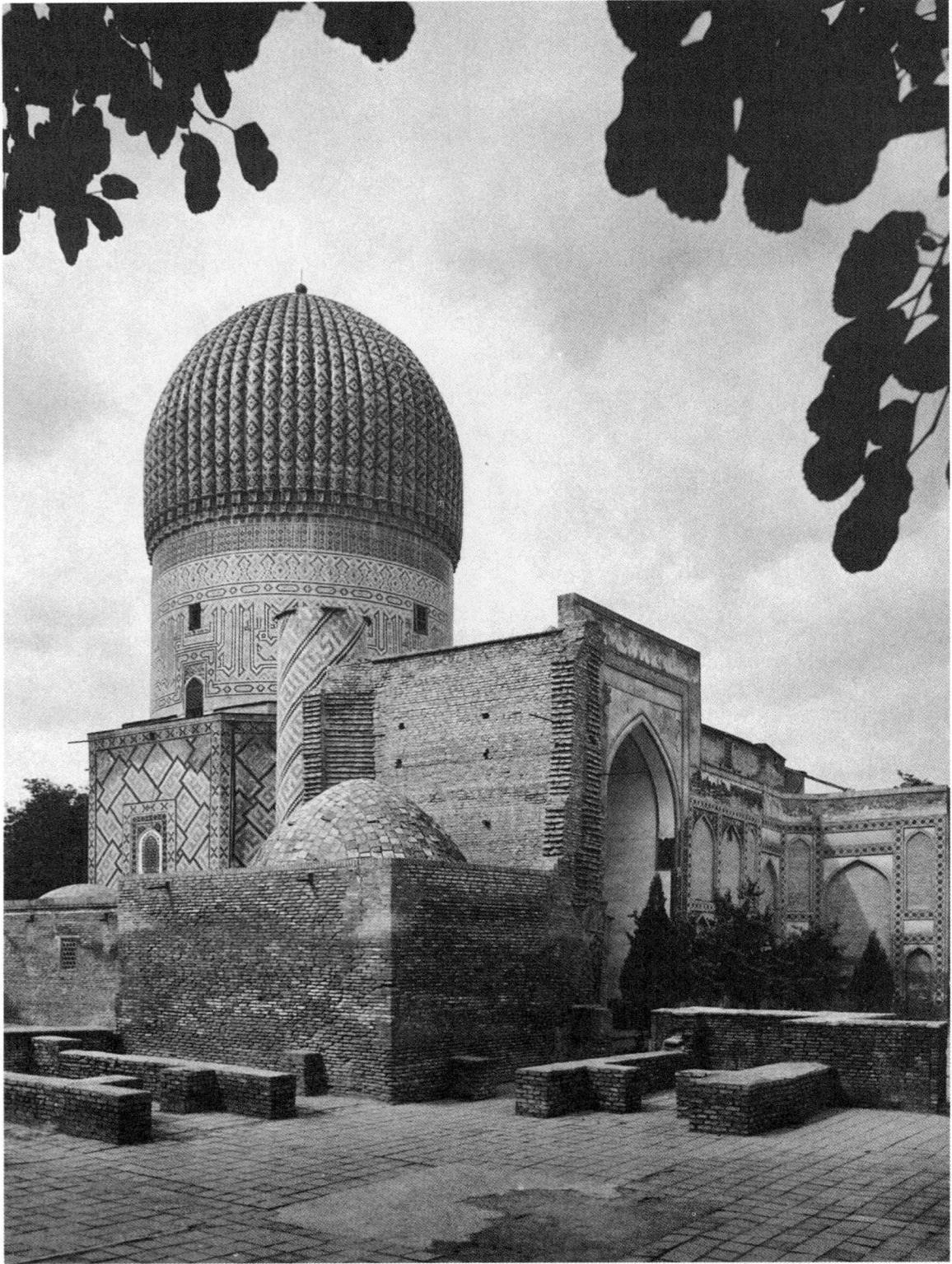

18-1 The Gur Emir, Tamerlane's tomb in Samargand, Uzbekistan.

18. CENTRAL ASIA AND THE MUSLIM COUNTRIES

Central Asia includes Kazakhstan, Kyrgyzstan, Tajikistan, Turkmenistan and Uzbekistan. The region is a transition zone between the European Russians to the north and the Asian Muslims to the south. Culturally, Central Asia is part of the same Muslim core as Iran and Afghanistan. The combined population is about 53 million. Because the national boundaries were artificially created in Moscow, they are now the subject of intense dispute.

The region is bilingual in Russian and several Turkic dialects. Pastoralism has been the traditional economy, and the expression "How do you do?" translates literally as "How is your livestock?"

Most of the territory is empty desert. The Caspian Sea and the eastern part of the Lower Volga River Valley mark its eastern limits. To the north is the great Siberian lowland. The east and south are bounded by some of the highest mountains in the world, including the Tien Shan and the Pamirs.

The high mountains prevent southern warm air currents from bringing heat or moisture to the land. Central Asia is in the rain shadow or lee side of the highlands and thus contains a topographical desert. The highlands capture some moisture, mostly from air currents originating in the Mediterranean in winter. These create a snowpack and add moisture to the glaciers of the high mountains. As the ice and snow melt in summer, the waters feed two main rivers, the Amu Darya and the Syr Darya.

Most of the streams that begin high in the southern mountains disappear into the desert sands. Only two survive; the Amu Darya and the Syr Darya which empty into the Aral Sea.

The 1,600 mile long **Amu Darya River** is formed by the junction of the Vakhsh and Pandj Rivers which flow from the Pamir Mountains. The Amu Darya flows through the Karakum Desert and provides most of the water for the 700 mile long **Karakum Canal**. The Tedzhen and Murgab Rivers also provide water for the canal. The Amu Darya was known as the Oxus River in ancient Persian literature and in the chronicles of Alexander the Great.

The Kara Darya River from Tien Shan joins Naryn Darya from the Altai Mountains in the Fergana Valley to form the 1,350 mile long **Syr Darya River.** The river flows through Tajikistan, Kazakhstan and Uzbekistan before it empties into the Aral Sea.

In recent years water from the two main rivers have been channeled into a series of irrigation canals. This consumptive use of water has severely depleted the amount going into the Aral Sea - which is really a lake. As a result, the Aral Sea has decreased in area and depth. Once a great fishing lake, the Aral is on its way to extinction. Boats are stranded hundreds of feet from the present shore. Today, the deepest part of the lake is 180 feet, down from 225. The average depth is 35 feet. The Aral Sea surface is 135 feet above sea level.

From 1961 to 1985 the Aral's level dropped 40 feet, its area shrunk by 30 percent and its volume by 50 percent. Salinity doubled, killing off most fish.

In 1982, no fresh water reached the Aral. In the following two years only a minimum amount was allowed to escape the irrigation channels and reach the lake. The lake level is decreasing three feet per year. Soon the Aral will be two lakes, one small lake fed by the Syr Darya and larger lake by the Amu Darya.

To make matters worse, the irrigated crops, especially cotton, rice and alfalfa, need heavy applications of fertilizers and

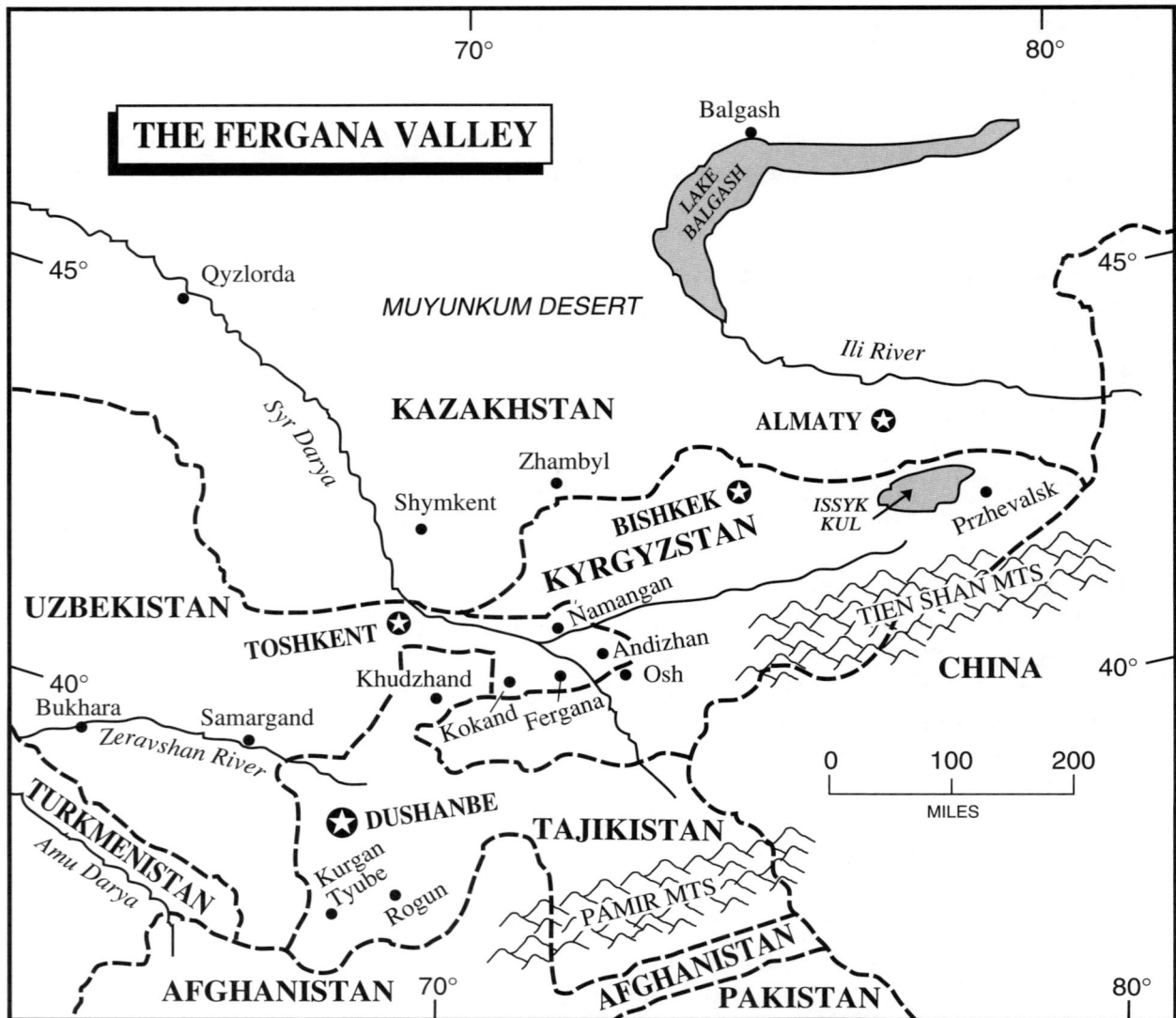

MAP 17   The Fergana Valley

pesticides to maintain production. These requirements increase each year. As a result the Aral Lowland is one of the most polluted places on earth. What water is left in the Syr Darya carries fertilizers pesticides industrial waste and sewage. Lung diseases and cancer rates are astronomical. Birth defects are among the highest in the world.

The dry dust of the former delta and the lake bed is constantly blown about by the wind. The dust contains pesticides and chemical fertilizer residue and these carcinogens are distributed to areas far from the Aral s shore.

Some cities in these Central Asian republics are among the most polluted in the world. Oskeman in northeastern Kazakhstan has lead and zinc smelters as well as workings in titanium magnesium cadmium and uranium enrichment. Soil air and water are also polluted with mercury and arsenic. The average age of male death was 55 in 1995.

152

18-1 The fertile Fergana Valley.

Caravan routes once crossed the Tien Shan mountains and entered the Fergana Valley of the Syr Darya River System. This gave rise to cities of enormous wealth - Samargand, Kokand, Bukhara. From here the ancient caravan route broke into two routes, one leading northwest to the Volga River and the other leading west to the Mediterranean Sea.

The Fergana Valley is divided among the republics of Uzbekistan, Kyrgyzstan and Tajikistan. It is overlooked by the Tien Shan range in the northeast and the Pamir Mountains in the south. The narrow Khodzhent pass in the west has historically served as an invasion route to the valley.

The Fergana Valley consists of steppe and desert. Irrigation made the Fergana's desert extremely productive which in turn enabled the population to increase, making it one of the most densely populated valleys on earth. The dense irrigation network is linked by the Great Fergana and South Fergana Canals. The valley is drained by the Syr Darya River.

Major cities in the valley include Kokand, Andizhan and Namangan in Uzbekistan, Khudzhand in Tajikistan and Osh in Kyrgyzstan. Uzbek controls most of the valley. A circular railway connects the cities.

There is considerable mining activity on the outskirts of the valley. Mineral deposits include iron ore, petroleum, natural gas and coal. Major cities are in both industrial and agricultural areas.

The valley's major agriculture products include irrigated cotton and alfalfa. There are also apple and peach orchards, vineyards and walnut groves. Mulberry plantations support a silk industry.

In the 13th century the Golden Horde of Genghis Khan invaded the valley and completely destroyed the cities. In the 14th century the armies of Tamerlane invaded and made Samarkand its headquarters. The city was about halfway between the Amu Darya and the Syr Darya.

The land changed hands among Persia, Turkey and the Arabs until the end of the 19th century when Russians moved in to take their turn.

The Bolshevik Revolution and the subsequent overthrow of the Czar created political instability. Eventually the Red Army took over and Soviet authority was established. However, most of the people in the region never really embraced communism.

Central Asia had always been a pastoral economy with small cities and trading outposts. The majority of rural people are still pastoral. Most areas graze sheep and cattle. Migration patterns were developed over the centuries in concert with precipitation. Goats are raised on the slopes in the mountainous south. In these mountains herders practice transhumance: they migrate up and down the mountains with the seasons.

Using the region's river systems, the Soviets created huge irrigation projects. Along mountain streams they built many hydroelectric stations. Railroads and airfields connect Central Asia's largest cities with Siberia and Moscow. Toshkent and Almaty grew to more than one million.

Russian immigrants moved into Central Asian cities to work in and manage many of the Soviet created industries. Today, more than ten million Russians live in the region making up one fifth of the population.

The majority of people are of Turkic descent, except for the Tajiks whose ancestry is Persian. They are followers of the Sunni Muslim religion.

While the people of Central Asia are Muslim they do not follow the main precepts of Islam. Almost none have read the Koran because it is written in classical Arabic, a language known only to a few scholars. When the Soviets came to power there were more than five thousand mosques in the region. Today there are about three hundred. Any call for a holy war by an Islamic fundamentalist would probably have little effect here.

The leaders of these republics are old communists who have changed their rhetoric to fit the present nationalism. They have maneuvered to keep themselves in power. Attempts to thwart this power in Tajikistan in 1992 met with strong governmental opposition. Nationalist groups wanted free elections and the old guard removed from power. Military aid from Russia helped defeat the insurgents. Nonetheless nationalism remains a powerful force in Central Asia.

All five republics have single candidate elections. In 1995, President Islam Karimov of Uzbekistan won a unanimous vote which was 99.6 percent of the turnout which gives him the presidency until the year 2000. If someone wanted to vote against him they had to mark a ballot in full view of local officials.

The five republics can best be described as fiefdoms similar to their status under the Soviets. The leader of Kyrgyzstan, Askar Akayev, dissolved parliament and rules without the handicap of elections and opposition parties. Saparmurat Niyazov, the leader of Turkmenistan has his portraits plastered all over the country, much in the fashion of the old communist bosses. Kazakhstan's Nursultan Nazarbayev also dissolved parliament and extended his term to the year 2000.

Some Central Asian leaders like Kazakhstan's Sultan Nurabeyev are starting to flex their muscles and become players on the world political stage. Kazakhstan is having more success with market reforms than Russia. Possessing nuclear missiles also adds to the country's international prestige. Treaties to dismantle the nuclear arsenal are being considered. In the future, countries like Kazakhstan will likely operate more like independent, sovereign nations as they resist Russian power.

When the Soviet Union dissolved in 1991 there was a move by nationalists to establish, once again, a unified Turkistan made up of the five Islam republics. The emotion was not lost on Turkey whose leaders perceived an opportunity to advance their country's influence. This seems logical, the area has a common language, history, religion and culture which has its roots in former Turkish expedition and settlement.

As of 1995, Turkey was involved with at least 200 projects in the region with an investment of about four million dollars. Some of these projects are oil deals which involves Kazakh pipelines on the northern Caspian shore. The pipelines would have to cross Russia to western Europe or cross Turkmenistan and Iran in order to reach western and Japanese buyers.

The oil problem between Russia and Turkey was intensified when Turkish airlines began flying to all the five capitals as well as Baky in Azerbaijan. Turkey , which is separated from Azerbaijan by Armenia has become actively involved in oil investments in Azerbaijan. In 1995, Turkey gave Azerbaijan more than 800 million dollars in humanitarian aid and permitted

almost ten thousand students from the six Muslim countries to study in Ankara universities.

Under the Soviets the Central Asian countries were in control of overlords sent from Moscow. They suffered from malnutrition, food shortages, abuse of pesticides, gradiose irrigation schemes and inadequate medical facilities. The legacy has its influence today. Central Asia has one of the highest infant mortality rates in the world. In 1994 the official Turkmenistan infant death rate per 1,000 births was 64. The actual death rate was probably much higher.

The cotton monoculture still demands heavy use of pesticides and fertilizers which have poisoned the drinking water. The region is finding it difficult to give up the cotton monoculture since it brings in the most cash to the region. New discoveries of natural gas and oil in Turkmenistan and Kazakhstan might give these countries incentive to change the agriculture dependency on cotton.

KAZAKHSTAN
(pop. 17,380 - 1,049,200 sq.mi.)

Kazakhstan is twice the size of Alaska and one of the largest countries in the world. Its capital is Almaty, also known as Alma-Ata.

Kazakhstan borders Siberia on its north, China in the east, the Kyrgyz, Uzbek and Turkmen republics in the south and the Caspian sea on the west.

Two deserts are in Kazakhstan: the **Kyzylkum Desert** (red sands) and the **Muyunkum Desert**. The Kyzylkum Desert extends into Uzbekistan. It is mostly rocky with shifting sand dunes. Irrigation produces wheat, cotton and rice.

The Muyunkum Desert, north of Zhambyl, is 200 miles long from east to west and 100 miles wide north to south.

Kazakh is a vast flatland with a mountainous section. Stretching over two thousand miles, it spreads from the lower eastern Volga River Valley and the Caspian Sea to the Altai Mountains in the east. Lowlands are in the north and west, hills in the center and mountains in the southeast. The capital city of Almaty in the south is separated by the Muyunkum Desert from the populous north.

Kazakh Uplands in the northeast separate streams into those that flow into the Arctic Ocean and those that remain in the desert basin. The northern uplands are steppe and desert steppe while the south is true desert.

Besides the Caspian Sea, Kazakh incorporates about half the Aral Sea and all of **Lake Balgash** (Balkhash), a large lake in the east encompassing 6,562 square miles.

Its rivers include the Ural, flowing from the Ural Mountains into the Caspian, the Syr Darya, flowing from the high Pamirs and emptying into the Aral Sea, the Ili, flowing into Lake Balgash and the Irtysh, flowing down from China to eventually join the Ob River in Siberia. Precipitation is low in most of the area. Where the Ili River flows into Lake Balgash the lake is fresh, but on the other end, where evaporation is high the lake is salty.

Most of Kazakh is desert and the only decent amount of precipitation occurs in the high eastern mountains. Even these receive less than 12 inches a year. In northern Kazakhstan winter snowfall is equal to approximately four inches of rain.

In the north the January average temperature is 4 degrees Fahrenheit while the July average is 68 degrees F. In the south, the January average is 18 degrees F. and the July average is 85 degrees F. (Temperature and precipitation data for Petropavl in the north and Balgash (85,000) in the south are given in the appendix).

Kazakh's pastoral economy, based on grazing and herding sheep, has existed for centuries. The nomads have worked out a pattern migration based on the availability of grass during different seasons. This way of life came into conflict with the communists who insisted upon settled farming and irrigation. Kazakhs resisted collectivization, slaughtering their livestock and hiding their grain. The Soviets sent the Red Army to enforce their new decrees, and in the process millions of Kazakhs perished.

Kazakh was one of the regions that suffered under the Soviet Virgin Lands Campaign a.k.a. Idle Lands Scheme. Agriculture was redistributed and intense irrigation projects constructed. The Virgin Lands Campaign reclaimed marginal lands which equaled more than all the arable land of Canada. A small Kazakh village, Aqmola, became the central city of the Idle Lands Campaign. It was renamed Tselinograd, "Virgin Lands City". Today, about one half of the Virgin Lands remain under cultivation.

The north's main crops are wheat, flax, hemp, millet and sunflowers. In the irrigated south, wheat, barley, rice, potatoes, cotton and vegetables are grown.

Pastoralism has returned to Kazakhstan. In 1994 there were about ten million cattle, 37 million sheep and about four million pigs. Pigs are the result of Russian influence, most Muslims do not eat pork. The wool and milk industries is considerable.

One of the famous products is **karakul wool**, produced from newly born lambs. The woolen skin is also known as Astrakhan, the city from which most of it is exported.

Farming is practiced in the north and on irrigated lands in the south. On the dry steppes, farmers watch warily for the **sukhovey**, a dry wind which blows north through Turkmenistan. It speeds up evaporation and transpiration, causing crops

KAZAKHSTAN AND NEIGHBORS

MAP 18 Kazakhstan and its neighbors.

to wilt. Grain harvests are severely affected by the sukhovey.

Nomads camp out, living in **yurts**, which is a tent of felt carpets draped over a skeleton of poles. When U. S. Vice President Albert Gore traveled to Kazakhstan in 1993, Sultan Nurabegev entertained Gore in his yurt.

The central Kazakh Plateau produces copper, coal and tungsten. Iron is produced in the northeast and zinc is mined east of Lake Balgash. Chromium, silver, Iceland spar, lead, manganese and nickel are also mined. Oil lies just north of the Caspian Sea. Phosphate rock and tungsten are on the Caspian eastern shore. Bauxite is produced at Arkalyk in the northern steppes.

Kazakh's major industries are steel, cement, shoes and textiles. Its chemical industries produce fertilizers, acids, artificial fibers, synthetic rubber and medicines.

A major source of power is the hydroelectric station at Zaysan on the Irtysh River. Natural gas is also produced on the northeast Caspian lowland. Recently two uranium deposits have been discovered west and south of Lake Balgash.

Kazakhs make up 42 percent of the country's population, Russians 36 percent. Prior to the dissolution of the Soviet Union,

18-2 The Hungry Steppe of Kazakhstan. An irrigation project is under construction in the background.

these numbers were reversed. There are also Germans (five percent) and Ukrainians (five percent). Minor groups are Uzbeks and Belorussians.

The turkic speaking Kazakhs are Muslims and the region is part of the Muslim core. The transplanted Europeans are mostly Eastern Orthodox. Russian is spoken by more than 70 percent of the population and German is spoken in many cities. Only about 44 percent of the people speak Kazakh.

Russians tend to live in the cities while the Kazakhs stay in the countryside. Several groups were exiled to the region during the great purges of Josef Stalin. During World War II, Crimean Tatars and Lower Volga Germans were moved here. Koreans were also sent to the area. Most of these people

have remained, but the Tatars want to return to the Crimea and reclaim their ancestral homes and lands. About 250,000 have done so.

Between 1949 and 1989 northeastern Kazakhstan became the Soviet Union's main proving ground for nuclear weapons. Over 500 atomic bombs were detonated south of the city of Semey (Semipalatinsk). People living within 60 miles of the test site are reporting an unusually high number of cancers and related diseases. Missiles with nuclear warheads remain and are presumably aimed at China.

Spacecraft and TV satellites are launched from a desert area, Baikonur, located between Qaraghandy (Karaganda) and the Aral Sea. This was an important facility to the Soviet Union. Russia has contracted a

18-3 Government buildings at Almaty, the capital city of Kazakhstan.

20 year lease at a cost of 115 million dollars a year.

Privatization of agriculture and industry progressed rapidly after independence but the process was suspended in 1993. An official currency called **tenge** was printed in 1994. In that same year, a free trade pact was made between Kazakhstan, Kyrgyzstan and Uzbekistan.

Almaty, also Alma-Ata (1,154,000), at the foothills of the Tien Shan Mountains, is the capital city of the Kazakh Republic. Originally, it was a Russian fort. Today, it is still mostly Russian. The name means "apple place". Leading industries include meat packing, leather tanning, tobacco processing, fruit canning and motion picture production. An industrial center, it is connected by four different rail systems. The city serves as a setting for many movies since the country's main film company works here. It also has an opera and a ballet company.

The city was heavily damaged by severe earthquakes in 1887 and 1911. It suffered a disastrous flood in 1921.

Qaraghandy , also Karaganda (615,000), and its suburbs contain about 50 coal mining communities. Its location in the middle of Kazakhstan gives it access to all parts of the country. It is a distribution center for most of the country's goods and an export center for its products. The city produces iron and steel, copper, flour, beverages and footwear. Small farm implements are also manufactured. The surrounding basin is a large producer of bituminous coal which fuels the giant Novo-Karaganda power station. Qaraghandy is deficient in water and heavy industry takes a lot of fresh water. This problem was alleviated somewhat by construction of a canal from the Irtysh River, a distance of 300 miles.

Shymkent, also Chimkent (394,000), in the south, has a direct railway connection to the Ural Mountains and Siberia. It is the center of a large zinc and lead industry and produces small machines, processed food, chemicals, pharmaceuticals and textiles. It is a center for the processing of karakul pelts. A new oil refinery was recently built to receive oil from Qaraghandy and Pavlodar.

Semey, formerly Semipalatinsk (336,000), is located in the northeastern part of the country on the Irtysh River. It has railroad connections with Siberia. Large freight depots for river and rail transportation are a major part of the city's economy. There are also metal products, silk processing, leather goods, ship construction for river traffic and food processing. It has the largest meat packing plant in Kazakhstan. Semey was once an important city on the caravan route between east and west. The name Semipalatinsk means "Seven Palaces" which is derived from the ancient ruins of what were once seven large buildings.

Oskemen, formerly Ust-Kamenogorsk (326,000), located at the junction of the Irtysh and Ulba Rivers in the extreme eastern part of Kazakhstan, uses its hydroelectric power to process local deposits of lead, zinc, copper and silver. It manufactures machinery and chemicals. Oskemen is an important railroad and highway crossroads in the foothills of the West Altai Mountains. Using " highway" to describe the roads may be a slight exaggeration.

Petropavl (245,000) is situated where the Trans-Siberian Railway enters Kazakhstan

and crosses the Ishim River. Its industries are based on agriculture and transportation. Products include leather, small motors, felt and agriculture machinery. The city is intimately tied into the Russian economy and the majority of Russian speaking residents would like to become part of Russia.

Pavlodar (334,000), located along the Irtysh River, has a large aluminum industry. It also has an oil refinery and a petrochemical complex. A heavy metal industry turns out tractors for the grain growing regions of the steppes. The aluminum industry derives cheap electricty from coal burning thermal units.

Zhambul, Dzambul (309,000) located in the extreme southern portion of the country is a major producer of phosphate fertilizers and has a large thermal reduction plant. Leather shoes are also a major product. It is a major trading center with Kyrgyzstan, especially the city of Bishkek.

Aqmola, formerly Tselinograd (280,000), also Akmolinsk, was the center for the Virgin Lands experiment devised by Nikita Khrushchev. On the Ishim River, it is a rail junction manufacturing agriculture products from the grain produced in its locality. It is also engaged in meat packing and produces some agriculture machinery.

Aqtobe, also Aktyubinsk (255,000) is the center of an important chromium industry in the northwestern part of the country, near the Russian border.. It also produces phosphate fertilizers from ores shipped in from Russia.

Qostanay, also Kustanay (230,000), on the Tobol River, is the major city for the grain region of north Kazakhstan and parts of Siberia. It is an important flour milling center.

Temirtau (215,000) is a major coal mining center located near Qaraghandy. It is located near the large Samarkand Reservoir whose waters are used in processing steel produced in its blast furnaces. It also has a small metallurgical industry. There is a large thermonuclear station near the city.

Qyzylorda, also Kzyl-Orda (179,000) is an oasis on the Syr Darya River. A large pulp mill produces cardboard and paper from the reeds growing in the river. It is located on the Tashkent-Orenburg Railway.

Guryev, also Atyrau (152,000) in Western Kazakhstan, is on the Ural River delta near the Caspian Sea. It is a fishing center and has a nuclear power station. It's port and railroad facilities are engaged in transporting products of the Emba Oil Field located nearby. It has a small oil refinery and a pipeline connected to Orsk in Russia.

KYRGYZSTAN
(pop. 4,771,000 - 76,642 sq. mi.)
KIRGHIZSTAN, KYRGYZ, KIRGHIZIA

Kyrgyzstan is about the size of Nebraska. Its capital is Bishkek. The country is bordered on the southeast by China, and on the north and west by Kazakh and Uzbek. Tajik borders it on the south and west.

Kyrgyz is a mountainous country at the junction of two great Central Asian mountain ranges, the Tien Shan and Pamir. The highest peak, Pobeda Peak on the Chinese border, rises to 24,409 feet. Tien Shan are the "Heavenly Mountains" and the Pamirs are the "Roof of the World".

More than half of the country is over 8,000 feet. Glaciers and permanent snow cover most of the highest elevations.

Here mountain slopes, intermontane basins and flat areas provide rich pastures for goats, sheep, cattle and horses. In the lowlands, irrigation produces cotton, sugar beets, tobacco, some fruits and grapes. Barley, wheat and oats are grown in areas not irrigated.

There are about one and a half million cattle on the pasture lands and over ten million sheep. The animals provide wool for the carpet and clothing industries and leather for footwear. Like most of Central Asia, there is a brisk silk industry. Opium poppies are also raised.

Natural resources include coal, lead, mercury, gold, antimony, tungsten, uranium, oil and natural gas. Industries produce agricultural machinery, textiles, sugar from beets and tobacco. Meat processing and leather are also important. Some metal refining is done but generally the ores are exported.

A large lake, Issyk Kul, is located in the northeast, almost on the Kazak border. It is the fourth deepest lake in the world. The name means "hot lake" because most of its water comes from thermal springs deep underground. This mixes with glacier meltwaters and keeps the lake temperature above normal. Water flowing from the lake forms the Chu River which is used for irrigation until it eventually disappears into the desert sand.

Kyrgyz has uranium deposits on the southern and western shore of Lake Issyk Kul. These are found in association with lignite coal deposits and are believed to have been a secondary deposit through hydrothermal processes. A small uranium processing plant is located south of Osh where uranium deposits are also found in association with lignite.

Kirghiz make up 52 percent of the population. Twenty percent are Russian and 13 percent are Uzbek. Kirghiz are a Sunni Muslim, Turkic speaking people. They are largely pastoral and only 38 percent of the country is classified as urban. Ukrainians are also a sizable minority with a quarter million people.

At one time, the Kazakhs were referred

to as Kirghiz and the people who settled in this region were known as Kara Kirghiz. The word Kara means "black" in the Turkic language. The Kirghiz are known for their story telling, and their history and literature abound with epic poems and folk songs.

There are about a dozen storytellers who go from village to village reciting the epic poem of the origin of the Kirghiz people. The poem takes four days to recite.

Kirghiz migrated to the region from the Upper Yenisey River where they had lived from the 7th to the 17th century. Famine and freezing cold weather brought them further south.

The Kirghiz came under the rule of the Kokand Khanate in the 19th century. This was a system of governing which placed one strong ruler, the Khan, in charge of a large territory.

The Kokand Khanate was annexed by Russia in 1876. It was an area of political unrest until the Red Army brought a measure of stability in 1922. During that same year a famine reduced the population by more than half a million.

Three very rare animals live in the high mountains : the Tien Shan bear, the red wolf and the snow leopard. The government and some international organizations are trying to protect these animals.

President Askar Akayev rules the country in the manner of a petty prince or mafia don. He has given himself absolute power. In 1993 he introduced a new currency, the **som** which violated the rules of the Commonwealth of Independent States. Some conflict erupted over this but it is unlikely the new money will be abolished.

In 1994 Kyrgyzstan joined Uzbekistan and Kazakhstan in forming a free trade pact. This will probably be extended to Tajikistan and Turkmenistan in the near future.

Bishkek (628,000) was the traditional name for this capital city located on the Chu River. The Bolsheviks renamed it "Frunze" after General Mikhail Frunze who helped establish Red Army control. When Kyrgyz became independent, one of its first official acts was to change the city's name back to the original.

A branch of the Turkistan-Siberian Railroad originates at Bishkek. It is the industrial and cultural center of the country. A large meat packing industry is found here along with a manufacturing operation that produces agricultural machine parts. Motor vehicles, textiles, building materials and clothing are also manufactured. Tanning and tobacco processing are also done here. A large hydropower plant is in the city proper.

The Uzbek khans of Kokand built a fortress here in 1846. The fort became the nucleus around which the city developed.

Bishkek has a university, an academy of sciences, several museums and a theater. Its tourist industry is developing slowly.

Osh (217,000) is at the headwaters of the Syr Darya in the eastern Fergana Valley. One of Central Asia's oldest settlements, Osh was a major silk producing region during the bustling days of the caravan trade. Silk production around Osh saved many Baghdad merchants the expense of going all the way to eastern China. An old city abuts the modern one. Today, Osh is a major producer of cotton cloth.

In 1990, fighting broke out in the city over land disputes between the Uzbeks and Kirghiz. Two hundred and thirty people were killed. Relations between the two ethnic groups remain tense.

Przhevalsk (99,000) is about one hundred miles southwest of Almaty, Kazakhstan. It is located on Issyk Kul, the "hot lake". The lake has become a tourist attraction because it is believed to have medicinal curative properties. Przhevalsk has a small metal industry and is the center of Kyrgyzstan's coal mining which also produces small amounts of uranium. Silk is also spun into thread and cloth here.

The city is named after General Nikolai Przhevalsky, an explorer who traveled widely in Asia. He discovered an Asian wild horse which is named after him, the Przhevalsky Horse.

TAJIKISTAN
(pop. 6,158,000 - 54,019 sq. mi.)
RESKPUBLICKI I TOJIKISTON

Tajikistan is about the size of Wisconsin. Its capital is Dushanbe, located in the western part of the country near the Uzbek border.

An autonomous district, Badakhshoni-Kuhi Viloyat, occupies 45 percent of the country. This has become a source of irritation to the government as this district demands true autonomy.

Tajik is bordered on the north by Kyrgyzstan and Uzbekistan, on the west by Uzbekistan, on the south by Afghanistan and on the east by China. Tajik is a mountainous country with the highest peaks in the Pamirs, the "Roof of the World". More than half the country is over 9,000 feet in elevation.

Mt. Communism at 24,590 feet and Lenin Peak at 23,405 feet are among the highest mountains on earth. These peaks will probably have different names soon.

The mountains are in the south and east: the southeast is a high dry plateau. In the north Tajik has a small section of the Fergana Valley. The hot, dry Gissar and Vakhash valleys are found in the southwest, not the kind of places where most people like to live.

The Amu Darya and Syr Darya Rivers begin in the Tajik mountains. The Great Gissar Canal has increased the cultivated land by over one million acres. Swift streams from the mountains are used to produce hydroelectricity.

Tajik's economy is based on agriculture. Main farm products are barley, maize, wheat, vegetables, potatoes, cotton, apples, peaches and grapes. Cotton is the main crop, and is part of the Central Asian cotton monoculture. Silk culture (sericulture) is an ancient enterprise that is still active.

Grazing slopes support about a million and a half dairy cattle and three and a half million Karakul sheep. Camels and yaks are also raised in small numbers.

The mountains are home to the rare snow leopard, Siberian horned goat and the almost extinct markhor. The mountains contain gold, coal, antimony, salt, fluorspar and other minerals in small amounts. Mineral springs support a modest health spa industry.

Industries include silk spinning, cotton ginning, fruit canning, leather tanning, wine making, carpet weaving, metal working and machine building. Cotton, wool, and silk textiles are also produced.

Lignite, mined in several locations but mainly at Kyzylkiya, is used in local industries. Uranium is found in the northern section of the country in association with vanadium deposits in volcanic breccia.

The highest dam in the world is at Rogun on the Vakhash River which flows into the Amu Darya. It is over one thousand feet high. Another large dam is located downstream at Nurek. Together these dams provide more electric power than Dushanbe and the surrounding towns can use; so the excess power is transmitted to nearby Turkmenistan and Uzbekistan.

Tajiks make up 65 percent of the population, Uzbeks 25 percent and Russians 2 percent. There are also Tatar, Kirghiz and Ukrainian minorities.

The Tajiks are an Iranian people following the Sunni Muslim religion. They

18-4 Chess players in Dushanbe, Tajikistan.

are descended from the inhabitants of ancient Sogdiana which was centered south of Bukhara. Two thirds of the population are rural and only a small portion of Tajiks live in the few cities.

The ancient caravan routes avoided the Pamir Mountains and missed most of present day Tajikistan. The people turned to cattle raising and handicrafts which they traded in the Fergana Valley.

Tajik, like the rest of Turkistan, was conquered by the Golden Horde under Genghis Khan. It became part of the khanate at Bukhara in the 16th century. Russia didn't take control until late in the 19th century. The ruthless exploitation of the land continued until the Soviet Union collapse.

When Tajik became independent in 1991 the United States sent a five person embassy staff to Dushanbe. A group wanting to merge with Uzbekistan and another group

wanting to get rid of the old communists began to arm themselves. Hostilities broke out and there was heavy fighting in the capital. The U.S. Embassy staff left the country. The communist party regained control and the dissidents, which included anti-communists and fundamentalist Muslims, were taken into custody.

About 900,000 Tajikistanis crossed into Afghanistan and many of these people then made their way to Iran. Nationalist feelings remained high and the Tajikistan leadership banned most political parties, public meetings and several newspapers. Five Tajikistan journalists were found dead under mysterious circumstances.

The insurgents, armed by Afghanistan, captured the capital city in 1992. But an infusion of Russian and Uzbek troops retook the capital. The Russians then sent in a quarter million soldiers and 25,000 of them still patrol the Afghanistan border.

164

18-5 Government buildings in Dushanbe, Tajikistan at the foothills of the Pamir Mountains.

When the civil war began there were 454,000 Russians living in the country. More than 400,000 of them fled in the first six months of fighting. Many Jews and Uzbeks also emigrated. This reduced the country's production by 35 percent and its main industry, aluminum production, completely ceased.

The expatriate Russians moved back to Moscow lowland region and today they live in extreme poverty. The promise of jobs and material aid never materialized.

Dushanbe (607,000), the capital city, is the major industrial and cultural center. The name is derived from "Monday" which was the day for the big market that drew people from many miles around.

Coal is mined nearby, as well as lead and arsenic. The city produces cotton, silk, phosphate fertilizers, leather, tractor parts, food products and wool textiles.

Dushanbe served as headquarters for the Emir of Bukhara who fought the Bolsheviks in 1919. It was called Stalinabad from 1929 to 1961.

The city has a highly regarded state university and an academy of sciences. Due to the civil strife, the city, like most of the country, is avoided by tourists.

Khodzhent, also Khudzhand and Khojand, (162,000,) on the headwaters of the Syr Darya River in the Fergana Valley, is a major center for silk production. Other industries include clothing, footwear and food products. Khodzhent, due to its location in the Fergana Valley, was located on the old caravan route between China and the Mediterranean Sea. The town marks the farthest eastern expansion of Alexander The Great's conquests.

Khodzhent was completely destroyed by the army of Genghis Khan. In 1936 it was renamed **Leninabad.** With independence it returned to its old name.

Many wood, leather and metal artisans practice their crafts in the city which bring high prices in the world market.

TURKMENISTAN
(pop. 4,100,000 - 188,417 sq. mi.)

Turkmenistan is slightly larger than Montana. Ashgabat, the capital, is located in the south center of the country. Turkmenistan is bordered on the north by Kazakhstan and Uzbekistan, on the south by Afghanistan and Iran and on the west by the Caspian Sea. Uzbek winds around it on the east.

Turkmen is mostly in the low Karakum (Garagum) Desert with some highlands to the southwest and southeast. Streams originating in these highlands disappear into the desert except for the Amu Darya which flows along the border with Uzbek. The small Murgab River originates in Afghanistan. A large arm of the Caspian Sea, the Kara-Boguz-Gol Bay, extends into Turkmen. Kara-Boguz-Gol means "Black Throat Lake". The level of the Caspian Sea is falling, and the size of the Bay has been halved in the last twenty years. Drying sediments from the bay are rich in Glaubers Salts.

The Karakum Canal runs east-west along the flanks of the foothills, providing water for irrigation and hydropower. The canal is 700 miles long and terminates at Ashgabat. If it is completed the canal will go all the way to the Caspian Sea.

More than 90 percent of the agriculture land is irrigated. Cotton is the main product. Two oases produce wheat, barley, maize, millet, sesame, melons, grapes, jute and alfalfa. Wheat and maize are also produced by dry farming methods on non-irrigated land.

The country is almost devoid of cattle and pigs but maintains a herd of about five million sheep. One of the products from the sheep is the Karakul hides for which the area is famous. The hides are taken from three day old sheep. Mature sheep provide wool for the carpet industry.

Camels are still raised, but the numbers do not begin to match those of one hundred years ago. There are some dairy cattle which are fed irrigated alfalfa and maize.

Turkmen's major industries include fish canning along the Caspian, meat processing, oil refining, cotton ginning, railroad car repairing and silk spinning.

Important resources are oil, natural gas, phosphate, salt, sulfur, iodine, copper, bromine, bentonite, lignite coal, barites, various salts, clay and gypsum. Natural gas is exported to Ukraine. There are twenty small hydroelectric stations scattered along the mountain foothills and the Karakum Canal.

Two important rivers, the Zeravshan and Kashka Darya, start high in mountain glaciers only to disappear into the desert sands. The 460 mile long Zeravshan River forms in the Pamir-Altai Mountain slopes and irrigates a belt about twenty miles wide on the last 200 miles of its journey. It passes through the Uzbek cities of Samarkand and Bukhara before it disappears into the sand north of Chardzhou.

The Kashka Darya is smaller than the Zeravshan. Nevertheless it creates several oases and irrigates fields of wheat, cotton, rice as well as orchards of peaches and apricots.

MAP 19   Uzbekistan and Turkmenistan.

Turkmen's heavy irrigation dependency has made it one of the most polluted places on earth. Fertilizers and pesticides dominate the dust of the air. Infant mortality in the country is more than 60 per 1000 inhabitants making it one of the highest in the world.

Turkmen has a major thermal power station at Mary and a smaller station at Ashgabat. These use natural gas piped in from Khiva to the north and oil from Krasnovodsk on the Caspian Sea. Natural gas underlying most of the country, is a potentially lucrative resource.

Turkmen's southern border is located over a fault zone creating geothermal power close to the surface. This is an untapped energy source, another great potential resource.

Turkomans make up 73 percent of the population. They are the descendants of medieval Oguz tribes to which the Seljuk and Osmanli Turks also belong. They still retain their tribal and clan divisions.

Russians and Uzbek are large minorities with about nine percent each. Other peoples are Kazakhs, Tatars, Ukrainians and Azeris. The Tatars were exiled here during World War II on Stalin's orders.

Eighty percent of the people are Sunni Muslim. They have little in common with the powerful Shiite Muslims of Iran.

167

18-6 Turkmen women in traditional costume.

although Iran has made many requests for Islamic unity. The Turkomans are under pressure from Iran, Turkey and Pakistan to form an economic unit with each of them.

Their language is Turkmen which belongs to the Turkic family. Russian is the second language and still the principal language of business and trade.

This barren desert land was originally part of the kingdom of ancient Persia. It passed to Arab domination in the 8th century. In the 11th century, it was ruled by the Seljuk Turks then conquered by the hordes of Genghis Khan in the 13th century. Tamerlane who became ruler in the 14th century ruled the territory until it came under Uzbek control.

Russia took over in the late 19th century. Large numbers of Turkomans fled to Iran and Afghanistan during the oppressive Stalin years.

When the Soviet Union invaded Afghanistan in the 1980s they sent in what they considered to be Muslim troops, many of them from Turkmenistan. The Soviets hoped the Muslims, who understood the culture, would quickly end the war. But most of the Turkomans had relatives living in Afghanistan and almost all of them defected.

Turkomen nationalists claim the entire Central Asia region including the other four republics are really Turkmenistan territory. They base their claim on the ancient kingdom known as Turkistan. These nationalists who remain quite active could be a threat to regional stability.

Turkmenistan society and politics is dominated by its leader, Saparmurad Niyazov, who has the power to dissolve any legislative body and supervise elections, if any. Practically any new building, college, ship, street or development is named after him. Large portraits of him hang everywhere.

In 1993, Turkmenistan created a new currency, the **manat**, which violated the rules of the CIS. The country decided to accept limited partnership in the CIS in 1993.

The country has several species of animal life found nowhere else. These include the caracal lynx, Central Asian cobra, three rare gecko and a desert monitor which is really a lizard that can grow to five feet in length.

Ashgabat (Ashkhabad) (430,000) was founded in 1881 as a Russian fortress. It is situated on an oasis near the Iranian border. The city was developed as a halfway point for stopping on the Trans-Caspian Railway from the Caspian Sea to Tashkent. The city, which is located on a major fault zone, was destroyed by an earthquake in 1948. It was then rebuilt.

Ashgabat performs administrative functions for the entire country. It produces textiles, small machines, glass, carpets, water pumps, leather, printing, small engines and even has a minor motion picture industry.

Chardzhou (Charjew), (164,000) on the Amu Darya River, is an inland port with shipyard facilities handling small vessels. It is the center of a cotton and silk industry. It also produces fertilizer from phosphate rock which is used in most Central Asian countries. Like the capital, Charjew was founded by the Russians in the late 19th century as a fortress.

Tashauz (Dashowuz) (100,000) is an important city in the north, close to the Uzbek border. Its position as an oasis connected with the Amu Darya River makes it a major source of vegetable products for the country.

Mary (92,000), on the Murgab River, stands alone in the southeastern part of Turkmenistan. It is an oasis in the Karakum Desert. Like most areas of the country, Mary is in a cotton growing region. The city is a rail junction exporting cotton and other products of wool, wheat and hides. There is a growing textile industry, and it is the center of a newly developed natural gas industry.

The modern city is built on the ruins of the ancient city of Merv and was known by that name until 1937. The recent construction of a thermal electric station has

18-7 The Karakum Canal flows through the desert from the mountains to Ashgabat.

made Mary an important energy provider for the rest of the country.

Krasnovodsk (65,000), located on the Caspian Sea, was once an important fishing center. It still has a fish canning industry, but today it is more important as a terminus for oil and natural gas pipelines and for the Trans-Caspian Railroad. The city, founded in 1869, is a breaking point for agriculture products. Products are sent here from the east, broken into smaller units then shipped to other cities.

The city has a very limited supply of fresh water and water is brought in daily from Azerbaijan across the Caspian Sea.

UZBEKISTAN
(pop. 23,100,000 - 172,700 sq. mi.)

Uzbekistan is about the size of Oregon and Washington combined. Its capital city is Toshkent, one of the largest cities in Central Asia.

Uzbek is bordered by Afghanistan and Turkman on the south, Kazakh on the west and north and Tajik and Kyrgyz on the east. The Karakalpak autonomous district is located within Uzbekistan.

The country encompasses about half the Aral Sea and contains most of the Amu Darya River system which flows down from the mountains. A small section of the Syr Darya headwaters is found in eastern Uzbek. Most of Uzbek is lowland composed of the Kyzylkum (Qyzylgum) Desert. In the southeast are the foothills of the Tien Shan or "Heavenly Mountains".

Desert fauna include the rare Saiga antelope and the desert monitor. The mountain fauna include the snow leopard and several varieties of mountain goats.

Much of the southeast is composed of loess (wind driven soil) which is fertile when irrigated. Agriculture production depends heavily on irrigation from the two rivers. The Syr Darya is used to irrigate the Fergana Valley with Kokand at its center. The Amu Darya waters irrigate some of the Kyzylkum Desert.

Cotton is the main crop grown on the irrigated lands. It is the center of the Central Asian monoculture. Cotton, at the expense of food crops, is exported to Moscow where it is the backbone of the textile industry.

When cotton is ready for harvesting, schools close and students begin picking. College classes are canceled and the army is called in and everyone picks cotton. There are some cotton picking machines but hand labor is still the norm. The government would like to diversify its agriculture and become less dependent on cotton. However, Uzbekistan is the world's leading exporter of cotton and it brings in hard currency, money needed to run the country. Cotton accounted for 80 percent of the country's income in 1995.

A big problem is the pesticides and fertilizers used to grow cotton pollutes drinking water and soil. Pesticide residue is also found on cottonseed which is the source of virtually all cooking oil. Thus the people are absorbing the pesticides through their drinking water and food.

Rice is also grown in the irrigated valleys. Other crops include wheat, maize, alfalfa, tobacco, sugar cane, and sesame. Grapes, apples, peaches and apricots are grown on the highland slopes.

The country raises about four million cattle and usually has about nine million sheep. Products include wool and Karakul sheep pelts. There is a thriving silk industry. However, cotton takes up so much land that the country must import two thirds of its grain, one half of its potatoes, one third of its meat and one fourth of its milk.

The large cities have begun to manufacture textiles from cotton, silk and wool. Uzbek also has food processing factories and more recently started manufacturing steel, tractors, cars and fertilizer.

Uzbek has a large natural gas reserve. The big producing gas wells are in the southeast corner of the country. Gas fuels most of the industries of Bukhara, Samargand and Toshkent. Lignite coal is mined in the southeast. The country also produces oil, zinc, gold, copper, tungsten, molybdenum, lead, fluorspar, wolfram, sulfur, limestone and clay. An oil field was recently discovered in the Fergana Valley.

Uranium has been found in the center of the Kyzylkum Desert in association with gold deposits. But large capital investment is needed before the uranium and gold can be exploited.

Twenty-two hydroelectric plants add to the electric supply provided by thermal plants. A large thermal power plant is on line at Syrdarya, south of Toshkent and a smaller unit operates at Navoi, west of Toshkent.

18-8 The Rigestan Square in Samargand, Uzbekistan. The buildings are theological schools.

The Aral Sea is rapidly drying up as a result of water diversion from the two rivers which flow into it. The intensive cotton industry has made Uzbek one of the most polluted places on earth. Pesticides and fertilizers, blown about by strong winds, have made Uzbek a leader in cancer and birth defects. The Aral Sea, which once supported an important fishing industry is almost a lifeless lake. Boats remain stranded two hundred feet from the present shoreline.

Freight transportation is mainly on two railroad lines. The Trans-Caspian Railroad begins in Toshkent and goes through Mary, Bukhara, Samargand and Ashkhabad before terminating at the Caspian Sea. The Kazalinsk Railroad begins in Toshkent and moves through the desert to Orenburg at the southern end of the Urals. This is the main route from Moscow to Toshkent.

Good highways connect the cities of Toshkent, Samargand and Bukhara. However, only one adequate road parallels the southern border to the small desert city of Nukus. Most of the country north and west of Bukhara is without roads but travel through the desert is not difficult.

Uzbeks make up 75 percent of the population. About 8 percent are Russian who live in the cities. Other groups include Tajiks (5 percent), Kazakhs (4 percent) Koreans, Ukrainians, Turkmens, Kyrgyz, Karakalpaks and Tatars. About 40 percent of the population is urban, high for Central Asia. Uzbeks make up significant segments of the population in neighboring countries.

During World War II, Stalin exiled Meshketians living in Georgia to Uzbekistan. They settled in the Fergana Valley and became a prosperous minority group. This has caused much ethnic strife and several nasty confrontations have erupted. Many of the Meshketians have tried to return to Georgia but they have not been welcomed there either.

The Uzbek language is related to the Turkic groups of Middle Asia and ancient Persian. Uzbek religion is Sunni Muslim, Russians are mostly Eastern Orthodox.

The **Karakalpak Autonomous District** makes up 37 percent of Uzbekistan, occupying the entire western portion of the country. However, it only accounts for about seven percent of the total Uzbek population. Its capital is Nukus.

Nukus (171,000) is in the Khorozm oasis area on the Amu Darya River. It processes alfalfa and food products.

The Republic comprises parts of the Kyzylkum Desert and the Amu Darya delta on the Aral Sea. Irrigation projects on the Amu Darya produce alfalfa, cotton, rice, maize and jute. Livestock includes cattle and Karakul sheep. Sericulture is an important enterprise.

Karakalpaks are a Turkic speaking people closely related to the Kazakhs. There are also minorities of Uzbeks, Kazakhs, Turkomans, Russians and Tatars.

Uzbekistan is the site of one of the world's oldest civilizations. It was first identified as the province of Sogdiana in the ancient Persian Empire. It was conquered in the 4th century B.C. by Alexander the Great. Turkish nomads came during the 6th century A.D. Uzbekistan was ruled by Arabs who introduced the Islamic faith in the 8th century. In the 12th century it was retaken by the Seljuk Turks of Khorezm. During the 13th century the forces of Genghis Khan overran the country.

Tamerlane conquered most of Central Asia and the Caucasus in the 14th century. He made his headquarters at Samargand in southeastern Uzbek, in the foothills of the mountains.

During these times, Uzbek was the major trade route between Europe and Asia. Marco Polo traveled through the area on his journey from Italy and India to China. The cities of Samargand, Bukhara and Toshkent prospered. Even by today's standards they were enormously wealthy.

The Uzbeks, remnants of the Golden Horde and known as Sarts, invaded the area from the north in the 16th century. Their name is derived from a leader, Uzbeg Khan, who died in 1340.

The Uzbek leader, Abdullah, extended his empire to Persia, Afghanistan and eastern Turkistan. This empire eventually broke into the khanates of Bukhara, Kokand and Khiva.

The khanates, weakened by internal fighting, gave Russia its opportunity. The whole region was conquered by Russia in the late 19th century.

Most of the Russians live in Toshkent. When the country became independent in 1991, 2.4 million Russians lived there. In 1995, emigration reduced this number to 1.7 million.

After the Russians began leaving and trade with Russia diminished the production of Uzbekistan decreased by twenty percent. Price controls were put into effect and privatization was curtailed. Private land ownership is still illegal.

In 1991, fledgling political parties were suppressed by the government. The main opposition leader, Abdumannob Pulatov was arrested and sentenced to three years in prison for slandering President Islam Karimov. He was arrested the day after the legislature ratified a constitution granting political and human rights.

18-9 Mechanical cotton harvesters in the irrigated valley of the Amu Darya River.

When the Tajikistan Civil War broke out, Uzbekistan refused to take in refugees. Most of the resident Tajiks live in Bukhara and Samargand. Some Uzbek troops were sent to back the Tajik government.

In 1994, Uzbek issued a new currency, the **somcoupon**. Even though this violated CIS rules, the country is still a member. It also has a free trade pact with Kyrgyzstan and Kazakhstan.

Despite the oppressive government the people of Uzbekistan have plenty to eat and open air markets are filled with food such as bread, lamb and spices of every kind. The crime rate is very low and the 115 different nationalities do not harass each other.

President Islam Karimov has rejected Islamic fundamentalism as a guide to his regime. He has, however, promoted himself for idolatry.

Toshkent, Tashkent (2,200,000), in the foothills of the Tien Shan mountains, is the largest and one of the oldest cities in Central Asia. It is the economic and cultural center of the region and an important air terminal, There are daily flights to the major Russian cities. A rail center, it is connected to all the main cities of the Aral Basin and Russia. It is the core city for all the Central Asian Republics.

Toshkent lies in a great oasis along the Chirchik River, tributary to the Syr Darya. Center of the cotton and rice trade, it has one of the largest cotton textile mills in the world. Tashkent also produces tobacco products, electrical equipment, furniture, pharmaceuticals, paper, pottery, hosiery and perfume.

Its old historical center features narrow, twisting streets, and numerous mosques and bazaars. The modern city was built by Russians and most ethnic Russians live here. A major earthquake in 1966 caused heavy damage.

The city has a subway system an academy of science, several colleges and several libraries.

Samargand, Samarkand (390,000), on the Trans-Caspian Railroad and the Zeravshan River, is one of the oldest cities in the world and the oldest in Central Asia. Ruins just north of the modern city date back to the 4th century B.C. The ancient Greeks called it Marakanda.

Samargand, conquered by Alexander the Great in 329 B.C., was the meeting point between Chinese and Western cultures. It became a part of the Arab world in the 8th century when it flourished as a trade center between Baghdad and China.

The tomb of the Arab scholar, Bukhari, is on the outskirts of the city, and is a major Muslim shrine. The old section of Samargand contains Registan, a great square which has some of the most splendid monuments in Central Asia. The most famous is Tamerlane's Mausoleum, the Bibi Khan Mosque, with a turquoise cupola erected by Tamerlane as a monument to his favorite wife. During his reign the city had tree lined streets, many palaces and gardens, and indoor plumbing.

Today, Samargand produces cotton and silk products, wine and tea. Metal products, motor vehicle parts, leather goods, and shoes are manufactured.

Bukhara, Bukhoro and Bokhara, (230,000), is located on the Shkhrud irrigation canal of the Zeravshan River. The city is a large cotton center with textile mills as well as ginning industries. It has the largest Karakul skin processing plant in Central Asia. It also has a well known carpet industry.

Like other ancient Uzbek cities, Bukhara was on the trade routes between east and west. It became a major Islamic learning center in the 9th century. The scholar Bukhari, after whom the city takes its name, traveled widely in the region. His philosophy was collected in *The Prophet*, regarded as the second book of Islam, second only to the Koran itself. Bukhari's tomb, as noted, is near Samargand.

Large Uzbek cities of the Fergana Valley include **Andizhan** (297,000), **Namangan** (310,000), **Kokand**, (185,000) and **Fergana** (205,000). All are connected to each other by a circular rail line. They are all engaged in food processing. Cotton , alfalfa, peaches, apricots, and mulberry trees are grown by irrigation in the Fergana Valley.

Karshi (160,000) in Southeastern Uzbekistan is located beneath the mountain foothills on the Kashka Darya River. It is an oasis growing wheat, cotton and mulberry trees for the silk industry. It was a stop on the old caravan routes. The mountain fed **Kashka Darya River** flows 200 miles through Uzbekistan before it disappears into the sand. It provides water for a network of canals and irrigation systems.

Angren (132,000), northeast of Toshkent, is in the center of the largest lignite mining site in Central Asia.

Bekabad (80,000) is a small but important city on the Syr Darya River south of Toshkent. It has a large steel mill and cement works. It receives its power from a hydropower station at Farkhand Dam on the Syr Darya.

19. AGRICULTURE

One in four Russians are engaged in agriculture, but less than ten percent of Russian land is under cultivation. The rest has almost no agriculture value. Non-agricultural lands include taiga, tundra, mountains and swamps.

Cultivated land forms the classic populated triangle. If Ukraine is included, the triangle points are St. Petersburg, Russia and Odesa, Ukraine in the west and Krasnoyarsk, Siberia in the east. The area north of the triangle is too cold for farming, south of the triangle it's too dry and the east is too mountainous. Scattered among the areas of cold, dry and mountains are small pockets of successful agriculture. But these are exceptions which take heroic efforts to coax crops from the thin soil.

Some of the dry areas are brought to fruitation by irrigation. Much of the low precipitation southern lands are in this category.

The natural vegetation of the plains region north of the Oka River is mixed forest. Over the centuries trees have been clear cut and the land put to the plow. These lands, especially those in the broad leaf region, have adequate humus in the soil which allows aeration to take place and moisture to remain in the topsoil where plant roots can get at it. Today, due to centuries of use, these soils need lime and fertilizer to be productive.

Almost all suitable land north of the Oka River has been cleared and cultivated. Much of it is ideal for hay which is used in the dairy cattle industry.

South of the Oka River, on the Russian Plain, are the most fertile soils - the black earth chernozems and the brown chestnut soils. Most of Ukraine has these excellent soils.

The steppe lands of Ukraine and southern Russia are mostly level or slightly hilly. These are easily cultivated with machinery. The steppes are found from Moldova to Central Siberia, and comprise the lands of northern Kazakhstan.

Steppe climate has periods of drought, about one dry spell every four years. This has been somewhat alleviated by irrigation along the Volga, Don, Dnieper and Dnestre Rivers.

Western Siberia farmers must battle winter cold, summer frosts, low precipitation and short growing seasons. If irrigation is used in these marginal lands, then agriculture production increases. However, irrigation has a tendency to increase salinity and alkalinity at the growing surface. This leads to salt crusts and infertility.

The steppe lands stretching from Moldova to the Urals are the heartland of agriculture in Eastern Europe. Here, the precipitation is adequate and cultivation is generally successful. The rate of crop failure increases toward the southern deserts. Farming south of Saratov on the Volga is a precarious occupation because of aridity. Astrakhan receives less than seven inches of precipitation annually. Irrigation projects are found along the lower courses of the south-flowing rivers.

In Siberia and northern Kazakhstan precipitation is unreliable. Barnaul receives 13 inches of precipitation annually which is enough to grow many grains. However, Petropavl on the plateau steppes receives 32 inches, quite adequate for agriculture. Barnaul's summer temperatures are ten degrees higher than Petropavl's and this offsets some of the disadvantages of lower precipitation. However, evaporation is

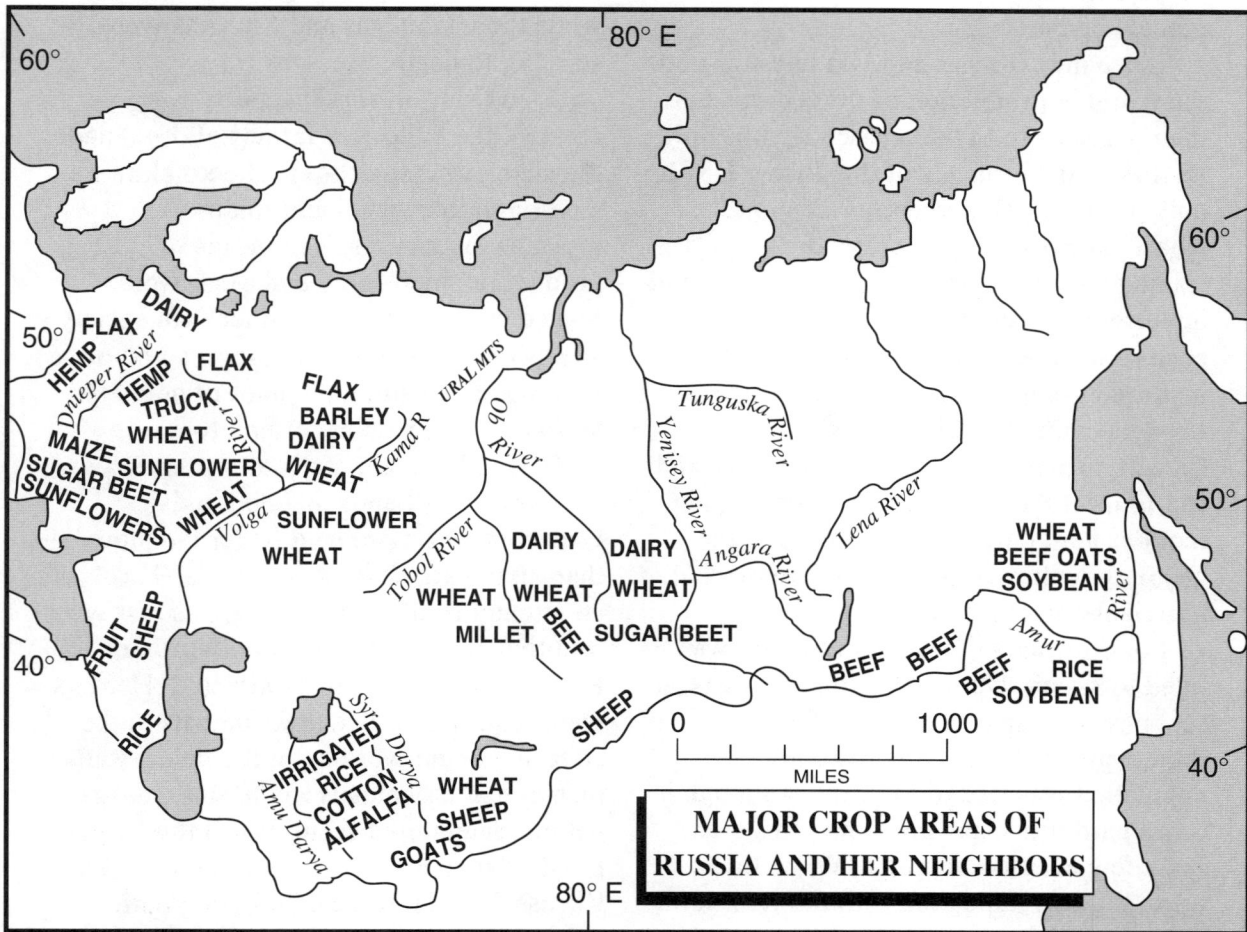

MAP 20   Major crop areas.

Map labels (reading across the map):

60° · 80° E · 60° · 50° · 40°

DAIRY · FLAX · HEMP · Dnieper River · FLAX · HEMP · TRUCK · WHEAT · FLAX BARLEY DAIRY · Kama R. · URAL MTS · Ob River · Tunguska River · Yenisey River · Lena River

MAIZE SUNFLOWER · SUGAR BEET · SUNFLOWERS · WHEAT · Volga · WHEAT · SUNFLOWER WHEAT · Tobol River · DAIRY · DAIRY · Angara River · Amur River · WHEAT BEEF OATS SOYBEAN

FRUIT SHEEP · WHEAT · WHEAT WHEAT · MILLET · BEEF · SUGAR BEET · BEEF · BEEF · BEEF · RICE SOYBEAN

RICE · Syr Darya · Amu Darya · IRRIGATED RICE COTTON ALFALFA · WHEAT SHEEP · SHEEP · GOATS

0   1000   MILES

MAJOR CROP AREAS OF RUSSIA AND HER NEIGHBORS

80° E

also greater and schemes such as wind breaks and dry farming techniques must be utilized.

In the Central Asian Republics, agriculture is heavily dependent upon irrigation. Much of the land is planted in cotton which is a surplus cash crop while food crops yields have dwindled in recent years. Rice production is increasing and may be the trend. Much of the irrigated land is planted in alfalfa for the livestock industry.

Dry farming methods are also employed in the piedmont areas of the high Central Asian Mountains. These methods involve planting without plowing, seed drilling,

heavy mulching and methods of evaporation control.

In 1980 the Soviet Union led the world in production of many important crops. Here is a comparison of production with the United States for three crops (numbers are in thousands of metric tons):

Wheat: **USSR** 98,000 - **U. S.** 64,492
Oats: **USSR** 14,200 - **U. S.** 6,642
Potatoes: **USSR** 66,900 - **U. S.** 26,400

In 1980 the USSR was the world leader in the following crop production: 22 percent wheat, 30 percent sugar beets, 27 percent barley, 37 percent rye, 30 percent potatoes,

177

33 percent oats, 53 percent flax and 25 percent hemp.

Since then, Russia and Ukraine still lead the world in production of these crops but their percentage has decreased significantly. By 1990 the farmlands of the former USSR only produced 18 percent of the world's wheat. The Soviet Union was the world's leading wheat importer and it was second in importing rice and maize. Today Russia needs a minimum of 25 million tons of imported grain annually to meet its needs. Imports come from the United States, Canada, Argentina, Australia, New Zealand and France. Paying for this imported grain requires hard currency and gold. For the major agriculture crop areas of Russia and its neighbors refer to the map.

For 300 years the Russian Empire was ruled by Czars. During this time the peasant economy was able to feed itself and even export food. A large peasant population was tied to the land. Although it was a hard life, many peasants prospered and a few even became rich. When times were difficult, immigration to the west took place, especially to the United States and Canada. Between 1880 and 1910 more than three and a half million Russian and Ukrainian immigrants came to the United States.

In 1928 Stalin began the first Five Year Plan in agriculture. Lenin had hesitated to nationalize agriculture but Stalin wanted individual farms made into large factory-type operations which became known as collectives. In Ukraine, successful farmers called **kulaks** resisted when their livestock and produce were confiscated for the collectives. More than ten million Ukrainians and three million Kazakhs died in a Stalin-made famine which was the result of confiscation of the food resources. Another five million Ukrainians were deported to obscure parts of the empire.

Stalin actually exported grain to Europe while the Ukrainians and Kazakhs were starving to death.

Two forms of rural property were created: the collective farm (**kolkhoz**) and the state farm (**sovkhoz**). The kolkhoz was a co-operative set up and run by the peasants themselves. The means of production, machinery and seed, were owned by the collective rather than society as a whole. The more important sovkhoz was organized along the lines of industry. Workers were paid according to a wage scale used for other state enterprises.

The Virgin Lands or Idle Lands Campaign put more land under the plow than all the arable land in Canada. This was an attempt to plow up the steppes that were traditionally used for grazing. Northern Kazakhstan was the most affected. Herders were required to give their animals to the state and begin working in the fields. Rather than give their animals to the state, most people slaughtered them. When the Virgin Lands Campaign was announced by Nikita Khrushchev, more than 300,000 youths volunteered to move from the Moscow region to Kazakhstan and Southern Siberia.

Irrigation canals were constructed in all arid areas with access to water. The Kara Kum (Garagum) Canal in Turkmenistan is over 700 miles long. A canal from the Irtysh River to Karaganda is over 300 miles long.

Deterioration of the agriculture base began in the 1970s. Improper agricultural practices started to catch up with the planners. Instead of farmers making decisions, bureaucrats in Moscow made them. Production quotas could not be coaxed from the land. Weather patterns began to change slightly and crop failure increased. The state farm and collective system began to collapse as the last decade of the century neared. There was a dearth of human spirit in the land.

19-1 Harvesting wheat on the steppe.

Stalin's system simply failed. In 1989, ten percent of the arable land in private hands produced 40 percent of the edible crop. This may be misleading because much of this crop was produced by seed, fertilizer, pesticides and machinery stolen from government supplies. People neglected the government lands to work their own plots. The personal calamity of Soviet farmers in the early 1990s is well documented.

There were long food lines in almost every city. Meat, eggs, potatoes were in short supply. More than one half of Russians were severely underfed during the winters of 1992 and 1993. Since then, the food shortage has been alleviated but many Russians must spend their entire incomes just to eat. Food is brought to Moscow from the Caucasus and sold in open markets. There is much conflict between Moscovites and these "blacks" from the south who are considered profiteers as well as outsiders.

Out on the state farms, there was no incentive to work. Payday, however small, arrived with or without effort. Farmers were paid less than industrial workers and this created envy and an attitude of "Why bother?".

Government bureaucrats determined when the crops would be planted and harvested. They paid no attention to factors like the weather. Autumn rains turned the potato fields to mud. There are few paved roads in the rural areas, and it was nearly impossible to harvest the crop and transport it. Alcoholism was almost 100 percent among the peasants. Fields were simply abandoned. In 1992 the army was used to harvest potatoes.

There was and still is inadequate storage facilities for grain. Estimates put the rotted wheat crop at 25 percent and the rotted potato crop at 20 percent from 1992 to 1994. Most collective farms have no storage facilities at all. The fresh fruit and tomato loss was estimated at 40 percent.

The Czars and Soviets did not build roads to any extent and the present government does not have money for roads. Most roads are used for the short haul. The major methods of transport are by rail and pipeline. River transport only accounts for 3 percent of the national transport.

Rail transport is acceptable for more durable foods such as grain and milled products, and to some extent potatoes. Most other farm products cannot be sent by rail. In 1995, farm products amounted to 4 percent of all railroad freight.

To improve Russian agriculture there must be a complete break with the Stalin-era collective and state farm systems. In 1994 only 6 percent of Russian farmland was privatized.

At the beginning of 1996, the Federation government boasted that 94% of all farms were in private hands. This was misleading and probably not true since the collective farms became the properties of the former communists who managed them under the Soviet system. Government regulation has such a stranglehold on farms that they remain state owned.

Armenia has privatized 82 percent of the land, Kazakhstan 10 percent and Kyrgyzstan 28 percent. Countries with less than one percent land privatization in 1996 include Belarus, Ukraine, Tajikistan, Moldova, Turkmenistan and Azerbaijan. In order for agriculture to improve, people will have to be able to buy land or receive long term leases for it. Personal investment in the land would ensure stewardship and individual responsibility.

As government owned factories close or become privatized, unemployment increased dramatically in Russian cities. In order to survive many urban dwellers are raising vegetables in small vacant lots and window boxes. Canning vegetables is common.

There is also an increase in the use of idle city lots for foraging by ducks, chickens and goats. This is especially true in the smaller cities.

Improving agriculture has been a top priority in government. Yet, Russia remains a heavy food importer. Real agricultural reform will probably not occur until well into the 21st century.

Russia has instituted many protectionist schemes for agriculture and farm products even though their own production is not enough to supply domestic demands. Protectionist legislation does increase production but when food is in short supply the situation might become critical.

One of the controversial items on the protectionist list is American chickens. The United States exported seven percent of its chicken production to Russia in 1995. Even though chickens are a backyard animal in rural Russian villages it cannot supply the urban population. Chicken farms, like those in the United States, do not exist. Various schemes, such as inspecting each chicken, have been insituted to cut down on imports.

The United States is the biggest exporter of seed to Russia and this is another area of controversy. Most of the seed purchased by Russia is corn and this crop does not do well in the cool climates of Russia. Seldom does corn reach maturity. Russia accused American firms of selling inferior seed in order to get rid of excess inventories and has defaulted on its debts.

20. ENERGY RESOURCES

Russia has more energy resources than any other country in the world. It has the world's largest natural gas reserves. Oil reserves are almost equal to that of Saudi Arabia, the world leader. Russia's coal reserves amount to one fourth of the world supply. The only other countries with comparable coal reserves are China and the United States.

Unfortunately, many of these Russian reserves are in inaccessible areas of Siberia and heroic expensive efforts must be made to bring them to the Russian and European markets. Some effort has already been made and a steady stream of fossil fuels is moving westward.

Russia is currently the only developed country in the world that can meet all of its own fuel and energy needs. As population and industry expand, it will be necessary to further develop these resources. If a country can be judged on the amount of per capita energy it uses, then Russia is fourth, after the United States, Germany and Japan.

Russia produces nearly one fifth of the world's primary energy and leads the world in oil and natural gas production. It is the world's largest exporter of those two fuels and is third in the production of coal, after the United States and China. However, present methods of oil extraction and outdated equipment have produced a steady decline in oil production since 1990. But natural gas production has increased steadily.

Russian fuel is exported to all the former Soviet Republics and some countries, like the three Baltic states, are very dependent on these fuels. Other countries receiving fuel exports are former Communist Bloc countries in eastern Europe - Romania, Poland, Czechy, Slovakia, Hungary and Bulgaria. Fuels are also exported to Germany, France, Italy, Austria, Sweden, Belgium, Finland, Netherlands and United Kingdom. As the Siberian fuel reserves are further developed there will be more exports to Japan. Several agreements between Japan and Russia will develop these fields, especially the oil reserves on the Sakhalin Islands.

The largest international trade project is the agreement between Russia and Western Europe for the natural gas pipeline linking Siberia's Urengoy gas field to Ukraine's Uzhgorod. From the western terminus in Ukraine, gas is distributed by pipeline to most of Europe. This pipeline is also connected to several pipelines centered near Orenburg in the southern Urals.

Russia's attempts to shift from a planned economy to a free market economy has created serious setbacks in many of the proposed fuel projects. Strikes and slowdowns in the Siberian coal fields have hindered production. Coal miners have discovered that they can be an effective political force; over 70 percent of all electricity in Russia is generated by burning coal.

Russia is the world's leading oil and natural gas producer, and one of the major exporters of both fuels. Oil and gas have been the key to the country's economic growth, and expansion of key industries is tied to the availability of these energy sources. The Moscow industrial area has shifted from the use of coal to the use of these fluid fuels.

The best data places Russia with about 12 percent of the world's total proven oil reserves. If the estimated reserves are accurate then Russia has about one fifth of the world's total reserves.

However, estimated or potential, oil reserves are not being exploited to full

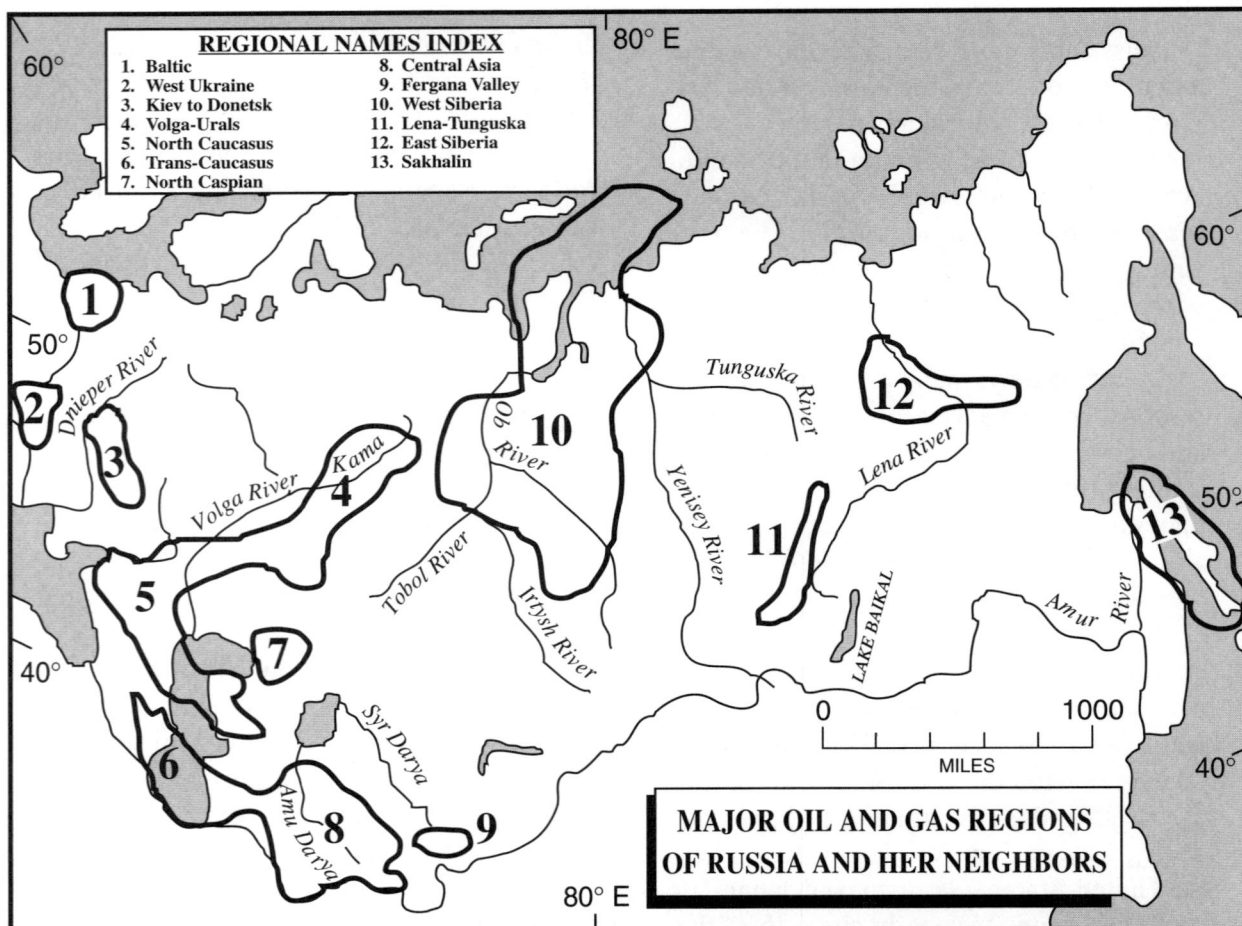

REGIONAL NAMES INDEX
1. Baltic
2. West Ukraine
3. Kiev to Donetsk
4. Volga-Urals
5. North Caucasus
6. Trans-Caucasus
7. North Caspian
8. Central Asia
9. Fergana Valley
10. West Siberia
11. Lena-Tunguska
12. East Siberia
13. Sakhalin

MAJOR OIL AND GAS REGIONS OF RUSSIA AND HER NEIGHBORS

MAP 21   Major oil and gas reserves.

potential. Current oil extraction is linked to systems already in place and Japanese, British and American companies have contracted to improve the antiquated systems.

Most of Russian oil production comes from the Volga-Ural fields stretching from the Kama to the Belaya River valleys west of the Urals. Future potential lies in the West Siberian Lowlands extending from the Kara Sea to Novosibirsk and encompassing almost the entire basin between the Ob and Yenisey rivers.

Other reserves include East Siberia around Yakutsk, the Sakhalin Islands, north of the Caucasus, Lena-Tunguska north of Lake Baikal and the Timan-Pechora area extending into the Barents Sea. Extracting these remote supplies will not be easy.

The biggest oil production in the Near Abroad comes from the Baky area of Azerbaijan. Other large fields have been discovered in Turkmenistan and Uzbekistan. The Ukrainian field from Kiev to Donetsk is a mayor oil producer and Ukraine is developing small reserves in its northwest.

182

Some oil is now extracted from deposits under the Baltic Sea off the coasts of Kaliningrad and Lithuania. Production from this field is expected to increase.

In 1994, the oil pipelines leading from the Pechora Basin to Yaroslav developed several breaks and tremendous amounts of oil leaked into the river system creating havoc with fresh water and wildlife. American oil companies repaired the leaks but it is evident that the entire pipeline system will need to be replaced. Present estimates put the leaking and wasted oil in all of Russia at 20 percent of extraction.

Russia has enormous natural gas reserves. The lowest estimates indicate at least 40 percent of the world's total reserve, but the location of these reserves are creating gigantic problems in extraction and distribution. The largest reserves are in the Arctic and construction costs are tremendous. About 80 percent of Russian reserves are in the Tyumen district north of the junction of the Irtysh and Ob Rivers.

Because the West Siberian field is believed to contain all the country's present gas needs as well as those for export there has been no effort to develop any other gas fields. Gas reserves are found in the same locations as oil reserves except for large gas deposits in the north Caspian region of Kazakhstan.

West Siberian gas and oil extraction are complicated by permafrost, occurring north of 64 degrees N latitude. Permafrost interferes with exploration, drilling and using concrete. Well casings have to be insulated to prevent collapse. It costs more to maintain extraction than it does to build the original facilities.

Western Siberia's oil and gas industry is an attraction to the marginally employed people of European Russia. About half a million people a year, more than one thousand a day, move here from the west.

This necessitates creation of suitable housing, shops, schools, health clinics and related facilities. People often end up disappointed and about 70 percent of them return to their former homelands in the west. This still leaves a net population increase of 150,000 annually.

Oil refineries are found in or near most major cities of the Russian Plain, Ukraine and the Caucasus. There is at least one refinery in each of the Central Asian countries. In Siberia large refineries are in Omsk, Achinsk, Angarsk, Komsomolsk and Khabarovsk.

Much of Russia's refining capacity is beset with problems. Modern cracking units which break down heavier fuels into lighter fuels such as gasoline and kerosene are lacking. The cumbersome units presently in operation are inefficient and lose about 10 percent of the usable product.

This lack of heavy-oil conversion capacity makes it difficult for refineries to produce the high-octane fuel needed in the aircraft transportation industry. High-grade diesel fuel is also difficult to produce. Since most of the heavy oil cannot be adequately refined, much of it is used in thermal electric power plants. These oil burning stations should be converted to coal and natural gas.

In refining crude oil the liquid must pass through a primary distillation process where it is separated into gases, gasoline, kerosene, diesel fuel and heavy fuels. These products are used as fuel or further refined to produce lubricating oils, high quality fuels and other finished products. The second refining process involves catalytic cracking, hydrogen treating, hydrocracking and lubricating oil production. Russia does not have enough of these secondary refining facilities.

The biggest waste of natural gas in the extraction process is the burning of gas as it comes up from the ground. Burning is an

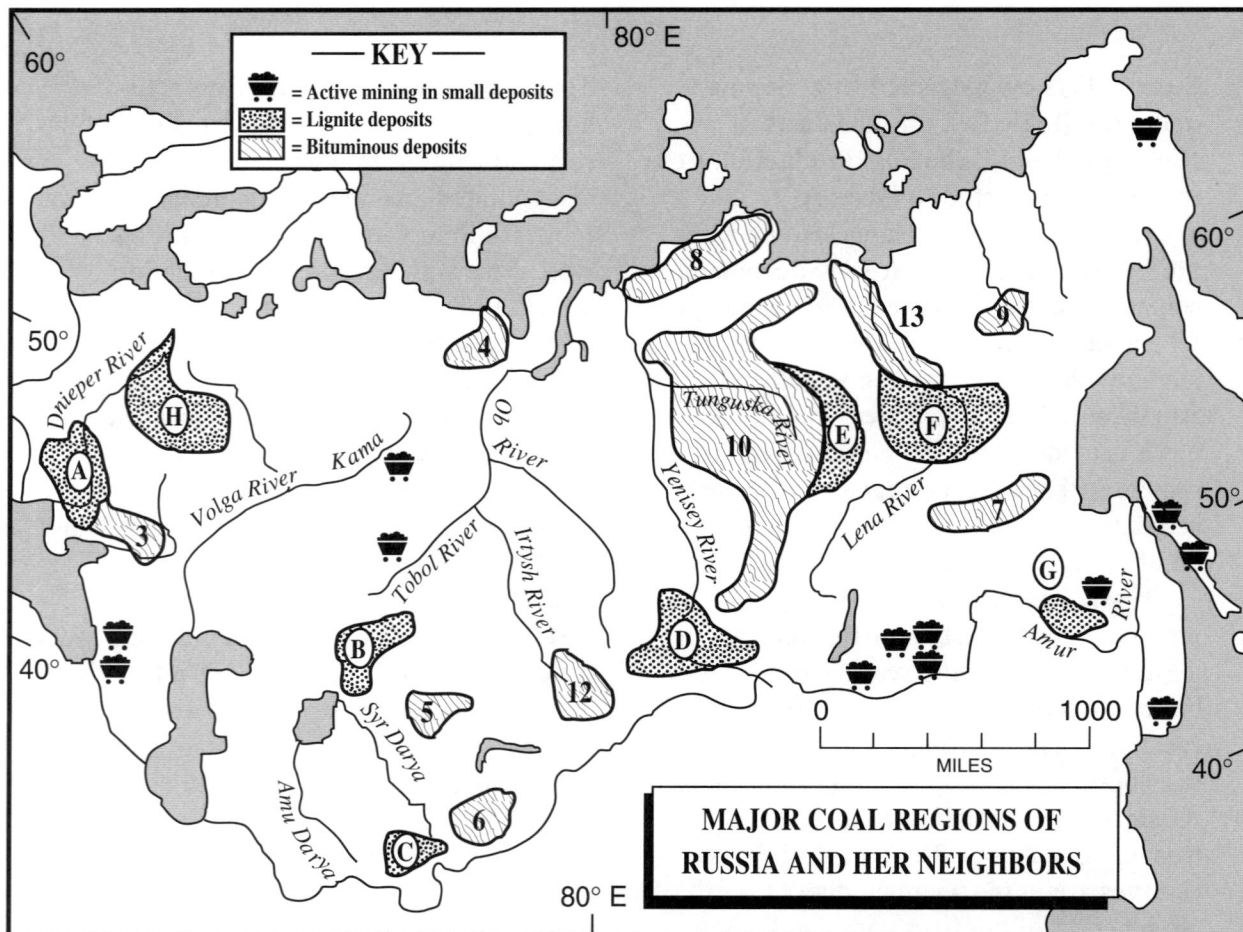

MAP 22   Major coal regions

Lignite Deposits: A. Dnieper Basin   B. Turgay Basin   C. Pamir Foothills   D. East Kuznetsk
E. East Tunguska   F. Lena Basin   G. Middle Amur   H. Moscow Basin

Bituminous Deposits: 3. Donetsk Basin   4. Pechora Basin   5. Karaganda   6. Kyrgyz Piedmont
7. South Yakuts Basin   8. Taymyr Basin   9. Zyryanka Basin   10. Tunguska Basin
12. Kuznetsk Basin   13. Lower Lena Valley

effort to obtain the oil associated with the gas. Much of this flaring occurs because people want the oil but not the gas. There are no facilities to capture the gas. Building gas treatment plants near the oil fields should eventually correct the problem.

Russia has expanded its capabilities to produce natural gas by-products such as propane, butane, sulfur and stable condensate. These products are useful to the petrochemical industry as well as for fuel. A large sulfur removing plant at Orenburg has helped to eliminate one of the basic environmental problems associated with burning gas - the creation of acid rain.

Twelve natural gas pipelines and five major oil pipelines transport fuels from Western Siberia to European systems. Pipelines are laid from October through May when the ground is frozen. After May, the ground thaws and becomes swampy. Pipelines are usually repaired during winter.

Oil and gas are convenient fuels. They are easily transported and leave little residue behind after combustion. But coal is heavy to extract and transport, and it leaves ashes behind after combustion. Coal, although hard on the environment, is the cornerstone of the Russian economy. It fuels the electric industry and the iron and steel industry.

There are many coal reserves in Russia and the Near Abroad. Highly desirable bituminous coal is found in the Kuznetsk basin, Tunguska basin east of the Yenisey, along the lower Lena River, in the Pechora basin and around Irkutsk. Bituminous reserves are also found in the Donetsk basin of Ukraine and in the Karaganda (Quaragandy) basin of Kazakhstan.

Less desirable but highly usable brown coal, or lignite, is found in large reserves south of Moscow, in the Yakutsk basin of the great bend in the Lena River, and along the TSR from Krasnoyarsk to Angarsk. Large lignite deposits are also found in Ukraine from Kiev to the Donetsk basin, around the foothills of the Pamirs in Tajikistan and in the Turgay basin of northern Kazakstan.

Russia exports much coking coal to Japan. Japan, with superior strip mining technology, is exploiting large Siberian reserves north of the middle Amur River, near the town of Neryungri.

A major problem in the coal fields is the shortage of labor. Few miners recommend the profession; the work is hard and dangerous and the rewards small. Lack of transportation facilities is another problem. Some railroad cars wait on sidings for six months before moving. A capitalist market economy would help solve these problems.

Coal seams are being mined at greater depths in the mines and the outlets from the mines are further away from the point of extraction. This necessitates long distance transmission of electricity from power stations to water pumping facilities deep inside the mines. This also increases the waste of time and energy in getting the coal to the surface. Siberian mines need a complete overhaul of equipment and management.

About 80 percent of the coking coal used in Russian industry is produced in the Kuznetsk basin. Most of the rest is produced on the Arctic shores of Pechora. The Donetsk basin in Ukraine is the largest producer of coking coal in the world, out-producing the Kuznetsk by about 15 million tons a year. The Karaganda coking coal production of Kazakhstan is about a third that of Kuznetsk. Most of the Karaganda coal is shipped to industries in the Ural Mountains. Bituminous coal of Donetsk, Pechora, Karaganda and Kuznetsk is all mined underground.

Russia has its nuclear generating capacity up to approximately six percent of the total electrical energy production. The country has extensive deposits of uranium and lesser deposits of thorium, the major nuclear fuels. These deposits are of two types, intrusive igneous deposits associated with metamorphic rock and hydrothermal deposits emplaced in sedimentary rock.

There are at least ten uranium-thorium deposits in Russia and twenty in the other former Soviet republics. The largest deposits are found north of the Pamir and Tien Shan mountains in the Fergana Valley and environs. A large deposit and processing center is located near Dnipropetrovsk in Ukraine. Large uranium enrichment facilities are located at Tomsk and Yekaterinburg. Plutonium production facilities are located at Tomsk, Krasnoyarsk and Chelyabinsk. In 1994 a plutonium tank exploded at the facilities in Tomsk creating serious environmental and health problems.

The biggest nuclear power plants producing electricity are located at St. Petersburg where there are four units in operation, the Kola peninsula with three units, Novovorenezhskiy on the Don river with five units, Kursk with three units, and

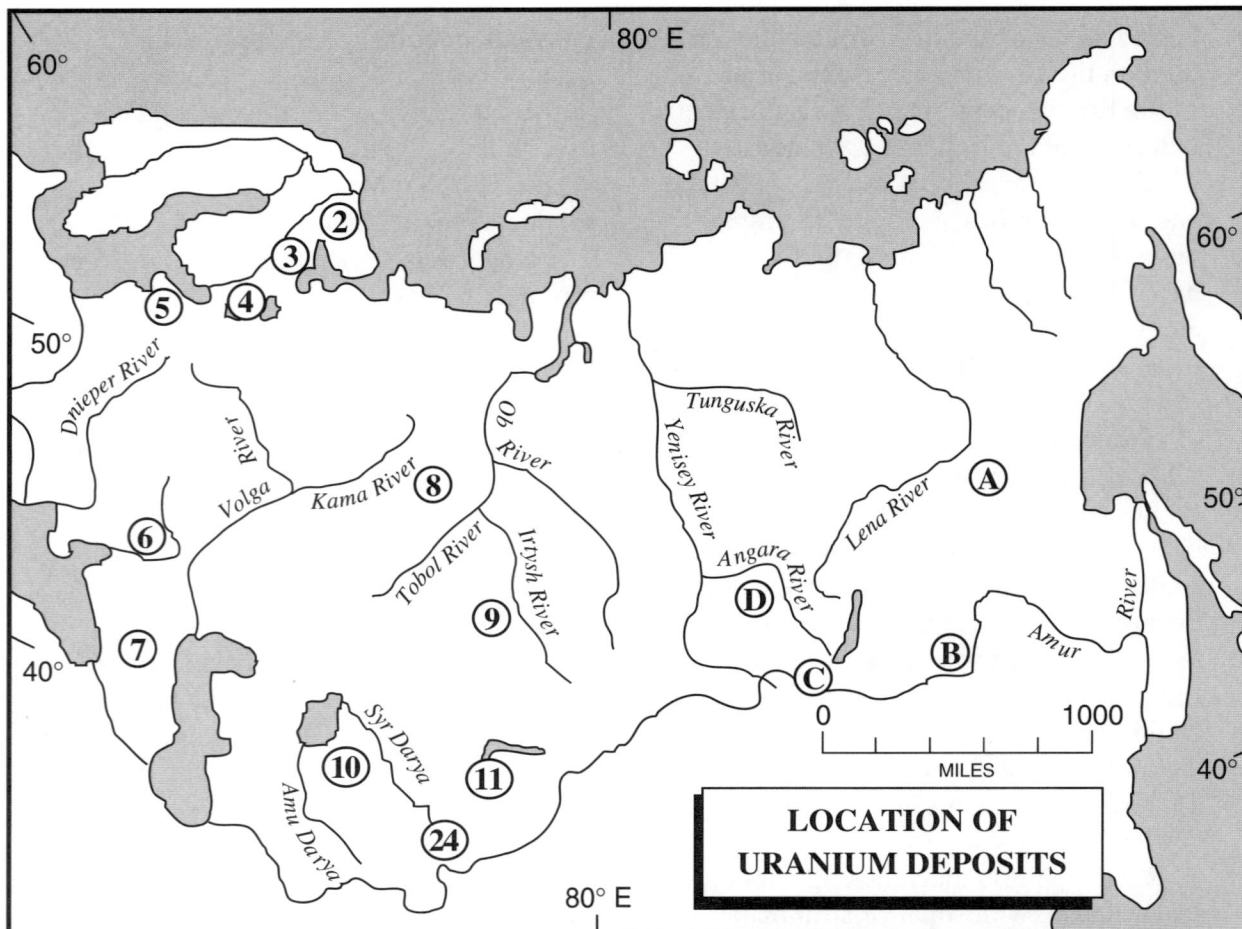

MAP 23   Location of uranium deposits

A. Aldan Plateau   B. Upper Amur Basin   C. Lake Baikal   D. Bratsk -with some thorium
2. Kola Peninsula -with some thorium   3. Chupa Karelia   4. Lake Onega   5. Gulf of Finland
6. Donbas   7. North Caucasus   8. Urals -2 mines   9. Middle Irtysh River Plateau
10. Kyzyl Kum Desert   11. Lake Balgash -2 mines
24. Foothills and Piedmont of Pamirs -11 mines, 5 processing centers

Uranium is found in association with other minerals such as iron ore, vanadium, phosphate rock, copper, lignite, gold and rare earths.

Beloyarskiy in the western Urals with three units. Ukraine has one unit at South Ukraine near Donetsk, two units at Rovno in the west and three units still operating at Chornobyl. One unit at Chornobyl was destroyed in the 1986 explosion. There are also two units operating on the outskirts of Yerevan in Armenia.

There are eight more units under construction in several major cities, notably Rostov, Kazan, Balakova, Kostroma and Nizhny Novgorod. Ukraine has units under construction in the Crimea, at Khmelnitskiy and at Odesa.

About 75 percent of Russia's electric power comes from thermal sources. Nuclear power accounts for six percent and hydroelectric power about 18 percent. Just about every major city in Russia and the Near Abroad has a thermal electric power

20-1 Laying gas pipeline in Siberia.

station. These burn coal, oil, peat and wood.

Despite the fact that Russia has tremendous hydroelectric potential there are serious drawbacks. Hydropower stations are expensive to build although their actual operation is cheap.

Russian engineering in the hydroelectric industry is legendary. They have built plants not only in Russia but around the world.

Large hydroelectric installations exist at Krasnoyarsk and Sayan-Shushenskoye on the Yenisey River, at Ust-Ilimsk, Bratsk, and Boguchany on the Angara River, at Tolyatti and Volgograd on the Volga River. Large installations of lesser production are at Votkinsk on the Kama River and at Zeya on the Zeya River. Stations are under construction at Bureya on the Amur, Zagorsk and Cheboksary on the Upper Volga.

Large hydropower stations are also found at Zaporozhye on the Dnieper of Ukraine, Inguri in Georgia, Chirkey in Dagestan, at Toktogul in Kyrgyzstan and at Nurek and Rogun in Tajikistan. The installation at Rogun has the highest dam in the world and the one at Nurek has the second highest. These two are fed by streams flowing down the Pamir Mountains.

Russia has large reserves of oil shale rock which has been a vital source of fuel in some areas. Although Russia leads the world in the exploitation of oil shales, it is a minor energy resource when compared to oil, natural gas and coal.

Major Russian oil shale deposits are found along the Volga River around Syzran and in Siberia north of Irkutsk. Smaller deposits are found on the Ob River in the north and along the Lena at Olenek.

20-2 The nuclear complex at Chornobyl, Ukraine.

Estonia has a sizable oil shale deposit which is its major mineral resource. The fuel is used in thermal electric plants, industrial furnaces and to drive locomotives. Most of the Estonian fuel is used at Narva and Tallinn to produce electricity.

Modest deposits of oil shales are found along the Dnieper River south of Kiev but these have not been adequately exploited. There are also deposits about one hundred miles northeast of the Caspian Sea.

Russia has large deposits of tar sands. These sands are found beneath the surface at depths of 600 to 1200 feet and heavy oil is recovered by heating the seams which are 6 to 15 feet thick. This heavy fluid is used to make grease, lubricants and heavy oils. Tar sands are found in the Volga River area,

Pechora Basin, Caucasus Mountains, the Fergana Valley, the north coast of the Caspian Sea and south of the Siberian Arctic. The Siberian sands will probably be held in reserve, at least for the foreseeable future.

Intensive use of peat for fuel occurred between Moscow and the Volga in the past. Today peat is still used but it is of minor importance. However, Belarus depends on peat for its major industries. Wood is also used for fuel, especially by rural people north of the Volga, from St. Petersburg to the Urals.

At a Krasnoyarsk demonstration plant synthetic liquid fuel is made from wood This experiment has been so successful that plants are being constructed in other parts of Siberia to utilize wood chips in the production of synfuels.

Russians have been experimenting for years with tidal power in the Sea of Okhotsk and the narrow inlet between the White and Barents seas. The French, who are the leaders in tidal power, constructed a tidal power station on the north slope of the Kola Peninsula which ties its power into the entire Kola grid. This is the only station in operation. Twenty such plants were slated to be constructed, but given the state of the Russian economy these may never be built. One future project requires the construction of a series of dams across the White Sea neck where tides rise more than 20 feet.

Russia has the greatest energy reserves in the world. She is already exporting fossil fuels for hard currency. But extraction methods and transporting systems are outdated. Renovation is necessary if Russians are to be competitive in the international marketplace.

Most of the inefficient power plants in the remote areas will have to be discontinued, and electric transmission lines will be needed to replace them. It is still feasible to build power plants in very remote, but highly productive areas such as Norilsk in the Lower Yenisey valley, above the Arctic Circle. Norilsk is an important copper, nickel and platinum mining center. It has three large power plants: two are thermal and run by natural gas, and one is hydro from a station at Snezhnogorsk further up the Yenisey. Norilsk is on a small tributary of the Yenisey.

Russia is handicapped by vast distances which separate the major population centers from the fossil fuel deposits. Efficiency in transportation is a major priority of Russia's energy industry.

When new industries develop, they are most likely to be located in the areas of old industry. These areas have the buildings already in place, the trained technical and labor force, as well as transportation routes, housing and food systems.

Russia is the leader in reserves of many metals, Russian policies can affect world metal prices. In 1992, Russian aluminum producers sold large inventories at 50 percent of the common world price. As a result, aluminum, which sold at 93 cents a pound in 1990, fell to 58 cents a pound in 1993. World aluminum companies suffered huge losses. By 1996, the effect of Russian aluminum unloading had stabilized and world aluminum prices moved upward once again.

The Oil Dilemma

Russia's oil companies have old equipment, bad management and refineries that are underperforming. No one has been able to identify the owners of the big companies but organized crime seems to be involved. The potential for enormous wealth is there.

Russia's laws are making western investors uneasy. These are "bizarre" tax liabilities and social welfare obligations. Oil companies are required to manage apartment buildings for their workers.

Russian spokesmen claim the oil reserves of each of their six biggest companies exceed those of the Shell Group which has the largest reserves of any private oil company at 8.6 billion barrels.

When crude oil is sold in Russia it must be 60% of the world price. It would be more profitable to export oil but the export tax negates this option. The export tax varies with the success of the company.

Despite the drawbacks many American companies have taken partnerships with Russian companies. These include Exxon, Texaco, Amoco, Conoco and Atlantic Richfield. Japanese companies are investing heavily in Sakhalin Island oil reserves.

21. ECONOMIC CONDITIONS IN RUSSIA

by Baher Ghosheh

Ironically, one of the major drawbacks of the Soviet system resulted from one of its most attractive features : guaranteed employment. Since the government provided employment to all able citizens, many were assigned to farms or factories where their labor was not needed. This resulted in disguised unemployment and underemployment. Since salaries were set by the government, workers had no incentive to work harder since their compensation would not change regardless of their productivity. This eventually transformed into low levels of productivity. Wages covered only the most basic needs.

Another major problem was the system's emphasis on quotas. Factories and farms sought to meet these quantitative numerical mandates without regard to quality of production. By the mid 1980s, eighty percent of Russia's industrial products failed to meet internationally accepted quality standards.

Gorbachev Reforms

Recognizing the short-comings of the state-run economy, Gorbachev set reforms in motion. Economic liberalization sought to tackle the problems of low productivity, shoddy products and the low standards of living. Towards that end, Gorbachev initiated reforms that encouraged productivity by providing incentives to industrial workers, farmers and managers. The results were apparent especially in agriculture where the government began leasing land to private farmers. Whereas the farmers did not own the land, they could keep a share of the surplus production and thus increased their earnings. This presented the Soviets with the possibility of reducing its dependence on imported grains. By 1989, the results were astonishing as private farms which accounted for a mere three percent of the tilled land produced thirty percent of total agricultural output. Private land produced fourteen times more food than state-run farms.

Gorbachev economic reforms were accompanied by political liberalization throughout the European Communist Bloc. By 1990, the political and economic ties between the Soviet Union and its partners weakened as the Eastern allies pursued closer ties with Western Europe. The fall of the Berlin Wall and closer unification between East and West Germany began the disintegration of the European communist alliances. Ultimately, rising nationalism with the non-Russian republics resulted in the collapse of the Soviet Union.

The break-up of the Soviet Union combined with economic liberalization resulted in major economic disruptions. The following are the most notable problems facing Russia and the Near Abroad at this time.

Problems of Supply

The Soviet economic system created a state of **"Forced Interdependence"** among the Soviet Republics. Within any one industry, inputs were required from different sources. Consequently when the republics became independent, industrial output drastically declined as shortages of inputs became prevalent. A major dispute erupted in 1991 as Ukraine, fearing food shortages at home, stopped shipments of wheat to Moscow. The Russians countered by curtailing their supply of oil and related products to Ukraine. While Moscow's bakeries faced severe shortages of wheat, Ukraine's airports were practically shut down as jet fuel ran out.

Trade Problems

As national economic interests replaced Communist camaraderie, trade problems became commonplace. In the past, Russia and the rest of the soviets traded with each other as well as distant like-minded countries. This spirit of assistance had little regard for profits and market forces. For years, the Soviet Union provided oil well below the international market price to its European allies. Much of the Communist trade took the form of **barter**, the exchange of goods and services for other goods or services. Today, all expect cash for their products and all want the highly prized hard currencies (U.S. dollars, German Marks, French Francs, Japanese Yen). Since the newly formed countries did not have significant reserves of these hard currencies, their trade levels quickly declined. Major disputes erupted over the form of payment among the former communist allies.

Even when these countries agreed to continue to use barter in doing business, questions arose as to the true value of each commodity. Furthermore, most of the newly independent republics sought to establish trade links with Western countries as a means of reducing their dependence on Russia, which some perceived as their former patron, dominator or colonial power.

Russians have employed barter in their trade with the United States, China and other countries. Russia had significant gold reserves which it traded away in exchange for desperately needed food products. Some surprising trade deals involved exchanging Russian vodka for American computers and a Russian nuclear power plant for Chinese rice.

Foreign Currencies

Economic liberalization allows Russians to make transactions in foreign currencies.

Under the Soviets, the ruble was the only currency citizens could use. The government strictly regulated the exchange of rubles for foreign currency and usually set an unrealistically high rate for the ruble vis-a-vis other currencies. Within months of relaxing currency controls, the ruble's value started a downward spiral that continues today.

Ruble vs. U.S. Dollar Exchange Rate
Rubles to one U.S. Dollar

1991	0.8 R
1992	140 R
1993	600 R
1994	3000 R
1995	5000 R
1996	6000 R

Source: Wall Street Journal, USA Today, U.S. News and World Report.

Clearly the table demonstrates, high inflation combined with the deteriorating value of the ruble led to impoverishment of many Russians. Hardest hit were Russian retirees who saw inflation eat away their life savings. Many had to sell their jewelry, house-hold furnishing and anything of value to make ends meet. The percentage of Russians living in poverty climbed from two percent in the 1980s to an estimated forty percent in 1996. Inflation continues today.

Rising Unemployment

The Soviet job security vanished with economic liberalization. Companies, factories and farms must pay attention to the "bottom line." Privatization has led to down-sizing as businesses try to minimize production costs. Official unemployment rates were reported at zero in 1991. Today, economists estimate the rate at about thirteen percent. Moreover, as government subsidies dry up and industries face tremendous difficulties, many of the remaining workers often go for months without pay. As of February 1996, coal miners and school teachers were owed wages for five months.

Widening Disparities

The economic opening allowed foreign investment to enter Russia and relaxed trade controls as regions gained more autonomy. For few Russians, this provided unprecedented opportunities. This selected few cashed in, legally and illegally, from the new found partnerships. Whereas the majority of Russians face extreme difficulty putting food on the table, the emerging elite drive fancy imported cars, wear elegant suits and spend on a dinner more than what the average Russian earns in a month.

The Brain Drain

The worsening economic situation within Russia drove millions of the well educated, highly skilled Russians to flee the country. Between 1990 and 1995 an estimated five million Russians emigrated to Western Europe, the United States, Israel and other countries that provided them with the promise of a better life. The emigrants included large numbers of scientists, doctors, engineers and other professionals.

Demographic Implosion

With Russians facing severe hardships and uncertain futures, many have stopped having children. Fertility rate, the number of children born to each woman, dropped from an average of 2.2 in 1989 to about 1.4 in 1995. Russia's population is shrinking at an alarming rate. In 1994 population decreased by 800,000 as deaths exceeded births. More alarming is the rapid deterioration of life expectancy as the average adult male now can expect to live sixty years, a level that is lower than life expectancy in South East Asia and parts of Africa. Between 1990 and 1993, Russia's birth rate (birth per 1,000 people) declined

from 14 to 9 while death rates increased from 12 to 14. By 1996 the official figures were 13 births per thousand and 11 deaths. The latest figures are the result of higher fertility rates among non-Russians. The crude birth rate for ethnic Russians in 1996 was 9 per thousand while the death rate was 14. Even at these levels the Russian population will not increase in the foreseeable future.

Health, Education and Social Services

The plummeting life expectancy, the rising rate of infant mortality and the diminishing levels of food intake are symptoms of the collapsed Soviet system. Many hospitals in Russia do not have adequate funding to replenish their supplies of medicine, purchase new equipment or even pay their health providers. The haves can still receive good health services in private hospitals and clinics. The vast majority of Russians however, go to state hospitals where everything is in short supply.

Alcoholism

Russia has historically had a serious problem with alcoholism. Heavy Drinking translates into billions of dollars in lost productivity. It also contributes to the plummeting life span of Russians. President Gorbachev attempted to deal with this problem by restricting the number of hours bars can operate and by imposing stiff penalties on employees who drink on the job. Those efforts however met with little success. Vodka, Russia's favorite drink, remains relatively cheap primarily because of government subsidies. Indeed vodka is **cheaper** than bottled water in Russia. One cannot help but wonder if the Russians drink heavily to cope with the harsh realities of life or whether their heavy drinking is the cause of their deteriorating standards of living. Although both conclusions are not mutually exclusive, the former seems to hold more credibility.

Rising Crime

The iron fist policies of communism kept crime at very low rates. Unfortunately, as central government control was relaxed, organized crime groups flourished in Russia. Russians today have to deal with sky rocketing crime rates. Murder, prostitution and theft is commonplace. The number of thefts in Russia increased by 400 percent between 1988 and 1992. Crime is fueled by both official corruption and the deteriorating standards of living. In March 1996, there were more than 4,000 police officers awaiting trial on charges of corruption.

Some Conclusions

The harsh current economic conditions in Russia resemble those prevalent during the Czar era. The tremendous wealth of the elite contrasted sharply to the miserable conditions of ordinary Russians. A visit to Moscow Armory clearly demonstrates the extravagant and ostentatious lifestyle the elite led. Today, disparities between the rich and poor are alarming.

One wonders what the future holds for this great nation that faces political instability and economic collapse. Ethnic rivalries can easily be stirred up in hard times and as each group or republic looks after its interests at the expense of collective well being of the commonwealth, the seeds of future conflicts are sown. The rising tide of nationalism within Russia and the newly independent states around it combined with economic problems associated with the collapse of communism and the human tragedies of ethnic purification policies undertaken by some new independent states can easily be exploited by radical political forces.

The 1995 elections for the Russian Parliament's lower house (DUMA) clearly revealed the deep seated resentment a suffering Russian populace has for the government that enacted the economic reforms. The Communist Party won the largest number of seats and was followed by the Nationalist Block. The Reform parties failed miserably at the polls. The elections may be a precursor of things to come. The Russians decry their loss of greatness, resent living in poverty and fear, grieve over the disintegration of the Communist empire and fear a second wave of disintegration within Russia itself. Indeed as Chechnya and Tatarstan demonstrated, the twenty eight million nationalities (non-Russians) that live within Russia desire some level of autonomy or total independence.

Some political forces within Russia are already calling for re-establishment, by force if needed, of the Russian/Soviet empire. The resources of other states (republics) could be seen as the key to Russia's economic growth and stability. Pride, greed and misery can unleash a new wave of violence in the former Soviet Union. The potential for another "Yugoslavia" at a much greater magnitude, cannot be underestimated. Whereas all seem to agree that things have to get worse before they get better, the world community must help Russia in this most difficult transition period. The price of inaction will be far greater for all. A second Communist revolution is indeed in the realm of the possible.

One of the bright spots in the Russian economy is the creation of a western style banking system. The Russian central bank has started to lend money to commercial banks and set interest rates which is a big step toward a stable economy. Strong support from the central bank will help to stabilize the ruble and hold inflation to an acceptable level.

22. RUSSIA IN THE 21st CENTURY

By Bonnie Henderson

As the new century dawns, scholars have already identified several trends that are shaping the 21st century: a world wide population explosion, revolutions in communications and finance, the rising power of multinational corporations that are increasingly operating independently of national governments, a second high-tech Industrial Revolution involving new technologies like robotics and genetic engineering, increasing dangers to the natural environment, the emergence of a "borderless world" in which trading partners are more important than military alliances, and the geopolitical phenomenon of new smaller countries replacing some of the old nation states.

The next century will be the consumer-driven information age. How will Russia and the Near Abroad, still so backward when compared to the United States, Northern Europe, and Japan fare in this brave new world?

It is now recognized that the old Russian Empire was probably the worst possible place to try to create a Marxist society. Czarist Russia was a multi-ethnic culture based on peasant agriculture and industrially backward. Imperial Russia was some 30 to 50 years behind the advanced Western nations. The government was an antiquated autocracy with all power concentrated in the Czar and a few of his ministers. While most of Europe had moved toward democracy Russia was still bound to an archaic medieval system.

When the communists came to power they were faced with two impossible tasks - - trying to establish a Marxist society while simultaneously trying to modernize an agrarian peasant economy. Seventy years of heavy industrialization and collectivized

agriculture did produce an initial economic boom, at least statistically, but the final result was a technologically backward, depressed economy that subsequently produced a negative Gross National Product (Graph 1).

It was the Soviet consumer who suffered the most. Even during the "boom" years the Soviet Union was never a consumer oriented society. Between 1929 and 1931 only 5 percent of imports were consumer goods. In 1940 the standard of living was lower than it had been in 1928 or even in 1913, four years before the Revolution. Consumer goods remained scarce right up to the dissolution of the Soviet Union in 1991.

Although the full extent of the Soviet Union's economic collapse was kept hidden from the West, the downturn became evident about 1976 in the waning years of the Brezhnev era. During the 1970s the Soviet Union became dependent on grain imports from the West. The cost of raw materials, especially oil, began to rise. In 1979 and 1980 GNP growth was little more than 2 percent. Industrial production declined to about 3 percent between 1975 and 1980. Agricultural output also fell, ending up the decade with a growth rate of about 2 percent. Per capita income declined to 2.6 percent per year in the second half of the 1970s.

During the 1970s hardships that had characterized Soviet life could no longer be hidden: declining health, an increase in the mortality rate, the low quality of consumer products, and the long lines to buy scarce goods. Stories filtered back to the West: the man who stood in line for ninety minutes to buy four pineapples, a woman who waited three and a half hours to buy

SOVIET GNP
Decline in Rate of Growth

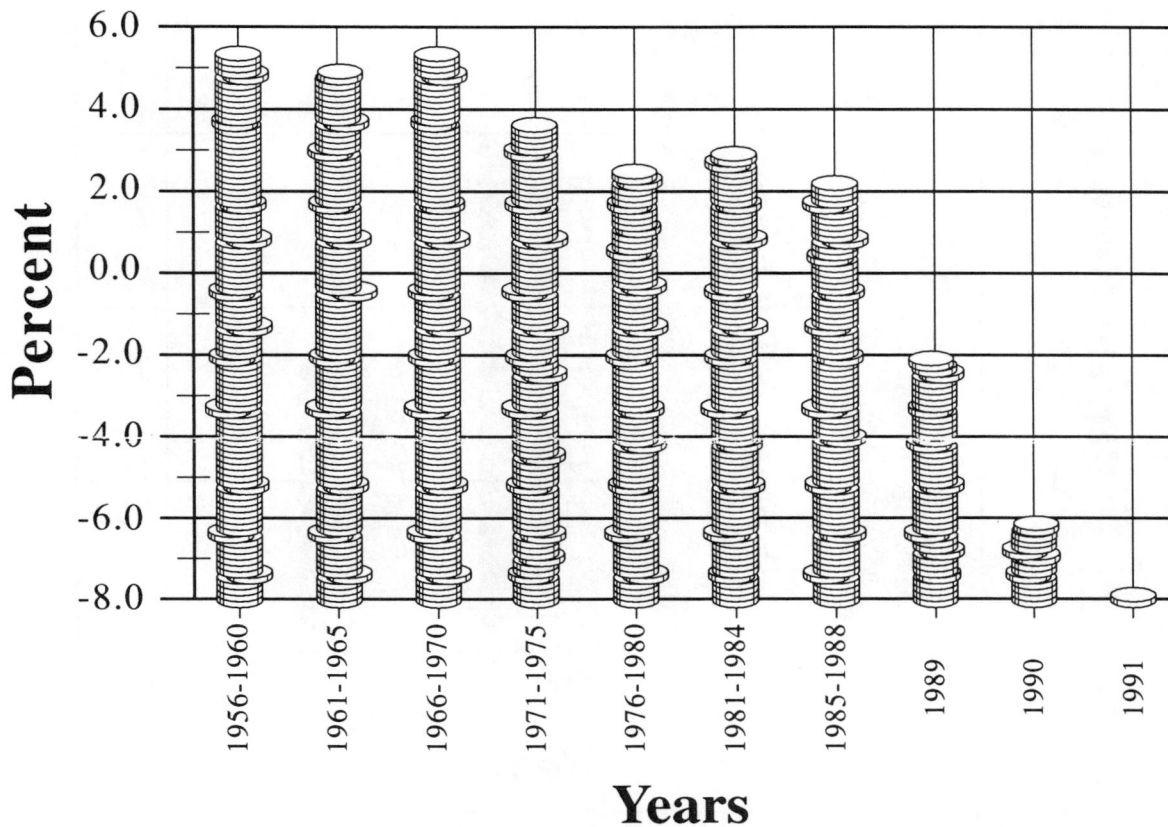

GRAPH 1 — Trends in the Soviet Gross National Product for thirty five years.
(Graph data is modified from Kennedy 1993 : 231 and Howe 1985 : 461)

three cabbages, an eighteen hour wait to sign up to buy a carpet at a future date.

After Josef Stalin came to power in 1927 he began a push toward rapid, heavy industrialization of the old agrarian economy. This was made possible by a plentiful supply of labor (both willing and unwilling), cheap energy, and almost unlimited raw materials. Then came the post World War II reconstruction period of the late 1940s and 1950s. Central planning and the setting of "targets" produced a heavy industry economy replete with iron and steel, cement, locomotives, machine tools, textiles, and tractors. Consumers and

the environment were ignored. The only people who prospered were the mafia-like bureaucrats and the military who got the lion's share of the factories, machine tools, and skilled workers. In addition, almost all scientific research and development went to the military. By the 1950s, 13 percent of the GNP was going to the military agenda. The result was a militarized economy which lasted until the end of the Soviet Union. (The United States experienced a negative GNP, -0.5%, in 1991 due to heavy defense spending).

During the 1960s the world economy began to change. Instead of emphasizing

The "Long Cycle" of the Soviet Economy

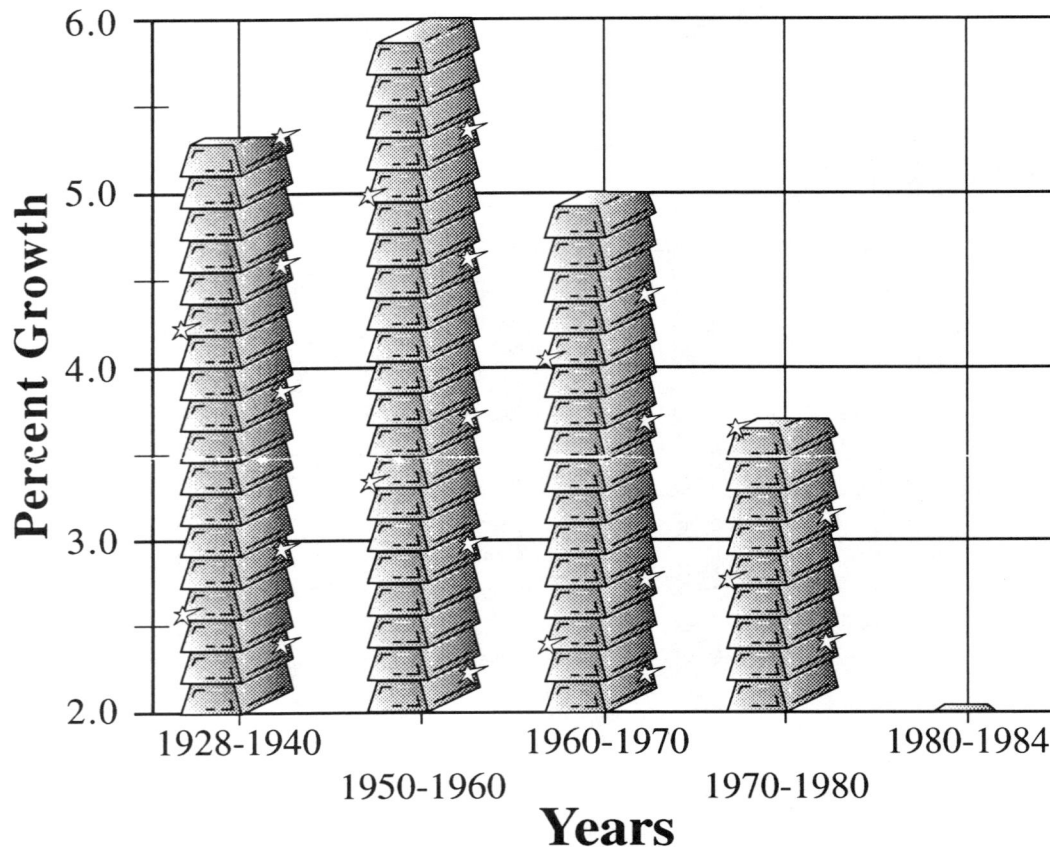

GRAPH 2 — The "Long Cycle" of decline in the Soviet Economy. The highest economic growth was experienced immediately after World War II.
(Graph data is modified from Kennedy 1993 : 231)

heavy industry, there was a shift to high tech consumer oriented goods: electronics, pharmaceuticals, automobiles, communications, and, most importantly, computers. The Soviet Union, with her tight police state, central planning, censorship, party controls, government monopoly, and ideology above all else, was left behind. Instead of modernizing her old industries, updating her infrastructure, reducing government subsidies, and decreasing military spending, the leadership looked inward and actually **increased** government subsidizing and military spending. The result was a moribund economy; trapped in a "long cycle" (Graph 2), and hopelessly tied to a 1930s style heavy industry economy. The Soviet Union was a superpower with a poverty base -- "Upper Volta with missiles".

Another problem was the very nature of the Soviet Empire itself. Instead of benefiting economically from her vast empire, the Soviet Union actually lost money on her satellite states. The Soviet Union supplied Eastern Europe with raw materials, especially fuels, at prices considerably below the world market value. For example, in 1980 Poland imported oil from the Soviet Union at half the world price. Subsidizing Eastern Europe cost the Soviets $5.8 billion from 1974 to 1978, $10.4 billion in 1979, and $21.7 billion in 1980. In 1980 The Soviets spent an estimated $4 to $5 billion on Poland alone, trying to prop up the Polish communist regime.

The Soviets also spent $3 to $5 billion annually on Cuba in order to keep Fidel Castro in power. Another Soviet sphere was parts of Africa where huge sums were also spent, particularly in Angola. All of this spending and subsidizing occurred during a time when the Soviet Union's own GNP had been steadily declining while her military spending kept increasing.

As the Soviet economy fell further and further behind, the Soviet people became more and more disillusioned, cynical, and apathetic. Alcoholism was (and still is) rampant. Wages became virtually meaningless because there was nothing to buy. "We pretend to work and they pretend to pay us," went the old joke. Workers, like the corrupt system itself, became increasingly inefficient.

Thus *perestroika* was born -- to free the hapless Soviet economy and to reduce the level of bribery, patronage, and corruption. In 1989 Mikhail Gorbachev announced he was cutting defense spending by 14.2 percent. He also began pulling troops out of Afghanistan, Hungary, and (then) East Germany. He warned there would be "unpopular, probably tough and even painful measures" ahead, and he hinted at wage controls and rationing. Tough measures were necessary, said Soviet economist Nikolai Shmelev, "or in two to three years there will be complete destruction of the consumer market."

But *perestroika* and *glasnost* could not save the wrecked economy, and the Soviet Empire started unraveling. On August 19,

1991, one day before he was to sign a treaty that would have granted virtual sovereignty to the republics, Gorbachev was seized during a coup attempt. Boris Yeltsin, the first democratically elected president of the Russian Republic, climbed upon a T-72 tank and declared the coup "reactionary and unconstitutional". Yeltsin emerged not only as a political leader but also as a leader of the economic reform movement. The reformers were determined to bring their country into the 20th century.

Their economic "shock therapy" was both bewildering and painful to the Russian people, particularly the old people who had to rely on their meager government pensions. Plunging from a centrally planned to a free-market economy resulted in hyperinflation and high unemployment with subsequent social unrest. The ruble's value plummeted (In July, 1996 the exchange rate was 5200 rubles for $1 U.S.). People who have them use American dollars, the preferred currency. Others use barter. More consumer goods are still traded rather than purchased. Russia still has no bond market nor other financial institutions through which she can borrow funds and raise cash. The creation of a federal bank will help. The banking system and stock markets are still in their infancies.

Given all her historical and current problems it is hard to see how Russia can enter the 21st century economy of robotics, biotechnology, lasers, optics, and telecommunications. A prerequisite for participating in this economy is the firm foundation of a computer based industry. But computers were an anathema to the Soviet regime who looked with hostility upon the free flow of information created by computers. Thus in 1987 there were only 100,000 personal computers in Russia compared to 5 million in the United States. In 1996 there were more than a half million personal computers in Russia. Russia's lack of modern telecommunications is one of the greatest obstacles to her transition to a market economy.

Right now Russia needs a lot of foreign capital as well as foreign expertise. The work force also needs extensive retraining. Another problem is the rapid invention and appearance of ever faster, ever more sophisticated computers in Japan and the West, making it that much harder for Russia to catch up.

Although pockets of prosperity are starting to appear, the average Russian's standard of living is low compared to the west and life is such a daily grind to make ends meet that it will be hard for such a society to transform itself. Even if the current economic reforms continue and catastrophe is averted, it will probably take Russia another decade or two just to be where North America, Western Europe, and Japan are **now.** The Russian people could end up paying for their 70 years of communism well into the 21st century.

The biggest problem with Russia's economy in the late 20th century is that it is controlled by what Russians call "Mafia". It is these criminal coalitions who can guarantee safety to people and businesses. Until the government can control the economy and the nature of business the only way free enterprise can succeed is through the criminal cartels.

The Mafia guarantees a supply of raw materials to industries, safe transportation and distribution of finished products and acceptance of a business at regional levels. Leaders of most regions are intimately tied into this system for it also guarantees the economic success of the region.

At the next lower level, crime is in the form of robbery, burglary and intimidation. Criminals in well organized groups sell narcotics, stolen raw materials and arms.

Criminals at this level have no allegiances and avoid dealing with local governments.

The lowest level of crime has unorganized criminals dealing in stolen property, murder, robbery and burglary. These criminals are the ones the police most often apprehend, beat up and incarcerate. Basically, the police avoid the upper level criminals because they are often in league with them, especially at the executive level.

Mafia control of the economy is not expected to go away anytime soon especially since they are far more efficient and organized than the government. Many Russians believe this situation will continue for ten to twenty years. A free market economy based on the rule of law is still a long way off and will have to wait until the new century.

Seven decades of collectivized farming created peasants with no incentive to work. Heavy government subsidies did keep food prices low (something Russians dearly miss) but they distorted the economic laws of supply and demand. Food production throughout the Soviet Union was uneven and unreliable (Graph 3). Although private plots accounted for only 10 percent of the arable land, they produced 40 percent of the crop and about one third of the livestock products. Before the Revolution Russia had been a food exporter, now she is a heavy importer. Payment for this imported food requires huge outlays of gold and hard currency.

A few innovative Russian farmers are trying to change all this, but they are meeting stiff resistance from the entrenched bureaucracy as well as jealousy from their neighbors who remain in the collectivized mind-set. The Stalinist legacy may take years if not decades to eradicate.

It is possible the biotechnology revolution could relieve some of the

Grain Production in the Soviet Union
1950-1988

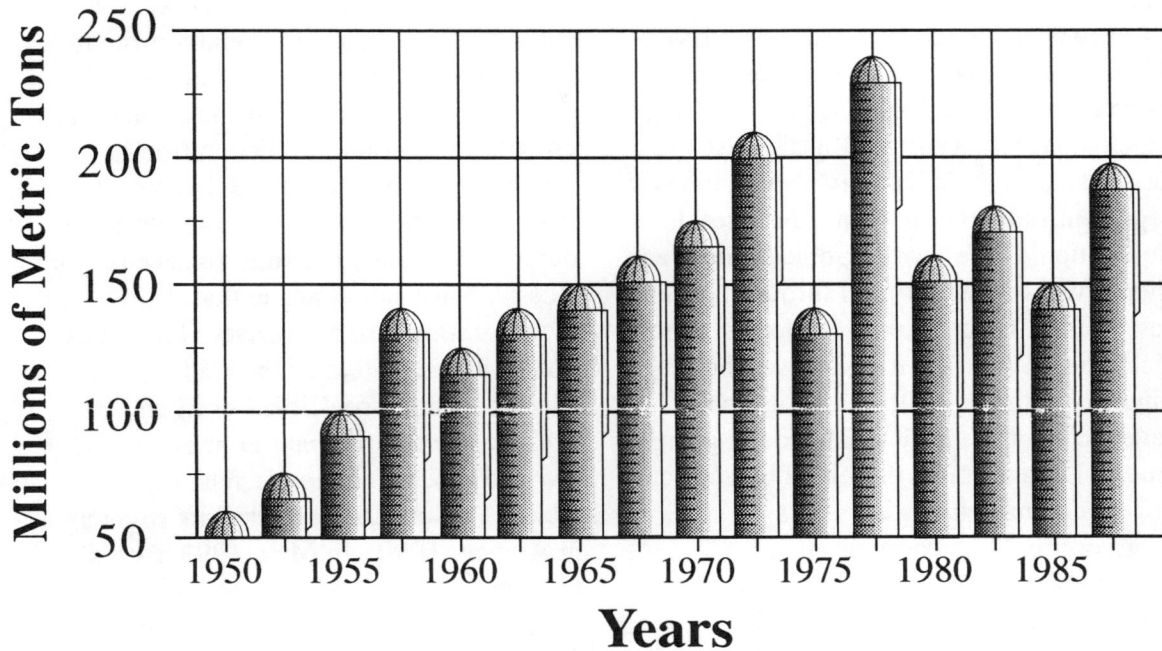

Millions of Metric Tons (y-axis: 50, 100, 150, 200, 250)

Years (x-axis: 1950, 1955, 1960, 1965, 1970, 1975, 1980, 1985)

GRAPH 3 — Soviet Grain Production. In the Last twenty years there has been serious shortages of grain. Russia needs at least 200 million metric tons of grain a year.
(Graph data is modified from Kennedy 1993 : 172 and World Resources)

agricultural problems. Genetically engineered crops that could, say, increase yields in colder northern regions or be made drought resistant in the south could be a godsend. But biotechnology requires modern laboratories, factories, and processing plants as well as highly trained scientists. Also, farming would need to be restructured -- better infrastructure, complete decollectivization, and an end to price supports. There is also the problem of the Russian peasants who make up one quarter of the population. How can they be made to fit in with biotechnology and other modern farming methods?

While the world population is exploding, Russia is actually experiencing a negative population growth. Infant mortality has been rising while life expectancy has been falling. This is due to a number of factors including environmental pollution, a high incidence of alcoholism and smoking, a high abortion rate (the average woman has six), poorly equipped hospitals, a scarcity of medicines, poor sanitation, and crowded substandard housing.

As early as the 1980s experts were noting the alarming trends in Soviet demography: a reduction of the birth rate coupled with an "incredible increase in the death rates beyond all reasonable past projections." (in Kennedy 1993:242). The life expectancy of Muscovites dropped by 10 years between 1970 and 1990. The labor force has been steadily shrinking. In the 1970s 22 million people were added to the labor force, in the 1980s 7.7 million were added, and in the 1990s only 5.7 million are expected to be added.

However, demographic trends are very different in the Near Abroad. The birth rates in the Muslim republics (2.5 -3.5) are much higher than that of Russians (0.7). By 2000 the ethnic Russian population will represent only 46.4 percent of the total population of the former Soviet Union, and then it will continue to fall throughout the rest of the 21st century. For the first time since the Revolution Russians will be a minority -- the so-called "demographic revenge" by the non-Russian ethnic groups. (In the United States there will be no racial nor ethnic majority by 2060).

Every republic contains ethnic minorities from the better known groups like the Ukrainians, Kazakhs, and Belorussians to groups like the Uzbeks, Tatars and Bashkirs. The Russian Federation alone contains over 130 different nationalities.

These groups differ not only in race and language, but also in religion and cultural customs. Many are antagonistic toward one another and some regions have a long history of ethnic turbulence such as the ongoing and bloody conflict between the Armenians and Azerbaijanis. The Soviet police state kept the lid on these simmering ethnic tensions but with the Soviet Union's collapse various ethnic conflicts soon broke out such as the 1992-1993 civil war between the Georgians and Abkhazians. In 1993 Bogdan Szajkowski identified over 204 ethnic/territorial conflicts in the former Soviet Union (in Geography 94/95:28). It is almost certain these conflicts will persist into the 21st century, raising the specter of border wars, perhaps spilling into neighboring countries as well as causing the mass migration of displaced refugees. In the Chechnya conflict which created over

400,000 refugees the first year of fighting, up to 4,000 people a day were leaving Chechnya.

The Russian Federation shows other signs of disintegration. The union republics of Tatarstan and Yakutia-Sakha have drafted their own constitutions. Tatarstan completely ignored the Federation's Constitution. In May, 1993 Tuva amended the Constitution to include its right to self-determination and the right to secede from Russia. Nationalists argue that Tuva's incorporation into the Soviet Union was just as illegal as that of the Baltic states. Bashkortostan proclaimed itself an "independent participant in international law and foreign economic relations" (Ibid:31). Tatarstan declared its sovereignty in August, 1990. In May, 1993 Tatarstan independently signed an economic cooperation agreement with Hungary for 1993-1998. Tyumen, which refused to sign the Federation Treaty in March, 1992, faces secession from two of its districts.

The 1994-1996 war between Russia and break-away Chechnya may be a sign of the problems to come in the future if Russia refuses to allow her republics to secede.

This breaking up of the Russian Federation into smaller autonomous countries is actually following a global trend: "the more democracy, the more countries" (Naisbitt 1994:34). By the beginning of the 21st century, there should be at least 300 nations in the world (compared with about 51 in 1945 and 172 in 1994), and there may be as many as 1000 by the end of the century.

To one degree or another, all of Russia's 21 republics have claimed autonomy, and her 67 smaller jurisdictions are pushing for similar independence. In July, 1993 Sverdlovsk declared itself independent and renamed itself the Urals Republic. Ten days later the Russian Far East (capital Vladivostok) declared itself an independent country. The republic of Karelia has its own parliament, laws, and economic policy. In Georgia's districts of Abkhazia and South Ossestia both want to secede and form their own independent countries.

The Russia of the next century will look entirely different from the Russia we knew in the 20th century.

Another urgent problem that will haunt Russia into the next century is the environmental damage caused by 70 years of Soviet industrial policy. While the nuclear disaster at Chernobyl and the shrinking of the Aral Sea are the best known examples, other environmental problems clamor for attention.

The Russian atmosphere is heavily polluted from carbon and other unrestricted emissions. Some industrial cities are so choked with pollutants the air is a health hazard. Magnitogorsk pollutes an area twice as large as Delaware. The city has a population of about 400,000. After retirement a man can expect to live only three more years. Two thirds of the children and one third of the adults are affected by respiratory diseases. . Four out of ten babies are born with birth defects.

Trees and whole forests are heavily damaged. Hundreds of thousands of acres of Siberian forest have turned into barren wastelands from unrestricted overcutting. Rivers and lakes are poisoned by industrial and chemical waste. Soil and ground water are contaminated from the helter skelter dumping of oil and nuclear waste, and by leaching from overfertilized fields. Soviet schemes to divert rivers for dams and irrigation have caused erosion and silting.

Seventy-five percent of Russia's water is considered too dangerous to drink, and the rest is considered substandard. Children of St. Petersburg suffer from skin allergies believed to be caused by contaminated drinking water from the river Neva. The Volga River has been described as a "turgid stream" (Sweet 1994:30). The Dnestre River, Odesa's source of drinking water, is heavily contaminated with agricultural chemicals. World Bank officials called the Black Sea "one of the world's most polluted bodies of water" (Ibid).

Unsound agricultural practices have contributed their share to the environmental degradation: erosion caused by reckless development of marginal lands, widespread (though illegal) use of DDT, careless use of heavy equipment, and overuse of fertilizers like phosphates, ammonia, nitrites, and chlorinated hydrocarbons.

There is also the worrisome problem of Russia's nuclear wastes caused by the Soviet practice of dumping radioactive wastes and reactors from submarines at sea. Chelyabinsk, a city in the southern Urals, may be the most radioactive spot on Earth because of contamination from its plutonium plant. Cleaning up this environmental mess will cost Russia billions over the next century.

Ironically, Mikhail Gorbachev, the last leader of the old Soviet Union, became president of Green Cross International, an organization formed to protect the Earth's environment. One of Gorbachev's top priorities was the military toxins created by both the Soviet Union and the United States during the Cold War. Russia has Chelyabinsk; the U.S. has the Rocky Mountain Arsenal and Three Mile Island.

As water supplies continue to shrink or suffer from contamination, disputes over water and water rights could exacerbate in the 21st century. A Ministry of Water in Moscow used to allocate water to each Central Asian republic. This department is now abolished and the water agreements no longer stand. Uzbekistan farmers upstream are now taking more than their share of water which means less for those living downstream. Meanwhile, there is still no relief in sight for the shrinking Aral Sea.

Ethnic tensions and disputes over water become even more alarming considering Russia, Ukraine, and Belorussia still have formidable nuclear arsenals. Ukraine, for example, has the world's third largest nuclear arsenal including 1,800 warheads, 176 long-range missiles plus bombers and cruise missiles. In 1995 the United States purchased Kazakhastan's missiles.

American policy toward Russia has not been judged a success. American backed reforms and loyalty to first Gorbachev and then Yeltsin did not make any real improvements in the lives of ordinary Russians. In 1992 inflation was running at 2500 percent, and although it did fall in 1993 it was still an unbearable 900 percent. The ruble has lost 72 percent of its value. Savings and pensions were virtually wiped out. While more goods have appeared in stores they are beyond the financial reach of many Russians. A GM car, for example, cost around $60,000 in 1994, an unimaginable sum to the average Russian who earned $1,112 in 1994. Russians complain that only criminals can afford to enjoy the fruits of capitalism.

Russia's military is increasingly discontented and frustrated. Many of these men have been demobilized but left without jobs or housing. Some observers believe the military is practicing a sort of shadow government. Acting unilaterally, the military intervened in Moldova, Tajikistan, and Georgia. Russian military officials also want to denuclearize Urkraine as soon as possible. In 1993 it was the Russian Defense Ministry, not the Yeltsin government, that announced it wanted a political settlement in the Bosnian War. In July, 1995 Russian military leaders made an agreement with Chechnya military leaders to end the fighting although no agreement

had been reached between the political leaders. Some western experts believe the military will take over in the next century if the politicians cannot bring stability.

President Yeltsin's Prime Minister, the conservative Viktor Chernomyrdin, was the former head of the Soviet Union's natural gas industry. Chernomyrdin was harshly critical of Western advisers who helped the reformers shape their policies. After taking office, he announced an end to the "era of market romanticism". The former military, industrial and agricultural spokesmen do not want socialist-era economic controls dismantled. Western analysts fear the government will increase subsidies to ailing state-owned industries, the same kind of unproductive propping up that was responsible for the Soviet Union's economic "long cycle" in the first place.

Yet for every trend there is a counter trend. Pockets of prosperity started to appear in 1994 as emerging capitalists and entrepreneurs experienced success in the new market economy. In 1994 a survey in *Argumenty I. Fakty*, a popular weekly newspaper, defined between 25 and 30 percent of Russians, about 50 million people, as middle class. In 1994 their monthly salaries were about 500,000 rubles (about $250). Five percent of the population, about nine million people, were in the upper middle-class category, earning more than 500,000 rubles a month. More than 2.5 million earn monthly incomes of $1,000 to $1,500. Russians now make up 80 percent of the customers in Moscow stores, especially supermarkets, which used to cater to foreigners. But other sectors of the economy, particularly the old state-run industries, remain in dire straits.

Some Western investors believe the negatives about Russia have been exaggerated. They believe the Russian economy is recovering, market demand is growing, opportunities abound, and that Russians have more money to spend than official statistics would indicate. These business people see Russia as a huge market that needs basic consumer goods; everything from housing to food processing to soap to shirts. They believe there are business opportunities with immediate growth prospects.

Other investors remain wary; citing the tales of crime, violence, the local mafias, rampant corruption, the shaky ruble, inflation and the fear of financial collapse. Capital flight from Russia ran about $1 billion a month in 1993-95. However, in 1996 inflation was only 18%, a positive sign for the country's future. Nevertheless, in 1996 China attracted 25 times more Western investment than has Russia.

In the 1996 presidential election Russians had a clear choice between voting for the past -- Communist Gennadi Zyuganov or the future -- Democrat and Reformer Boris Yeltsin. The Russian electorate chose Yeltsin by a margin of 13 percentage points. While Yeltsin is far from the ideal democrat or reformer, his victory did show that democracy and a free market are taking root. By the summer of 1996 there were indications that most segments of Russian society were fulfilling their material desires albeit at a modest level.. This probably helped Yeltsin and hurt Zyuganov although the Communist candidate did well in central Russia (the "Red Belt"). Yeltsin did best in the cities and the Far East and Siberia whose independent-minded citizens are forging economic ties with Asia and Alaska.

What these contradictions mean for Russia in the 21st century is unclear. Right now the country is undergoing enormous change and painful transition. But it does seem apparent that American style democracy and a free market economy will not fully materialize until well into the 21st century.

Former republics like Ukraine, Kazakhstan and Georgia will likely increase in international importance. Parts of the Russian Federation itself will continue to act independently of Moscow and may try to break away altogether like Chechnya did. Any western euphoria over the Soviet Union's collapse is being replaced by the hard realities of the new geopolitical diversity in the space that was once the Soviet Empire.

Overall, living standards have improved since 1991. There are products in the markets and people somehow find money to buy them. There is definite growth in a middle class. While pensioners, some rural residents and the indigent are poor there is work and income for those willing to look for it. New businesses in Russia are progressing well and foreign investment is accelerating.

As the taxing bodies have discovered there are no accurate statistics on the business community. The situation encourages hiding rather than disclosing the real financial condition of companies. However, a casual inspection of businesses in larger cities such as Novosibirsk, Tula and Omsk indicate a healthy investment in the future.

Democratic reforms in politics and lower level management directives are becoming law. It is only a matter of time until the old communists are gone and a new breed of politician takes over. The country has become too complex and decentralized for effective control from the top. The Duma will have to assume more power and effectively run the country. In the present political climate, it would be impossible for Russia to return to a dictatorship. There is room for optimism in the New Russia.

Astrakhan cloth synthetic weaving used to resemble the karakul wool hide

BAM Baikal-Amur Mainline, railroad beginning at Tayshet in Siberia and ending at Sovetskaya Gavan on the Tatar Strait.

Belo, Beloye white

Bolshevik means "majority". Name adopted by the radical left wing of the Russian Social Democratic Labor Party. Name used to identify the followers of Lenin who overthrew the Czarist regime.

Bolshoy, Bolshoya large, big

Boyar wealthy merchants, they had much power during the times of Ivan III and Ivan IV

Buran snowstorm

Chernozem fertile black soil, usually associated with steppes

Chyorni derogatary term used by some Russians in reference to people from the Caucasus

C.I.S. Commonwealth of Independent States. An organization made up of eleven republics of the former Soviet Union.

Cold War estranged United States and Soviet relationship after World War II. Fueled by different ideologies: Communism vs capitalism.

Collectivization forced socialization of privately owned farms initiated by Stalin. The seized farms were then reorganized into giant state owned collectives. Initially caused much misery and death for the peasants.

Communism theory of classless and stateless society of workers   and peasants. Proposed by Karl Marx and Frederick Engels.

Czar (Tsar) absolute ruler of Russia before the Soviet Union was created. Russia was ruled for over 300 years by Czars.

Democratization popular participation in the electoral processes.

Duma legislative body, literally "house". The first Duma appeared in 1905. Disintegrated after the Bolshevik Revolution. Reappeared in 1993.

Gangri mountain, peak

Gavan harbor.

Glasnost openness and candor on national issues.

Golden Horde   Mongol state comprising most of Russia during the 13th and 14th centuries.

Gora   mountain.

Gorod (grad) town or settlement.

Gulag prison system of the former Soviet Union where forced labor was practiced and conditions were harsh.

Hanseatic League League a mercantile league of medieval German towns. The system moved into Slavic coastal towns and Novgorod in the 13th century.

Imperial Russia Russia the Russian Empire under the Czars.

Lesostep steppe with wooded areas

Livonian Knights also Livonian Brothers of the Sword. German military and religious order founded in 1202 by Bishop Albert of Livonia (Estonia and Latvia) for the purpose of conquest and Christianization of Baltic Lands.

Karakul breed of sheep, type of lambskin.

Kazaki cossack. Peasant-soldiers first organized in the 15th century.

KGB Committee For State Security, secret police. Originally the NKVD.

Khanate district administered by a local chieftain, emir or khan.

Khrebet mountain range.

Kol, kul lake

Kolkhoz collective farm.

Kombinat industrial complex, an attempt to make a region self sufficient in production.

Komsol Soviet youth organization, Communist Youth League.

Krazno beautiful, red

Khrushevskies hastily built multi-story housing, project started by Khrushchev

Kulaks allegedly prosperous peasant targeted by Stalin.

Kum (Gum) sand, desert

Kustarny cottage industry such as rug weaving.

Leostep wooded steppe

Loess fine textured soil material deposited by wind.

Long cycle the long period of decline in the Soviet economy. The result of government subsidies, collectivization of agriculture, military spending, corrupt bureaucrats, and the obsolete theories of Marxism/Leninism.

Marxism/Leninism economic theory based on the collective (state) ownership of resources and means of production. Competition and the laws of supply and demand were eliminated, and replaced by central planning.

Mensheviks minority, associated with liberalism.

NATO North Atlantic Treaty Organization. Security group of western nations formed to counteract former Soviet and Warsaw Pact threats.

Nagorno plateau

Narodni, Norodniki populist, common people.

Near Abroad term Russians use for the former Soviet republics.

Nizhnii, Nizhniy lower.

Novy, Novaya new.

Oblast large administrative unit in the former Soviet Union, region or province.

Okrug Autonomous area in former Soviet Union , low status administrative unit, part of a kray or oblast.

Ostrov island

Ottepeli temporary warm spell in winter.

Ozero lake

Permafrost frozen soil, top may thaw but bottom remains frozen.

Perestroika restructuring of economy, introducing profit and loss into management.

Podzol ash gray soil, formed beneath trees in cool climates.

Povolzhye general reference meaning "along the Volga".

Proletariat the working class, wage earners

Purga Arctic blizzard.

Rayon lowest status administrative unit in the former Soviet Union

Rasputitsa spring thaw and slush.

Ruble unit of Russian currency.

Russian Federation the organization of post-Soviet Russia, including republics, regions, territories, autonomous areas and federal cities.

Russification an attempt by the Soviets to unify the Union with a common language and culture. Russian, of course.

Serfdom system of political and economic servitude which tied peasants to the land. Serfdom was abolished by Czar Alexander II in 1861.

Sericulture silk enterprises.

Severny northern

Shiite Muslim fundamentalist Muslim, strict code of behavior.

Siberia vast geographical reign of Asian Russia. Comprises the northern third of Asia. An area rich in natural resources.

Sierozem desert soils.

Socialism state management of agriculture and industry. Involves a government bureaucracy and the payment of subsidies.

Solonchak saline soils.

Solonets alkali soils.

Sopka volcano

Soviet Bloc the former Soviet Union and its Warsaw Pact allies.

Sovkhoz state farm.

Steppe dry grassland.

Sukhovey hot, dry wind in the steppes.

Sunni Muslim moderate follower of Islam.

Syelos village.

Taiga (tayga) northern forest, mostly evergreen.

Tamerlane (1336 - 1405) strong Mongol leader who conquered most of Middle Asia and the Caucasus in the 13th century.

Teutonic Knights German military and religious order founded in 1190 during the Third Crusade. Their cities were involved in the Hanseatic League. The Knights held territory in Germany until 1809.

TSR Trans-Siberian Railroad. Built between 1892 and 1905.

Veliki large, upper or great.

Virgin Lands Campaign the cultivation of idle lands and grazing lands. Development of marginal lands under the Soviets.

Warsaw Pact mutual defense treaty signed in 1955 by Albania, Bulgaria, Czechoslovakia, East Germany, Hungary, Poland, Romania and the Soviet Union.

Xerophytic plants adapted to desert conditions.

Yurt felt tent erected on a wooden or pole frame.

Yuzhny (Yugo) south or southern.

Zapovednik nature preserve

Zemlya land, earth.

Appendix II
SELECTED RUSSIAN RULERS OF THE PAST

Year of rule: A.D.

862   Rurik, a Scandinavian, united the Slavic tribes around Novgorod.
972   most of the Slavic tribes moved south to Kiev.
988   Vladimer I, Duke of Kiev, converted to Greek Orthodox.
1019 - 1054 Yaroslav, his daughters married kings of France, Hungary and Norway.
1294 - 1303 Daniel Nevsky, first Duke of Muscovy.
1328 - 1341 Ivan I, known as "Moneybags" was the first to rule from Moscow.
1380   Dmitri Donskoi, Dmitri III, defeated the Tatars.
1462 - 1505 Ivan III, the first to be called Czar.
1547 - 1584 Ivan IV, Ivan the Terrible, conquered much land.
1584 - 1598 Feodor I, the empire was really ruled by Boris Godunov.
1613 - 1645 Michael Romanov became Czar at age 17, the first Romanov.
1682 - 1725 Peter I, Peter the Great, was the 5th Romanov.
1725 - 1727 Catherine I, wife of Peter the Great.
1741 - 1761 Elizabeth, Peter the Great's daughter. Had more than 15,000 dresses.
1762 - 1796 Catherine the Great, Catherine II, She was formerly princess of Anhalt
            Zerbst of Germany.
1801 - 1825 Alexander I, defeated Napoleon.
1825 - 1855 Nicholas I, put down Decemberist Revolt
1855 - 1881 Alexander II, freed the serfs in 1861.
1894 - 1917 Nicholas II, the last Czar, abdicated in 1917.
            He and his family were murdered in Yekaterinburg July 16, 1918.

SOVIET UNION LEADERS

1917 - 1924 Vladimir Lenin, founder of the Soviet Union
1927 - 1953 Josef Stalin, absolute dictator
1953 - 1964 Nikita Khruschchev, started market reforms
1964 - 1982 Leonid Brezhnev, ruled during the "Period of Stagnation."
1985 - 1991 Mikhail Gorbachev, the last leader of the Soviet Union.

RUSSIAN FEDERATION

1991 -   Boris Nicolayevich Yeltsin, the first president popularly elected

LATITUDE AND LONGITUDE OF SELECTED CITIES
The first number is latitude (degrees North), the second is longitude (degrees East),
rounded to nearest whole number.

RUSSIA

Arkangelsk 64 - 40
Astrakhan 46 - 48
Barnaul 53 - 83
Chelyabinsk 55 - 61
Chita 52 - 114
Grozny 43 - 46
Izhevsk 57 - 53
Irkutsk 52 - 104
Kazan 56 - 48
Kemerovo 56 - 86
Khabarovsk 49 - 135
Krasnodar 45 - 39
Krasnoyarsk 56 - 93
Magnitogorsk 53 - 59
Moscow 56 - 38
Murmansk 69 - 33

Naberezhnye Chelny 56 - 52
Nizhny Novgorod 56 - 44
Norilsk 69 - 87
Novaya Zemlya 72 - 55
Novokuznetsk 54 - 87
Novosibirsk 55 - 83
Omsk 55 - 73
Orenburg 52 - 55
Penza 53 - 45
Perm 58 - 56
Pskov 58 - 28
Rostov na Donu 47 - 40
Ryazan 55 - 40
Rybinsk 58 - 38
Samara 53 - 50
Saratov 52 - 45

Simbirsk 54 - 48
St. Petersburg 60 - 30
Tolyatti 58 - 49
Tomsk 56 - 85
Tula 54 - 37
Ufa 55 - 37
Ulan Ude 52 - 108
Vladikavkaz 43 - 45
Vladimir 56 - 40
Vladivostok 43 - 132
Volgograd 49 - 42
Vologda 59 - 40
Voronezh 52 - 39
Yaroslavl 57 - 39
Yakutsk 62 - 130
Yekaterinburg 58 - 72

THE NEAR ABROAD

Almaty, Kaz 43 - 71
Ashkhabad, Turk 40 -58
Baky, Az 40 - 37
Bishkek, Kyr 43 - 75
Chisinau, Mol 47 - 29
Chornobyl, Uk 51 - 30
Dnipropetrovsk, Uk 48 - 34
Dushanbe, Taj 39 - 69
Kaunas, Lit 55 - 24
Kharkiv, Uk 50 - 36
Kiev, Uk 50 - 30
Lviv, Uk 50 - 24

Minsk, Bela 54 - 28
Odesa, Uk 46 - 31
Qaraghandy, Kaz 50 - 73
Qostanay, Kaz 53 - 64
Riga, Lat 57 - 24
Samargand, Uz 40 - 67
Sevastopol, Uk 45 - 34
Tallinn, Est 59 - 25
Tbilisi, Geo 42 - 45
Toshkent, Uz 41 - 69
Vilnius, Lith 55 - 25
Yerevan, Arm 40 - 44

Latitude of some North American places

| Washington DC 39 | New York 41 | Toronto 44 | Seattle 48 |
| Montreal 46 | Quebec 47 | Edmonton 53 | Anchorage 61 |

AVERAGE MONTHLY AND TOTAL YEARLY AVERAGE
TEMPERATURE AND PRECIPITATION FOR SELECTED CITIES
Temp = degrees Fahrenheit, rounded   Precipitation - inches

	Jan	Feb	Mar	Apr	May	Jun	Jul	Aug	Sep	Oct	Nov	Dec	Year
For comparison: Chicago, Illinois continental, hot summer													
T.	26	27	37	47	58	68	74	73	66	55	45	39	51
P.	2.0	2.1	2.6	2.8	3.6	3.3	3.4	3.0	3.1	2.6	2.4	2.1	33.0
For comparison: Montreal, Canada continental, wet, warm summer													
T.	13	15	25	41	55	65	69	67	59	47	33	19	42
P.	3.7	3.2	3.7	2.4	3.1	3.4	3.7	3.3	3.5	7.3	3.4	3.7	40.4
Archangel continental, cold winter													
T.	8	10	17	30	42	53	60	55	46	34	21	12	32
P.	0.9	0.7	1.1	0.7	1.2	1.8	2.5	2.4	2.1	1.6	1.2	0.9	17.1
Astrakhan desert steppe, low precipitation													
T.	19	23	33	48	64	72	76	74	63	50	30	27	49
P.	0.5	0.4	0.4	0.7	0.7	0.8	0.5	0.5	0.5	0.5	0.6	0.6	6.6
Barnaul continental, warm summer													
T.	-1	2	15	34	52	64	68	63	52	36	17	5	34
P.	0.7	0.5	0.5	0.6	1.3	1.6	2.0	1.8	1.1	1.2	1.0	0.9	13.2
Irkutsk continental, cold, dry winter													
T.	-5	0	15	35	48	60	64	59	47	34	13	-1	18
P.	0.5	0.3	0.3	0.6	1.1	3.3	4.0	3.9	1.9	0.8	0.2	0.6	20.7
Moscow continental, cool summer													
T.	13	16	24	38	53	60	65	61	50	39	27	18	38
P.	1.7	0.9	1.2	1.5	1.9	2.0	2.8	2.9	2.2	1.4	1.6	1.5	21.6
Novaya Zemlya tundra ave. summer temp. below 50 degrees F.													
T.	-2	2	2	11	23	33	42	42	34	25	10	4	20
P.	0.3	0.3	0.3	0.3	0.6	0.8	1.4	1.7	1.7	0.9	0.5	0.5	9.3
Omsk continental, cold,dry winter and warm summer													
T.	-3	0	12	36	52	63	66	61	51	36	15	2	33
P.	0.3	0.2	0.3	0.7	1.2	2.1	2.8	1.8	1.3	0.9	0.6	0.5	12.7
St. Petersburg continental, sea influence, warm summer													
T.	18	18	24	38	50	60	65	62	52	41	32	24	40
P.	1.4	1.3	1.0	1.3	1.6	2.1	2.7	3.0	2.3	2.0	1.8	1.4	21.9

	Jan	Feb	Mar	Apr	May	Jun	Jul	Aug	Sep	Oct	Nov	Dec	Year

Vladivostok continental, sea influence

| T. | 7 | 14 | 26 | 40 | 49 | 55 | 63 | 68 | 61 | 48 | 30 | 16 | 40 |
| P. | 0.7 | 0.7 | 1.1 | 1.7 | 3.1 | 4.1 | 4.6 | 5.9 | 5.7 | 2.8 | 1.5 | 0.6 | 32.5 |

Yakutsk continental, dry, very cold winter

| T. | -46 | -33 | -9 | 17 | 41 | 60 | 66 | 59 | 43 | 17 | -20 | -40 | 13 |
| P. | 0.2 | 0.2 | 0.1 | 0.2 | 0.5 | 1.1 | 1.3 | 1.7 | 0.9 | 0.5 | 0.4 | 0.3 | 7.4 |

Almaty, Kazakhstan continental, very hot summer

| T. | 18 | 23 | 35 | 51 | 61 | 69 | 74 | 72 | 63 | 50 | 32 | 22 | 48 |
| P. | 1.0 | 1.3 | 2.5 | 3.8 | 3.9 | 2.3 | 1.4 | 0.9 | 1.0 | 1.8 | 1.9 | 1.4 | 22.9 |

Balkash, Kazakhstan desert with very hot dry summer

| T. | 50 | 59 | 60 | 72 | 83 | 91 | 95 | 94 | 87 | 76 | 73 | 52 | 73 |
| P. | 1.0 | 1.1 | 1.1 | 0.7 | 0.3 | 0.0 | 0.0 | 0.0 | 0.6 | 0.1 | 0.8 | 1.0 | 6.1 |

Petropavlovsk, Kazakhstan continental cool summers

| T. | 18 | 18 | 22 | 31 | 38 | 46 | 54 | 56 | 51 | 41 | 28 | 22 | 36 |
| P. | 2.4 | 1.2 | 1.8 | 1.7 | 1.6 | 1.8 | 2.9 | 2.9 | 5.2 | 3.3 | 2.7 | 4.7 | 32.2 |

Kharkov, Ukraine continental, moisture all year, warm summer

| T. | 19 | 20 | 29 | 46 | 59 | 66 | 70 | 68 | 57 | 45 | 33 | 25 | 45 |
| P. | 1.4 | 1.3 | 1.3 | 1.3 | 2.0 | 2.4 | 2.9 | 1.9 | 1.3 | 1.6 | 1.5 | 1.5 | 20.4 |

CONSTITUTIONAL MEMBERS OF THE RUSSIAN FEDERATION

Republics

Adygeya	Chechen	Kabardin-Balkar	North Ossetia
Altai	Chuvash	Kalymkia-Khalmg-Tangch	Tatarstan
Bashkortostan	Daghestan	Karelia	Tuva
Buryatia	Ingush	Khakassia	Udmurtian
		Komi	

Territory

Altai	Khabarovsk	Krasnodar	Krasnoyarsk	Maritime	Stavropol

Region

Amur	Kamchatka	Novosibirsk	Tambov
Arkhangelsk	Kemerovo	Omsk	Tver
Astrakhan	Kirov	Oryol	Tomsk
Belgorod	Kostroma	Penza	Tula
Bryansk	Kurgan	Perm	Tyumen
Chelyabinsk	Kursk	Pskov	Ulyanovsk
Chita	Leningrad	Rostov	Vladimir
Ivanovo	Lipetsk	Ryazan	Volgograd
Irkutsk	Magadan	Samara	Vologda
Jewish Autonomous	Moscow	Saratov	Voronezh
Kaliningrad	Murmansk	Sakhalin	Yaroslavl
Kaluga	Nizhni Novgorod	Smolensk	
	Novgorod	Sverdlovsk	

Autonomous Area

Aga Buryat	Evenk	Koryak	Ust-Orda Buryat
Chukchi	Khanty-Mansi	Nenets	Yamal-Nenets
	Komi-Permyak	Taimyr (Dolgan-Nenets)	

Federal Cities   Moscow   St. Petersburg

Note: Sverdlovsk Region has changed its name to Ural Mountains and the areas along the Ussuri River to the coast have begun using the name Maritime Province. At this time, this is in violation of the constitution.

Appendix VI
Population, Crude Birth Rate, Crude Death Rate, Infant Mortality Rate
Russia and the Near Abroad Countries (1996)

Country	Population (rounded millions)	CBR	CDR	Infant Mortality / 1000
Armenia	3.6	23	7	26
Azerbaijan	7.8	22	7	34
Belarus	10.5	13	11	19
Estonia	1.7	14	12	17
Georgia	5.7	16	9	23
Kazakhstan	17.4	19	8	40
Kyrgyzstan	4.8	26	7	46
Latvia	2.8	14	13	21
Lithuania	3.9	14	11	16
Moldova	4.5	16	10	30
Russia	150.0	13	11	26
Tajikistan	6.2	34	7	60
Turkmenistan	4.0	30	7	68
Ukraine	52.0	12	13	20
Uzbekistan	23.1	29	6	52
Iran	65.0	35	7	55
Poland	38.8	13	9	12
Sourth Korea	45.6	16	6	21
Turkey	63.4	25	6	46
United States	263.9	15	8	8

To calculate the annual population increase of a country by births and deaths:
    CBR - CDR multiply by the number of 1000s in the country.
        Estonia: 14 - 12 = 2   2 x 1,700 = 3,400 per year

To calculate the number of years it will take a country to double its population if the data does not change appreciably: CBR - CDR/10 converts to percent then 70/% = Doubling Time   Moldova: 16 - 10 = 6   6/10 = .6   * 70/.6 = 116.6 years
    * 70 is the number of years it would take to double a number at 1% annual growth.

BIBLIOGRAPHY AND REFERENCES

Akchurin, Marat 1991 SOVIET MUSLIMS, SEEKING REFORM, NOT REVOLUTION: The World & I, October 1991

Alexandrov, Yuri 1995 GHOSTS OF THE PAST: RUSSIA'S LANDMARKS : *Russian Life,* August 1995

Anderson, Jack and Michael Binstein 1994 SADDAM COURTS RUSSIA'S ZHIRINOVSKY: Times-News, Erie PA Jan 23 1994

Avineri, Shlomo 1991 THE BREAKUP OF THE SOVIET UNION: The Brookings Review, Spring 1992

Bahree, Bhushan 1993 SIBERIAN GAS OFFERS UNTAPPED PROMISE: The Wall Street Journal, April 16, 1993

Belt, Don and Sarah Leen (photo) 1992 BAIKAL, RUSSIA'S SACRED SEA *National Geographic*, June 1992

Bogert, Carroll 1993 SELLING OFF BIG RED*: Newsweek* March 1, 1993

Bradshaw, Michael J. (ed.) 1991 THE SOVIET UNION: John Wiley & Sons, Inc and Belhaven Press London

Carmichael, Joel 1990 A HISTORY OF RUSSIA, Hippocrene Books, New York

Central Intelligence Agency 1985 USSR ENERGY ATLAS

Channon, John and Robert Hudson 1995 HISITORICAL ATLAS OF RUSSIA: Penguin Books

Chernow, Barbara A. (ed.) 1993 THE COLUMBIA ENCYCLOPEDIA : Fifth Edition, Houghton Mifflin Co.

Clark, Miles and James P. Blair (Photos) 1994 A RUSSIAN VOYAGE, *National Geographic*, June 1994 Vol 185, No.6

Combes, Colleen 1995 IS THERE A FUTURE FOR THE PAST (TOURISM), *Russian Life*, November 1995

Combes, Colleen 1996 ARCTIC PARADISE, SOLOVETSKY ARCHIPELAGO, *Russian Life* July 1996

Cutler, Blayne 1994 WELCOME TO THE BORDERLANDS: Geography 94/95, Dushkin Publishing Group, Ninth Edition

DeBlij, H.J. and Peter O. Muller 1992 GEOGRAPHY REGIONS AND CONCEPTS: John Wiley & Sons, Chapters 1 and 2.

Doder, Dusko and Peter Essick (photo) 1992 THE BOLSHEVIK REVOLUTION: *National Geographic*, Vol 182, No. 4 Oct.1992

Edwards, Mike 1993 A BROKEN EMPIRE: *National Geographic,* Vol 183 No. 3 March 1993

Edwards, Mike 1996 THE FRACTURED CAUCASUS: *National Geographic*, February 1996, vol 189, No. 2 pp 126 - 131.

Elliott, Dorinda and Andrew Nagorski 1993; AFTER THE SHOWDOWN: *Newsweek* April 5, 1993

Garreau,Joel 1992 THE KEY TO UNDERSTANDING THE FORMER SOVIET UNION: Washington Post, National Weekly Edition, February 11, 1992

Goldman, Minton F.(ed.) 1992 COMMONWEALTH OF INDEPENDENT STATES: The Dushkin Publishing Group, Inc.

Greenall, Robert 1995 KALMYKIA, *Russian Life* September 1995
Greenall, Robert 1995 LOUDER FLOWS THE VOLGA, *Russian Life* October 1995
Greenall, Robert 1996 THE PEOPLE'S WILL (ELECTIONS), *Russian Life* June 1996
Greer, Colin 1994 THE WELL BEING OF THE WORLD IS AT STAKE:
    interview with Mikhail Gorbachev, Parade Magazine, January 23, 1994
Hodgson, Bryan and Natalie Fobes (photo) 1992 HARD HARVEST ON THE BERING
    SEA: *National Geographic*, October 1992
Hodgson, Bryan and Sarah Leen (photo) 1994 KAMCHATKA, RUSSIA'S LAND OF
    FIRE AND ICE: *National Geographic*, April 1944
Holzman, Franklyn D. 1982 THE SOVIET ECONOMY: Foriegn Policy Association, No.
    260, Sept/Oct 1982
Holzner, Lutz and Jeane M. Knapp 1987: SOVIET GEOGRAPHY STUDIES IN OUR
    TIMES: The American Geographical Studies, The Univ of Wisconsin-Milwaukee
Hooson, David 1966 THE SOVIET UNION: Wadsworth
Howe, G. Melvyn 1983 THE SOVIET UNION: Longman Scientific & Technical, Essex
    England
INFORMATION PLEASE ENVIRONMENTAL ALMANAC 1994, World Resources
    Institute,Houghton Mifflin Company.
Kandel, Paul 1993 SEEKING A LASTING ROLE FOR RUSSIA: World Press
    Review, reprint from Nezavis Imaya Gazeta, June 1993
Kennedy, Paul 1993 THE ERSTWHILE USSR AND ITS CRUMBLED EMPIRE :
    and THE AMERICAN DILEMMA: in Preparing For The Twenty First
    Century, Random House
Kotlyakov, V.M. 1991 THE ARAL SEA BASIN: *Environment* Vol 33, No l.
    January/February 1991
Laqueur, Walter 1990 STALIN, THE GLASNOST REVELATIONS: Charles Scribner's
    Sons
Lincoln, W. Bruce 1994 THE CONQUEST OF A CONTINENT, SIBERIA AND THE
    RUSSIANS, Random House
Matlock, Jr. Jack F. 1995 AUTOPSY ON AN EMPIRE: Random House
Naisbitt, John 1994 GLOBAL PARADOX, Avon Books
Onaran, Yalman 1993 DEMOCRATIC REFORM: The Christian Science Monitor,
    February 25, 1993.
Ostling, Richard 1988 WILL BELLS CHIME AGAIN?: *Time Magazine*, April 4, 1988
Pitzl, Gerald R. (ed) 1994 GEOGRAPHY: Dushkin Publishing Group, Inc 1994/95 Ninth
    Edition
Powell, David 1991 THE REVIVAL OF RELIGION: Current History, October 1991
Reid, Alex 1996 ANCIENT RUSSIA AND ITS WATERWAYS, compiled for Odessa
    America Tour group: Mineola New York 11501
Remnick, David 1993 LENIN'S TOMB, Random House
Repenko, Paula 1993 RUSSIANS ABROAD STAND THEIR GROUND: World
    Press Review October 1993 reprinted from "Liberation".
Riche, Marth Farnsworth 1994 WE'RE ALL MINORITIES NOW: in Geography 94/95
    The Dushkin Publishing Group,Inc
Satter, David 1989 WHY RUSSIA CAN'T FEED ITSELF: *Reader's Digest*, Oct. 1989

Schmemann, Serge 1991 THE SOVIET STATE,BORN OF A DREAM, DIES:
    The New York Times, December 26, 1991
Shelton, Judy 1993 A BOLD STEP TO SAVE RUSSIA , *Readers Digest* July 1993
Shupe, John F. (Cart),William Graves (Ed) 1993 MAP, RUSSIA AND THE NEWLY
    INDEPENDENT NATIONS: *National Geographic Society*, March 1993
Siternoff, Howard and Tanya Samofalova 1995 RUSSIA BY RIVER,Rikki-Tikki-Tavi,
    Inc, St. Petersburg
Specter, Michael 1994 A RUSSIAN OUTPOST NOW HAPPILY EMBRACES ASIA,
    The New York Times
Stanglin, Douglas et.al.1992 RUSSIA IN RUINS; *U. S. News and World Report*
    December 7, 1992
Stewart, John Massey 1991 THE NATURE OF RUSSIA, Cross River Press
Stresemann, Gustav 1993 THE RUSSIAN FEDERATION, Statistisches Bundesamt,
    Wiesbaden
Sudoplaltov, Pavel 1994 SPECIAL TASKS, Little, Brown and Company
Sweet, William 1994 ENVIRONMENTAL CRISIS IN THE FORMER SOVIET
    BLOC, WHOSE PROBLEM?: in Great Decisions, Foreign Policy Association. NY
Szajkowski, Bogdan 1993 WILL RUSSIA DISINTEGRATE INTO BANTUSTANS?:
    in Geography 94/95, Dushkin Publishing Group
Talbott, Strobe 1992 CAN RUSSIA ESCAPE ITS PAST?: *Time Magazine* Dec.7,1992
Tarica, Andrew 1996 KAMCHATKA, *Russian Life* August 1996
Tomikel, John 1965 BASE MAPS OF THE WORLD: Allegheny Press
Tomikel, John 1991 - 1996 RUSSIAN NOTES: Allegheny Press
Tomikel, John and Bonnie Henderson 1994 RUSSIA AND HER NEIGHBORS,
    Allegheny Press
Watson, Russell and Dorinda Elliott 1993 STATE OF EMERGENCY: *Newsweek*
    October 11, 1993
World Almanac 1996, Funk & Wagnalls
World Resources 1990/91: Oxford University Press
Yeltsin, Boris 1991 THE LAST DAYS OF THE SOVIET UNION: reprint from Ogonyok
    Magazine, The Pittsburgh Post Gazette, March 25, 1991
1990 USSR AND EASTERN EUROPE, END OF AN ERA: in Great Decisions, Foreign
    Policy Association, Inc. New York
1991 TOXIC WASTELAND: *U.S.News & World Report,* April 13,1992
1992 BREAKUP OF THE SOVIET UNION, U.S. DILEMMAS: in Great
    Decisions, Foreign Policy Association, Inc New York
1996 A NATION OF 'PLOTTERS' (DACHAS), *Russian Life* July 1996
1996 HERE COMES THE NEVESTA (Marriage in Post-Communist Russia)
    Russian Life August 1996

216

ABOUT THE AUTHORS

John Tomikel is assistant professor of geography at Edinboro University of Pennsylvania. A world traveler, he is the author of 21 books and 6 exercise manuals. Dr. Tomikel earned a bachelors degree from Clarion University, a masters degree from Syracuse University, a masters degree and a PhD from the University of Pittsburgh. He writes a weekly column for the Erie Morning News and is involved in specialty editing for Allegheny Press.

Bonnie Henderson earned a masters degree in cultural anthropology from the University of Pittsburgh and a masters degree in cultural geography from California University of Pennsylvania. She spent a summer at UCLA under a grant from the National Endowment for the Humanities. She was an instructor at the Community College of Allegheny County, Duquesne University and Penn State University: McKeesport. She authored numerous newspaper feature articles and is senior editor for Allegheny Press.

MAP 24 Major cities of Eastern Europe.